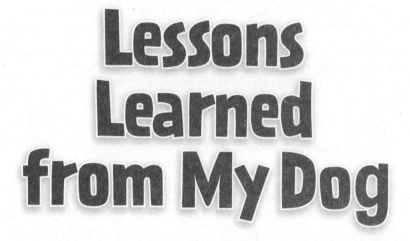

Chicken Soup for the Soul: Lessons Learned from My Dog
Amy Newmark

Published by Chicken Soup for the Soul, LLC www.chickensoup.com
Copyright ©2023 by Chicken Soup for the Soul, LLC. All Rights Reserved.

The publisher gratefully acknowledges the many publishers and individuals who granted Chicken Soup for the Soul permission to reprint the cited material.

Front cover photo of dog courtesy of iStockphoto.com (©Nynke van Holten), photo of microphone courtesy of iStockphoto (©nito100)
Back cover and interior photo of dog with hat courtesy of iStockphoto.com (©Dorottya_Mathe), photo of Jack Russell Terrier courtesy of iStockphoto.com (©Obradovic), photo of dog with books courtesy of iStockphoto.com (©cynoclub)
Photo of Amy Newmark courtesy of Susan Morrow at SwickPix

Cover and Interior by Daniel Zaccari

Publisher's Cataloging-In-Publication Data

Names: Newmark, Amy, editor.
Title: Chicken soup for the soul : lessons learned from my dog / Amy Newmark.
Description: Cos Cob, CT: Chicken Soup for the Soul, LLC, 2023.
Identifiers: LCCN: 2022946911 | ISBN: 978-1-61159-098-2 (print) | 978-1-61159-335-8 (ebook)
Subjects: LCSH Dogs--Anecdotes. | Human-animal relationships--Anecdotes. | Dog owners--Anecdotes. |
Dogs--Humor. | Conduct of life. | Essays. | BISAC PETS / Essays & Narratives | PETS / Dogs / General | HUMOR / Topic / Animals
Classification: LCC SF426.2 .C45 2023 | DDC 636.7--dc23

Library of Congress Control Number: 2022946911

PRINTED IN THE UNITED STATES OF AMERICA
on acid∞free paper

30 29 28 27 26 25 24 23   01 02 03 04 05 06 07 08 09

Lessons Learned from My Dog

Amy Newmark

Chicken Soup for the Soul, LLC
Cos Cob, CT

Changing the world one story at a time®
www.chickensoup.com

Table of Contents

❶

~Be Ready for Adventure~

❷

~Be a Friend~

❸
~Step Outside Your Comfort Zone~

❹
~Be Open-Minded~

❺
~Find Your Purpose~

❻

~Find Your Inner Strength~

❼

~Live in the Moment~

❽

~Miracles Happen~

❾

~Sometimes You Just Have to Laugh~

❿

~ Get On with Life ~

⓫
~Saying Goodbye with Gratitude~

Chapter
1

Be Ready for Adventure

Ridiculous Sometimes Works

In order to really enjoy a dog, one doesn't merely try to train him to be semi-human. The point of it is to open oneself to the possibility of becoming partly a dog.
~Edward Hoagland

Like most young pups, my little Beagle/Jack Russell mix grand-dog was an escape artist extraordinaire — from his harness, from the gate around my patio, and from me. While most people might be able to catch a runaway puppy, I use a mobility scooter, and its maximum speed is only four miles per hour — no comparison to Dan, who seemingly could go from zero to sixty in five seconds if something caught his eye. Fortunately, while doggie-sitting one day, I discovered a surprising alternative to speed for catching him.

When we returned from a walk, I opened the door to my gated patio to let Dan out to get a drink and then went about preparing lunch. A few minutes later, I realized he had not returned inside. He was nowhere. Gone! While fretting and pondering what to do, I glanced out my kitchen window and spied him running loose in the common area between my community's townhomes in pursuit of a rabbit. I gasped. It would not have been such a concern except that I am just a half-block away from four lanes of busy traffic, and I silently prayed his prey would find a safe haven in the opposite direction.

I quickly jumped on my scooter without a clue as to what I would do. And then I noticed his harness and leash on the counter. I quickly grabbed them in hopes that, if I did catch him, I would have a way to bring him home.

I rode on the sidewalk until I saw him again, running behind other townhomes. I instinctively shouted, "Dan!" He turned to look, and I knew I had one shot at making him come to me. Panicked and unprepared, I wondered, *Now what do I do?* Suddenly, an idea popped into my head, followed quickly by, *This will never work.* But what other choice did I have?

I grabbed his harness and leash from my lap and dangled them so he could see. "Walk?" I asked. I silently cringed, thinking how ridiculous it looked for a woman on a scooter to hold out a harness and leash to a dog who was already running free. To my complete surprise, it worked! Dan ran over to me ready for another walk, which he knew would only happen if he wore the appropriate "attire." That is when I learned a lesson: There is no such thing as ridiculous if it works.

—Vicki L. Julian—

The Expulsion

*Discipline isn't about showing a dog who's boss;
it's about taking responsibility for a living creature
you have brought into your world.*
~Cesar Millan, Be the Pack Leader

"Expelled from dog-obedience school!" That was the headline I envisioned by the time I drove Trooper, my Welsh Springer, home from our first, and last, day of school. I was embarrassed and angry. How, fifteen minutes into our first day of dog-obedience class, could I find myself heading home, kicked out of school?

In a time long before Cesar Millan, the dog whisperer, and before it became fashionable to have your dog trained in the social graces, I found it necessary to have Trooper properly trained in the basics. Not the roll-over, give-paw, or even sit basics. I'm talking about the no-bark, no-jump, no-pull, no-acting-crazy basic boot camp for dogs. My husband and I had tried for months but we just couldn't get through to him. We began to think that adopting a "forever pet" might not be forever for us. Perhaps the old adage "you can't teach an old dog new tricks" was true, but Trooper was only two years old when we adopted him — certainly not a pup but still only a teenager in people years.

I had been thrilled to read in our local newspaper that a woman was offering dog-obedience classes. The ad said she would teach our dog how to behave. Wow! That was for me. I could see it: In four short weeks, Trooper and I would be walking the neighborhood. Heads held high. He at my side. No pulling, no sniffing. I mailed in my seventy-five dollars.

The dog-obedience trainer called to set up an interview with us. "An interview?" I asked. She explained that she needed to meet Trooper before accepting him, and I made an appointment with her for the next day.

The following day went well with the trainer, and I was happy that Trooper and I passed inspection. After being given a thumbs-up to proceed with a four-week course in socialization, she supplied me with a shopping list of assorted items I needed to get: a new collar and leash, even a *Dog Training for Dummies* book for me to read. All of this could be purchased from the trainer for an additional seventy-five dollars. *It's only numbers,* I said to myself. Anything for my precious Trooper.

On Friday evening of the following week, Trooper and I left home for our first class. I was hopeful. The clock read 7:00 P.M. when we arrived.

There were approximately eight dogs of assorted sizes and breeds. Forming a semi-circle, all were quiet and heeling at their masters' sides. We joined the semi-circle. Trooper, jumping and barking. Me, red-faced, pulling and tugging, occasionally uttering, "Shhhh." Across from me stood an English Setter. His eyes bore down on Trooper with a look of disgust and disinterest on his face. A Boxer on the other side of Trooper, looking smug and self-righteous, backed away, apparently afraid he might catch something.

"Excuse me. Excuse me," the trainer shouted over the cacophony. I looked up to see that she was talking to me. "I'm sorry, but can you take your dog outside to calm him down a bit?" I grabbed Trooper's leash and dragged him out to the back yard for a time-out. After gaining some control, we returned to the training room. All was quiet for the moment. The clock read 7:11 P.M.

Several barks and a few shoulder-dislocating tugs by my four-legged Cujo later, the trainer asked us to leave... permanently. I looked at her in disbelief as she explained that Trooper was too disruptive, preventing the other "students" from learning. I begged for another chance and reminded her that her class was on socializing. That's why we were there. She was unforgiving. I grabbed my dog equipment and dog-training book, and we left, heads down, tails between our legs. The clock read 7:15 P.M.

— Nancy Hesting —

The Disappearing Leash

The belly rules the mind.
~Spanish Proverb

t was a stifling summer night with humidity out of this world. My husband David and I felt miserable, even outside on the porch where it was cooler. As we sat complaining about the heat, David came up with a great idea.

"Why don't we watch a movie? Something with snow and cold. That might cool us off a bit."

After searching our shelves, we picked out a movie and headed upstairs to watch. The story took place in Canada and featured plenty of cold, snow, and Huskies. Halfway into the movie, we found that instead of cooling us off, the story made us miss our lovable, goofy Huskies. We'd put them outside in their large kennel for the rest of the night since our cabin did not have air conditioning.

Like two crazy people, we paused the movie, raced downstairs to get our Huskies' leashes and headed out with them for a walk. Despite the beastly weather, the dogs were ecstatic. They'd never gone on a walk in the dark before, and the night sounds of the forest excited them. They pulled us along with wild abandon. Eventually, the dogs wore us out, and we found ourselves getting them home around midnight.

We removed their leashes and filled their water buckets with fresh, cool water. Then, David and I headed inside to finish our movie.

The next morning, I found Eska still wearing her collar — minus the leash. Normally, the collar and leash fastened together, and I always removed them as one piece. I unfastened Eska's collar and thought nothing of the missing leash until it was time to walk the dogs. David and I spent the next several hours searching everywhere, including the kennel, in case one of the dogs had buried it.

That day, our two sons had returned from their Japan trip and offered to join us in the search. But Eska's leash had disappeared without a trace.

Days later, my sons called me outside. In the middle of the kennel sat a huge, fresh pile of dog poop that resembled a volcano. Upon closer inspection, it appeared that the dog responsible for this dump had swallowed an extra-long snake — bright blue in color.

Using my fingers to plug my nose, I grabbed a stick and removed the lengthy leash, shocked to find it still in one piece. How Eska survived swallowing anything that long is still a mystery. As a precaution, I phoned the vet, who thought she'd be okay since the entire leash had passed.

Over the years, we'd had a long list of items that our Huskies consumed — socks, hair ties, stuffed toys, cardboard, to name a few — but the leash made Husky history. In true Husky fashion, the ordeal didn't faze Eska at all. Under the circumstances, we felt lucky and grateful that, in the end, everything had come out okay.

— Jill Burns —

Woodland Lights

A dark night, lightened up by thousands
of glowing fireflies... It's magical.
~Ama H. Vanniarachchy

The workweek was finally over and my husband and I were able to sit down to relax and watch a movie. Through the low volume, I could hear the clink and clank of our sleepy Bloodhound Hunter's collar jingling as my husband rubbed lovingly at his ears. Our other Bloodhound, Opie, was snoring away on his bed, snuggled up with his freshly washed blanket, as content as could be.

"Grrrrrrrrr." Hunter suddenly sat bolt upright, staring at the back patio door and grumbling in an alert manner. Opie perked up his head and jerked his gaze toward our back door as well. I hit the Pause button on the movie, and we paid attention to our security team. There was silence for a few moments as we watched and listened.

"Booooof! Boooof!" Hunter let out a couple of whispering barks, which was his way of issuing a warning to us that something was amiss outside. He stood up and walked protectively over to the door, growling intermittently. Opie got up to join him and started growling alongside his big brother.

"Wait, I think I just saw something," I whispered to my husband, as a distant light caught my eye from our back yard.

"I'm going to go grab a flashlight," my husband said. He went quickly to our bedroom. I walked stealthily over to our two hounds, and Hunter became adamant that I remain behind him. He tried to herd me away from the door, all the while acting as our lookout.

"Look! There!" I whisper shouted as my husband came back into the room wielding a flashlight. "A light keeps coming in and out of the trees out there beyond the yard."

"Where?"

"Over there," I said. I pointed, trying to best indicate where I had last seen a light out yonder in the woods. "Look! There it is again!"

"Yep, there's definitely something out there," my husband said, making his way to our back patio to shine a light out in the yard.

"Bark! Bark! Barooooooo!" My hounds were going bananas by this time. My husband shone his flashlight here and there, but we couldn't see any movement or anything, just a light that became visible through the densely wooded trees here and there.

"It's getting closer!" I remarked as I saw the light begin to appear now within the foliage and flowers in our back yard.

"I don't see anything," my husband replied. But Opie and Hunter were sure that was incorrect, and there was definitely some threat that needed addressing out in their back yard.

"Aaaaah!" All of a sudden, the light gleamed into my peripheral vision, and I let out a faint, high-pitched screech of surprise. Lights began popping up all over our back patio, and the hounds went berserk. I began laughing hysterically as I realized what was going on.

"What is it?" my husband asked.

"It's... fireflies!" I said through my laughter. My husband joined me in laughing at the "big threat" we had discovered outside. But, more than anything, we were laughing at our silly hounds who were still going bonkers over the sporadic flashes of light from a multitude of fireflies.

We had just recently moved to the Midwest from Colorado, where we had grown up without the incredible, glowing treat of these spectacular beetles. In the city where we came from, it was definitely a concern when you saw lights outside your home, and our dogs were well-attuned to warn of such behavior. But here in the country, it seemed the big threat now was fireflies.

— Gwen Cooper —

Lucy and the Green Ball

Dogs do speak, but only to those
who know how to listen.
~Orhan Pamuk, My Name Is Red

Our Cavalier King Charles Spaniel, Lucy, had lost her beloved green ball and she was acting quite glum about it. My husband Dave and I were beside ourselves. Even though Lucy could drive us bonkers with her insistence that we play ball with her, it had become a vital part of our evening ritual.

We searched for days. No ball. We tried to get her to play with her other toys, but nothing quite did the trick.

"We've got to find another ball just like it," Dave said. "And when we do, we'll buy out the store!"

At a nearby pet shop, I purchased four balls for Lucy. Granted, none was exactly like the green ball, but surely she would like one of them. The first was small and orange and would fit perfectly in her mouth. The second was pink and delightfully textured with rubbery spikes. The third was green (the right color) with orange material inside that crackled when one bit on it. The fourth and final ball was blue and bouncy. It looked just like the old ball except, of course, it was blue.

Dogs are color-blind, aren't they?

We started with the orange ball. Lucy quickly discarded that one. We tried the pink. Same thing. The green ball with the orange stuffing? She barely nosed it. It all came down to the blue ball. Surely, surely, she would love it.

She had to!

She did display a bit of her old exuberance when Dave first threw it for her. She mouthed it. She brought it back several times. She even made it squeak! I began to think we had solved the problem.

"Go back and buy out the store," Dave got as far as saying.

But then Lucy went back to lying on the floor with her head between her paws, and her sweet brown Spaniel eyes looked up at us as if in mourning. "Oh, woe is me. Life will never be the same. My best friend is gone. Gone forever," she seemed to say.

There was nothing we could do to help her.

Nothing!

There's almost nothing worse than being with a cherished dog in mourning. So, I fled the scene. I went upstairs to put away the laundry while Dave escaped to the grocery store. As I was rolling pairs of socks into their own little balls and wondering if Lucy would like to play with one of these, suddenly, out of the depths of our sad, old house, came a sharp, excited, high-pitched bark. I knew that bark — it was a green-ball bark. Had Lucy found "the ball"? Had she, after all these days, discovered its hiding place on her own? She couldn't have! She was probably barking at one of the cats.

She barked and barked and barked.

"All right. All right! I'm coming!" I went downstairs, and there she was in the dining room — barking at the sideboard.

"What is it?" I asked.

She stared hard at the sideboard.

"We've already looked there. I am not about to get down to look beneath it again. I've got a sore back. A pinched nerve. My sacroiliac is inflamed!"

Her stare could have bored holes in that sideboard.

She would stand there all day if I didn't do her bidding. I finally said, "Oh, all right. But this is useless. And if I end up in the hospital having back surgery, it's all your fault."

I slowly got down on my hands and knees and then, painfully, turned onto my stomach to see what she was staring at.

There, buried deep in the dust and pet hair that had accumulated beneath the massive wood sideboard with its shelves of family heirlooms, was Lucy's small green rubbery treasure.

Oh, the joy! The madcap romp! The green ball flying this way and that — day after day after day — bouncing off walls, down the basement steps, under chairs and tables. And, all the while, our Lucy's ecstatic barking drowned out the dismal evening news and everything was right with the world.

— Sally M. Keehn —

Naughty by Nature

I feel sorry for people who don't have dogs. I hear
they have to pick up food they drop on the floor.
~Author Unknown

Rosie came into our lives as a nine-year-old rescue after it didn't work out with her previous foster home. Over the years, we'd fostered many dogs, but none had walked into our house like Rosie. Usually, foster dogs are skittish. They hang back until they figure out the routine and their place in the house. Rosie came into our house like the only thing it was missing was her. Even though she had been given up and discarded, she never doubted that she owned the room.

Rosie was unfazed by impromptu light-saber battles and the antics of our two small boys. She fit right in and became an instant member of our family. It went so well that we wondered what trouble she had gotten into at her previous foster home. Then, food started disappearing from places where Basset Hounds with short legs shouldn't be able to reach, like countertops and the kitchen table.

With two kids and two dogs, things tend to be a bit chaotic, and we thought perhaps we were imagining things. That was until I found Rosie standing in the middle of the kitchen table with an unrepentant look on her face and a lunch plate that had been licked clean.

It was on.

She would strike fast and stealthily, like a ninja. I'd come out of the bathroom and find the mug of tea next to my work computer completely empty, the cup still upright, and not a drop of tea spilled on the table. I learned that she liked peppermint tea the best, especially when I added cream and sweetener. But when I made Rosie her own cup, she wasn't interested. She liked my tea. Forbidden fruit is always sweeter.

Food continued to be snatched from the kitchen table even though we made sure to push the chairs in tight. How was she doing it? With her short Basset legs, she wasn't tall enough to jump up there. Then one day I heard the scrape of a chair sliding across tile. I shot up to find Rosie under the kitchen table pushing the chair out with her nose. Nothing is out of reach if you want it badly enough.

One Thanksgiving, after seeing our guests to the door, we turned back to find Rosie on the dining room table licking leftovers off the plates. Caught in the middle of being naughty, she didn't look abashed or ashamed. She continued her feast, making sure to get every possible morsel as we pulled her off the table.

As time went on, Rosie honed her skills to become a garbage thief that raccoons and bears would envy. I don't know that she liked eating the garbage as much as she liked spreading it around the kitchen. One by one, Rosie defeated every child-proof cabinet lock we found, even the ones I had a hard time opening. We ended up keeping the garbage on the kitchen counter. Even then, she'd still get into it sometimes.

When the garbage was no longer a challenge, she graduated to the pantry. While we were gone, Rosie liberated cereal boxes, pasta boxes, bread — whatever she could reach by stretching her long body. Always generous, she was happy to share her bounty with Sully, our other dog. We'd come home to empty chewed-up boxes on the floor, and of course garbage scattered across the kitchen and two dogs looking guilty. Well, one dog. Rosie never looked guilty. Her big brown eyes conveyed love and joy but never guilt.

I'd heard of treat puzzles for keeping dogs busy and out of trouble when they were alone. The one I bought had twelve compartments that all had to be opened a different way. Some had doors that slid to the left, some to the right. Some required multiple steps. It was not an entry-level treat puzzle. Chuckling to myself, I filled each compartment and set it down on the floor, waiting to see what she'd do. Rosie watched as Sully went after it first, carefully working each square before giving up, satisfied that he'd gotten all he would get out of the treat puzzle after he opened a few of the doors. It took him about fifteen minutes. I filled it up again and set it down in front of Rosie. She picked it up and banged it upside-down against the wall. When all the treats fell out, she scarfed them down and waited for me to refill it. Thirty seconds and done.

When she got sick, it meant more vet visits and medication. As much as she loved eating garbage, Rosie would not willingly eat a pill. No matter what food I hid it in, she always found the pill inside and spit it out. I tried everything I could think of, including smashing it up and mixing it in with peanut butter. Nothing worked. It wasn't until I left a bread-wrapped pill in the middle of the kitchen table and left the room that she jumped up on the table and ate it. I watched from the hallway, proud and excited that I had finally outsmarted the dog after all this time.

Cancer made her skinny and tired. It happened so gradually that at first we didn't realize how bad it had gotten — because she never lost her big personality. As thin as she became, she never stopped getting into mischief. We still had to keep the garbage on the counter and the childproof locks on the pantry. Her tail never stopped wagging. Saying goodbye to Rosie was one of the hardest things my family has done. Years later, we still feel her absence in our house, even though many dogs have passed through. She lived in the moment, found joy everywhere, even when she was in pain, and didn't let things like childproof locks stop her from getting what she wanted. Rosie taught me that a little audacity goes a long way.

— Meadoe Hora —

Chicken Soup
for the *Soul*

Lost and Found
and Lost

There are three things we cry for in life:
things that are lost, things that are found,
and things that are magnificent.
~Douglas Coupland

"Cara, Cara, come home," I called as I stumbled along our street in Deep Cove, a densely forested and rainy region near Vancouver, British Columbia. I could hear my husband and two girls ahead and behind calling, "Cara, Cara, come home!"

My heart sank as we completed the final leg of our search grid with no sign of Cara. Along the way, we had plastered posters on every available telephone pole. Lost dog. A photo of Cara's sweet face. A little fringe of partially cut tabs at the bottom with our phone number. Exhausted with worry, we stumbled home to wait for news of our beloved dog.

More than ten days had passed since Cara went missing. Huddled together on the sofa, the four of us tried to make sense of it.

Perhaps she had been hit by a car and crawled into the forest to die. Or was killed by a coyote.

A wooly white Shih Tzu/Bichon cross, she indiscriminately greeted everyone with affection. How could that beautiful soul be lost forever?

To our astonishment, our vet called a few days later. "Cara has been reported found by the SPCA in Coquitlam," she said.

How was this possible? Coquitlam is thirty-five kilometers from Deep Cove.

"We're on our way!" I exclaimed. We were whooping with joy and getting ready to leave when the phone rang again. "There's an update from the SPCA. They told us the owner had just been there," our vet advised.

There was a moment of stunned silence. It wasn't us. And if it wasn't us, who was it?

Still later, the vet called a third time and gave us a name and possible location of the party who had claimed Cara. She suggested we call the police.

"Do you think we should?" I asked my husband. It seemed a bit extreme. We lacked experience with dognapping, so we somewhat hesitantly made the call to the local detachment.

The constable arrived that evening around 5:00 P.M. He was going off shift but said he would rescue our dog.

"Under no circumstance are you to go and try to get her yourselves," he said. "It could be dangerous."

My husband chafed, but we complied.

The TV was on, but no one was watching it when the doorbell rang at 11:00 P.M. My husband threw open the door. On the front porch, haloed by the streetlamp behind him, stood the constable. Clasped to his broad chest was our beautiful dog.

My heart surged with joy. Our daughters thundered down the stairs and collapsed on the hardwood floor in the front hall, racked by sobs of relief. We crowded around, anxious to caress Cara's fur and reassure ourselves that her return was not a figment of our imagination.

The constable told us that he had found Cara chained to a large stake in the back yard of the dognapper's house. The woman protested that she thought the dog was lost — that she had rescued her. Leaving, he advised her there would be a further investigation.

Some days later, the constable called with more details. The dognapper, who lived in Coquitlam, was the flag person on a construction crew working near our house.

Somehow, Cara had escaped from the dognapper's clutches and, like Lassie, started her journey home. Evidently, she didn't know that to reach us she would need to navigate many kilometers of unfamiliar streets, cross the Burrard Inlet over a busy six-lane bridge, and thereafter find her way to Deep Cove.

Possibly drawn by the scent of the thick stands of western hemlock and other coniferous species in the conservation area on the western edge of Coquitlam that might have reminded her of the trees in her own yard, Cara found herself on the network of paths that crisscross the nature park. There she encountered two elderly ladies walking their dogs. She greeted them affectionately and followed them all the way to their car.

The two humans she chanced upon were avid dog lovers. They noticed she was collarless and lacked dog tags but was healthy and well-groomed. With no owner in sight, they took her to the SPCA.

Evidently, the dognapper knew enough to check with the SPCA about a lost pet. What she didn't know was that Cara had an identification number tattooed in her ear. (The number look-up system triggered the call from the SPCA to our vet.)

On providing an accurate description of Cara, the dognapper was told, as the shelter was full, that Cara had been taken home by the two women who found her. One of the women left her home address but in the SPCA parking lot, they had decided it made more sense for Cara to go home with the other woman.

Lacking this information and armed with the address on file, the dognapper set off to collect "her" lost dog.

The next few minutes were a testament to the power of a dog to inspire humans to greatness.

After the SPCA alerted the woman on file that the person coming for the dog was not the owner, she phoned her friend to hatch a plan. The dognapper had already been to her house and was on her way to her friend's home to collect Cara. They had a chance to outwit the dognapper, but it would require nerves of steel.

"The SPCA told me I need to see your ID," the second woman prevaricated to the pretend owner standing at her front door. She scanned it for details and then gave up Cara. The moment the door closed, she called the SPCA. In turn, we provided this information to the police.

***

A few weeks after Cara returned, the dognapper telephoned. I don't know how she got our number, perhaps from our Lost Dog poster.

She told me she never saw any posters, and no one ever asked her crew about a lost dog. She had wanted a dog and Cara had seemed to like her and had jumped right into her car. She had paid $200 for a collar and leash.

When the constable called to provide the findings of the police investigation, he had asked, "Do you want to press charges?"

My husband and I deliberated. We felt blessed to have Cara back through such an unlikely sequence of events. There were so many dog lovers involved in our happy ending: the constable, our vet, the SPCA staff, the two ladies.

Cara would not ask for revenge. We did not press charges.

—Jan Pezarro—

That Stinks

Sometimes, when you get in a fight with a skunk,
you can't tell who started it.
~Lloyd Doggett

Our dog Bonnie was an Australian Shepherd, a breed known for their extraordinary ability to herd livestock. She was superb at her craft and excelled doing it. Unfortunately for us, she loved to herd skunks.

We seemed to have an endless number of skunks in our yard despite having a fence around the perimeter to keep them out. Once they breached the fencing, the little stinkers were experts at concealing themselves behind the plants and bushes. We always seemed to spot them in their hiding place only after we had let Bonnie out. She would capitalize on our oversight and joyfully flush out the animals, nudging the critters along as her ancestors had done with cattle before her.

"Noooo!" Lou and I would yell in unison when we saw her start to chase after a skunk. Our desperate cries for her to come back always fell on deaf ears. That dog was on a mission. We were defenseless to try and stop her; herding was in her DNA. The only thing that would finally stop her was when the skunk, tired of being chased, sprayed her with its pungent fragrance.

"This has got to stop," my husband said to me after yet another stinky encounter. "This is the third time in three weeks that she's gotten sprayed. We need to look more carefully before she's let out into the yard. I'm tired of having to constantly bathe her."

I agreed and made a promise to him to be more vigilant. He was right. These encounters all could've been avoided if we had just paid closer attention.

A few days later, I was awakened by Bonnie at two in the morning. She needed to go to the bathroom. I slipped out of bed quietly, not wanting to wake up Lou. As we got to the door, I grabbed a leash and put it on her. "Not this time," I whispered to her. "I know better. You're staying with me."

I did a quick look out the back door for skunks. I saw none. Satisfied, I stepped out with her and waited for her to do her business. As she sniffed around, I half-closed my eyes from drowsiness. Suddenly, I was awakened by being jerked and pulled to the ground.

In the darkness, I could barely make out the scene in front of me, but I knew exactly what had happened. The stench of rotten eggs overwhelmed me. Bonnie had found another skunk, and this time she had included me in her adventure! The skunk had sprayed both of us. My eyes started to burn and tear. I could feel myself getting nauseous from the stench. I managed to get myself up, gather her and head toward the house.

I entered the house as quietly as I could. I didn't want to wake my husband and have to explain that the dog had gotten sprayed on my watch.

As I crept up the stairs, Lou's voice yelled out, "OH, MY GAWD! DID SHE GET SPRAYED AGAIN?" I cringed and realized there was no hiding it. How could I? The skunk's scent had permeated the air in the house and woken him from a deep sleep.

"Yes," I answered sheepishly as I ushered her into the bathroom so we could clean up.

I washed the dog and myself until there was no more hot water. Satisfied that I had gotten all the smell off us, I climbed back into bed and tried to get some rest. It had been a long night, and I had to be at work the next day.

The next morning as I sat at my desk, I shared the story of our skunk encounter with my boss.

"Ah, that explains it," he said.

"Explains what?"

"The skunk smell coming from you."

"Seriously?"

"Yep, you stink!"

"Maybe I should go home."

"Yes," he said as he playfully grabbed his nose and pinched it. "Maybe you should."

I took his advice and went home. I spent the day showering and using an assortment of odor-neutralizing concoctions until the smell was finally gone.

I wish I could say that was the last time that Bonnie ever got sprayed by a skunk. It wasn't. It was, thankfully, the last time that I did.

— Kathy Diamontopoulos —

Lizzie Meets Lassie

Why does watching a dog be a dog fill
one with happiness?
~Jonathan Safran Foer

Every dog has its day. For my dog, Lizzie, that day came when I took her to the W Hotel in New York City to meet Lassie.

It was a once-in-a-lifetime opportunity to see a genuine superstar, a very special canine who not only has achieved fame for her talent and heroics but is beloved by children and adults across the globe. I could tell Lassie was thrilled. And a little bit awed.

After all, Lizzie did win the blue ribbon in the Pooch Who Can Smooch competition at Puttin' on the Dog, the annual talent show and Adopt-A-Dog fundraiser that is held in Greenwich, Connecticut. It regularly draws about five thousand people, many celebrity judges and several hundred canine contestants.

Lizzie has also been the star of numerous columns that have appeared in newspapers across the country and around the world. She has even been on the public radio show *Marketplace*. But she has never let fame go to her pretty head and has remained sweet and unaffected.

Lassie has done all right for herself, too. She is a Hollywood icon whose latest movie is *Lassie*. (The producers chose the title so people wouldn't mistake her for Lizzie, I guess.) She's even an entrepreneur with a line of pet food, biscuits and treats called Lassie Natural Way.

When Lizzie and I walked into Suite 1805 at the W, Lassie was sitting on a couch surrounded by her entourage, including her trainer

Carol Riggins, her veterinarian Dr. Jeff Werber, and her agent John Fraser.

Lizzie and Lassie hit it off right away, greeting each other with kisses on both cheeks, Hollywood style. It was nice to see that these two major stars wouldn't be getting into a cat fight.

Lizzie, true to her standing as Pooch Who Can Smooch champion, was air-kissing everyone in the room.

"You might want to trademark Lizzie's air kisses," said Fraser, adding that he'd be honored to be her agent, too.

I must confess that I was hoping Lizzie would land a movie deal. (Her first film would be, of course, *Lizzie*.)

But then reality set in. "Lizzie's beautiful, but she's a little too pleasantly plump," Werber said diplomatically. "In order for her to look good walking down the red carpet, she'd have to lose a few pounds."

Naturally, he recommended that Lizzie change her diet and start eating Lassie Natural Way products. They seem to have helped Lassie keep her girlish figure.

But when Riggins offered Lizzie a treat, she politely declined. Maybe her feelings were hurt. To show Lizzie how good the treats are, I ate one. Actually, it wasn't bad. I only wish I had a beer to wash it down with, but I was told that Lassie only drinks water.

Riggins put a treat on Lassie's nose. On command, Lassie flipped the treat into the air and snapped it up. What talent! Then I tried it. Riggins put a treat on my nose. On command, I flipped it into the air, but it bounced off my mustache and fell to the floor.

"You need more practice," Riggins said.

As all this was going on, scenes from Lassie's new movie, which got a special screening at the Tribeca Film Festival, were playing on a screen behind us. Lassie wasn't even watching.

"She's already seen it," Fraser explained.

I asked if Lassie ever got tired of saving Timmy on the old TV show.

"The stupid kid was always falling down a well or getting trapped in a cave, and Lassie would have to run for help," I noted. "She played those scenes with great enthusiasm."

"Lassie is a good actor," Fraser said.

I asked about persistent rumors that Lassie really isn't a girl.

"I told you she's a good actor," Fraser replied with a wink.

She's also very sweet. And, like Lizzie, unaffected by her fame and talent.

After we all posed for pictures, and Lassie gave Lizzie a pawto-graph, it was time to leave. The two stars said goodbye with one last air kiss. Then Lassie settled back onto the couch for a beauty nap while I chauffeured Lizzie back home.

As both of them will tell you, it's anything but a dog's life.

—Jerry Zezima—

The Golf Outing

You are wise to remember that a well-developed
sense of humor is the pole that adds a balance
to your steps as you walk the tightrope of life.
~William Arthur Ward

I kicked off my flip-flops and felt the soft spring grass below my feet. I sank into the Adirondack chair, cloaked in the shade of our backyard maple tree. I had my dog at my feet and stroked his fluffy head while I read a book. I took a deep breath and smiled contentedly while sipping my green tea. It was the end of May, and the weather was flirting with summer.

This was the first day I had to myself in months. We were in strict, stay-at-home mode since March, when COVID started to spread in Westchester County, New York, where we live. We made the most of staying in our family pod, reading books, playing games and cooking together, but I was ready for a relaxing day alone.

As the weather changed, we started spending more time outdoors. My husband offered to take our boys on a golf outing that afternoon, leaving me home with my seventy-pound Bouvier des Flandres puppy named Sirius Black.

Sirius is a herd dog, and he thinks his family is his herd. He wants to be around us all the time. If I sit down, he's at my feet. He's not a dog that runs away. Our yard adjoins a golf course. He sees golfers walking or carting along all the time and never even meanders in their direction.

But just as I settled into my shady chair, a maintenance golf cart zipped by my yard. The maintenance carts have loud engines and make a sudden noise that cuts through the quiet. Sirius had never heard it before and popped up, barking. He bolted after the cart.

The cart was flying across the course, and my dog sprinted after it, barking loudly. Barefoot, I darted after Sirius, screaming "HOLD" and "TO ME" to no avail. Golfers were watching me, pausing their games to avoid striking me as I ran across the fairway. Someone didn't see me at first and yelled "FORE!" Thank goodness, he missed us.

Meanwhile, the maintenance man had no idea that a giant dog was chasing him, unable to hear anything over his loud engine. Finally, a golfer waved him down and indicated for him to look back. When he did, it was clear from his expression that he was terrified. I was mortified. I kept running barefoot after them, calling my dog, trying not to notice all the people staring at us.

The golfer could see that the maintenance man was frightened and offered to drive the cart toward me to lead the dog back to me. When we finally met, I grabbed Sirius by the collar, thanked the golfer and apologized profusely. I yelled an apology to the maintenance man, and then I yelled a louder apology to everyone in general. Then, I did a walk of shame back toward my house, clutching my dog's collar as we trotted along.

And then, it happened.

I begged him not to do it. "Oh God. Please, Sirius. No, no, no."

Right there, in the middle of a fairway, as all the golfers patiently waited for us to get out of the way, Sirius pooped! I didn't have my shoes, let alone a poop bag. "I am so sorry!" I bellowed, as my face went hot.

When I made it home, I called my husband.

"I hope you all had a nice golf outing today because Sirius had his own outing, and we are never leaving this house again!"

— Kelly Bakshi —

Mud Run

Let's choose to do something really difficult,
something that saves lives, and let's do
that thing with people we love.
~Donald Miller

As the rain came down in buckets, Mom ran around shouting, "I can't find Penny. I can't find Penny!"

"Okay, calm down," I urged her as I stuck my feet in my shoes. I told my two younger sisters to stay in the house in case the dog came back so they could call her inside from the door.

With that, Mom and I took off, calling out "Penny!" as we went searching frantically.

At the time, we lived on a five-acre farm, so I thought to myself, *Well, this is going to be fun. There will be no dry clothes tonight.*

"Penny! Penny!" We called to her over and over, wondering if we could even be heard above the noise of the storm. Mom and I split up.

Finally, I heard Mom yelling as she came running. While huffing and puffing, she said, "She's having the puppies!"

In shock, I asked, "What? Where?"

Between breaths, Mom pointed and said, "Down alongside house one!" (That would be the chicken house to you non-farm folks.) Mom continued, "She's dug a hole in the side of the embankment. But the water is rising fast! I'm afraid they're going to drown!"

Good old Penny had dug a hole in the middle of a seven-foot-deep irrigation-ditch embankment.

Well of course she did.

"Show me where!" I yelled over the rain. Mom took off and I followed her.

Penny would not let us get anywhere near her or her puppies. I told Mom to get Penny out of there and get her back to the house.

Mom shouted, "She'll probably only come if we have one of her puppies!"

Naturally.

Urgently, I insisted that Mom follow my lead. "Get Penny up here with us and hold onto her. I'll go down, snag a pup, and hand him up to you. Then you do whatever you have to in order to get them both out of here."

I stepped back, and Mom finally coaxed Penny to climb the bank. Mom grabbed her by the collar and held on. Penny was snarling and growling. Mom tried to soothe her. "It's okay. Terry's just trying to help your babies."

I walked down the muddy embankment at an angle in a feeble attempt to keep my footing.

Down I went. I could hear the whimpering of pups. What I could not discern was whether or not I heard any water moccasins. Or any other water-loving snake, for that matter. *Damn dog* was all I could think as I said a short prayer, stuck my hand into the black hole, and pulled out a handful of fur. I was struggling to get back up in the dark with all the mud. It was slippery.

I handed Mom the first pup, and they all took off.

At that time, it was my first real chance to look down and assess the situation. It wasn't good. Like I said, we were at the back of the property, which is a hike on a good day.

Sigh.

We had to repeat the process seven more times.

On the final uphill slipping-and-sliding, I finally lost my balance. There was nothing to grab onto. We were headed for the bottom of the fast-moving ditch.

Mom reached down and grabbed me by my wrist while yelling, "Hold on!" She was trying to pull me up. I was trying to get my footing while holding a wiggly puppy tucked into my ribs like a football.

Once I made it back up to the top, I passed the final fur ball off to Mom.

"Are you okay?" she yelled.

I dropped to all fours. I was exhausted. I just nodded my head and motioned for her to go on without me. Once I caught up to the new puppies and their momma, I saw that my mother had had a stroke of genius.

Dad had a camper top that went on the back of the pickup truck. It was lying in the grass since it was off-season. Mom had popped open a little end door and stuffed Penny and the babies in there.

"They'll be safe and dry until tomorrow morning," Mom said as she pulled me toward the house.

Yeah, and then Penny and I were going to have a serious talk about safe sex.

— Terry L. Cooper —

Chapter
2

Be a Friend

12

Morning Inspection

*Animals are such agreeable friends — they ask
no questions; they pass no criticisms.*
~George Eliot

My husband and I were doing some yard work one day when we heard a chorus of meowing coming from beneath our front porch. Upon inspecting the underside of our hollow concrete staircase we discovered three tiny, black-and-white kittens nestled together. Although tempted to take the furry babies inside, we opted to wait and see if the mother returned. We kept a close watch on the porch until we were certain that the mewing critters had truly been abandoned.

Naturally, our next course of action was to get the kittens inside and fed, although there was one problem that my husband and I had to think about: Carver.

Carver is our one-year-old, floppy-eared Coonhound/Beagle mix. While friendly to dogs and people alike, Carver has always demonstrated the desire to prey upon any living thing smaller than his head. So, naturally, my husband I were cautious about bringing three young kittens into our house. Per advice that we looked up on the Internet, some people suggested that we calmly introduce our dog to the cats. After keeping the babies in a warm, blanketed basket for the night, we opted to show Carver his new roommates in the morning.

The result? He loved them. Immediately demonstrating gentleness, Carver carefully sniffed and nudged at the kittens; any worries about his predatory instincts went out the window. Even after putting the three cats down on the ground, Carver doted over them and watched them keenly as they tumbled around and played together. The kittens quickly warmed up to the brown giant that towered over them as well. They even began to follow him to his bed and attempt to cuddle up to his face.

While my husband and I are still in the process of finding homes for two kittens (we've decided to keep one), we've been keeping the trio in a bedded cage in the living room at night. We open the cage in the morning and let the kittens wander out on their own. Carver has developed a weirdly adorable ritual when this happens.

As we open the cage and the cats start to head out, Carver will go to one of them and begin to sniff at it, poking and prodding its body with his nose. Sometimes, he'll give it a lick or partially lift it into the air using his snout, as if checking the underside of the animal. When he completes this routine with the first kitten, he'll promptly move onto the second, and then the third. My husband and I have since referred to this process as Carver's "morning inspection" of the cats, and he has done the same thing without fail for weeks now. What he's inspecting for, I don't know, but it is certainly adorable, and we always laugh at it.

The cats don't seem to mind or are at least indifferent to it. They'll sometimes paw at Carver's nose or shoot him a look of annoyance as he does it. My husband likens it to parents giving their kids a once-over before they head out for the day. I'm not sure what it could be either, but I know dogs are pack animals, and Carver has very much accepted the kittens as members of the family. Maybe he's just checking on the babies and has strong paternal instincts? Who knows, but for now the cats get a doting big brother and his daily ritual of morning inspections.

— Brittany O'Connor —

13

Love at First Nuzzle

A kind gesture can reach a wound
that only compassion can heal.
~Steve Maraboli

My wife and I had recently retired and were looking for a dog. A small, old dog.

What we ended up with was entirely different.

She was curled up on a mat in the far corner of her 5'x6' cubicle at the Upland Animal Shelter. We had passed her three times already, oblivious that a dog was in there. My wife saw her first and called out. Long, spindly legs unfolded, and a beautiful yellow Lab ambled over to the metal mesh, stuck her nose through and nuzzled my wife's fingers.

And that was all it took. Love at first nuzzle.

She had been picked up two weeks before by the Upland Police Department. I say "picked up," but in reality she had jumped into the patrol car when they opened the door. The shelter's vet told us she weighed eighty pounds and was probably only two years old.

So much for a small, old dog. We now had a young, big dog.

My wife named her Scout after the little girl in *To Kill a Mockingbird*. She was house-trained, obedient and, aside from the time she bolted through our screen door to chase a skateboarder down the street with me sprinting after her in my PJs, a model pet.

Perhaps it was because she had been abandoned that led to her being such a gentle soul. If an animal on TV appeared to be in any kind of distress, Scout would stare forlornly and make a low, guttural distress call, prompting us to quickly change the channel. Her patience and forbearance toward our two grandchildren, who were terrified of dogs, won them over to the point that they would curl up on her oversized bed and nap with her.

But it was Scout's ability to charm a grumpy, recalcitrant neighbor that convinced my wife and me that we had adopted a truly special dog.

Her name was Imogene Van Pelt. When we moved into our new home, we were warned by the Neighborhood Welcome Wagon that Ms. Van Pelt was not to be trifled with and, whenever possible, to give her a wide berth. Unfortunately, this latter bit of advice was simply not feasible. She was my next-door neighbor.

Each day, Ms. Van Pelt would assume a lordly presence on her front porch swing and glare at all who dared pass. For months, I tried to get her to warm up to me, helloing and smiling and waving. In response, all I got was that impenetrable, steely, cold glare.

That is, until we got Scout.

I made it a practice to take Scout on morning and nightly walks, as much for my middle-aged weight gain as for Scout's olfactory enjoyment. And I scrupulously avoided Madame Van Pelt's domain — until one night when darkness obscured her diminutive presence on the porch swing, and I dared to cross that forbidden threshold.

"Who's that?" a scratchy voice asked.

"Oh, uh, good evening, Ms. Van Pelt," I stammered. "Didn't see you there. It's me. Your next-door neighbor."

"Not you. I know who you are, hollering and waving your arms at me like a crazy man. Who's that with you?"

"Why, it's Scout. She's a yellow Lab. My wife and I adopted her from the Upland Animal Shelter."

"Scout's a boy's name."

"My wife named her after the little girl from *To Kill a Mockingbird*. Are you familiar with the novel?"

Ms. Van Pelt snorted. "Course I am. Not a nitwit, you know."

By this time, Scout had heard her name mentioned more than once and assumed that this must be about her. She gave a steady pull on her extendable leash and inched toward Ms. Van Pelt.

"Is she going to bite me?"

"No, Ma'am. She just wants to say hello."

"Got her shots?"

"Yes, Ma'am. Current on all her shots."

Scout was now directly before Ms. Van Pelt, staring, looking for some sign of approval. When none came, Scout moved cautiously forward and gently laid her head on Ms. Van Pelt's lap, nuzzling her with her long snout.

There was a moment of silence. And then I heard a quiet, delicate voice whispering, "There there girl. You're a good dog. Good dog."

Through the dim, receding light, I could vaguely make out Ms. Van Pelt stroking Scout's head and neck.

And that was all it took. Love at first nuzzle.

From then on, whenever Scout and I passed Ms. Van Pelt's house (or Imogene, as she now preferred to be called), Scout and I would stop — or, rather, Scout would stop and pull me in the direction of Imogene who was forever perched on her porch swing. We would say our obligatory hellos, but mostly Imogene would focus her attention on Scout, stroking her fur and speaking softly to her. And Scout would relish the attention, begging for more by scooping up Imogene's hand again and again with her long nose, adding the occasional lick for emphasis.

And then one day…

It was Saturday, and, as my day off dictated, I was mowing the lawn. I had almost finished when my wife came out to review my progress. "Hey, where's Scout? I thought she was out here with you."

I did a quick once-over of my surroundings, looking in her familiar napping spots.

Nothing.

"Here girl," I called, adding a whistle for good measure.

Nothing.

"The gate's open," my wife quickly observed. "Do you think she got out?"

Becoming anxious, we searched everywhere — under the patio,

behind bushes, the side of the house.

Nothing.

And then, something suddenly occurred to me. "I think I know where she might be."

A quick reconnaissance confirmed my guess. Scout was next door. And here was the truly surprising thing: She was sitting, quite comfortably, on the porch swing with her new friend, Ms. Imogene Van Pelt.

"Looks like we've found our furry fugitive," my wife quipped as we approached.

"Figured you might come looking for her," Imogine laughed. "We've been having a merry time, Scout and me. Already made arrangements to meet next Saturday, assuming that's agreeable to Mom and Dad."

Which, of course, it was.

Now, every Saturday and sometimes during the week, I escort Scout next door where she assumes her position next to Imogene, sitting there like the queen she is, with the porch swing swaying gently back and forth.

As for Imogene, she has become quite the celebrity. The neighbors have become accustomed to seeing an eighty-pound Lab sitting next to an elderly woman on a porch swing. They pass by, exchanging pleasantries with Imogene, who returns their kind words with ones of her own. And she smiles. The grumpy, recalcitrant woman is no more.

And Scout? She is what she has always been, what most dogs are: a lover, a forgiver, an extender of unconditional love to anyone with a kind word, a warm heart and a gentle stroke of the hand, changing the world one nuzzle at a time.

— Dave Bachmann —

Made for Each Other

Being a hero to someone, even if it is a dog,
is a feeling like no other. Though it can be frustrating,
it can be the most rewarding thing to give someone
a second chance at a happy life.
~Elizabeth Parker, Finally Home

Standing in the curve of her bay window, my sister smiles as she watches a short, elderly woman wearing a bold green bandanna, walking slowly and carefully into the wind, holding tightly to a leash with her purse over one arm. At the end of the leash is a small, black dog with an odd, prancing gait. Together, the two walk to the end of the block and stop at a postage-stamp-sized church yard where the older lady waits patiently as the dog makes use of the lawn.

When she is finished, she waits patiently for her companion to make an about-face, and together they slowly head back in the direction that they came. They make good time, obviously eager to get out of the cold wind. Soon, the slam of the downstairs door notifies us that they have returned.

I follow my sister to the door and hear the clattering of the dog's claws as she scrambles up the stairs, followed by Grandma's slower, heavier tread. My sister opens the door and waits patiently for them to appear. Grandma, red-faced from exertion as well as the chilly wind, ascends the stairs behind Casey, who waits for her on the landing. It took Cheryl a long time to get Grandma to remember to release Casey's leash before scaling the stairs. These two are devoted to each other and, despite the private, enclosed stairway, Grandma is afraid to let go of the leash until she is sure that Casey is safe.

Stepping into the apartment that she shares with my sister, Grandma makes the same announcement that she always does after returning.

"Shooey ding dong," Grandma says, wiping her nose. "It's colder than a witch's…"

"Elbow!" Cheryl quickly finishes with a grin.

Grandma flashes a devilish smile as her hazel eyes sparkle. They both know that it's not the witch's elbow that is cold, but still they enjoy the familiar banter.

Grandma removes the leash from Casey's collar and gently rubs the dog's soft, black ears. It seems that Grandma and my sister's little dog Casey were made for each other. Grandma and the little Cockapoo each had unfortunate vascular accidents. Grandma had a stroke, which permanently impaired her short-term memory, while Casey had a violent allergic reaction to inoculations, which resulted in her being of limited mental abilities, but theirs was a symbiotic partnership. Each complemented the other. Grandma was unable to remember so many things, including the short routes she walked daily. So, while Grandma watched out for cars and other dangers, Casey led her safely home every time.

When my sister discovered the benefits of the relationship, she began to send them out together for walks and potty runs. At first, she followed at a safe distance, but when she was certain that the simple route had imprinted upon them both, she sent them out alone. She didn't want them to discover her spying upon them because Grandma needed to feel self-sufficient after a lifetime of independence, and Casey, as all dogs do, just needed to be needed.

After some time, my sister began to feel secure enough to observe them from her bay window. If necessary, she could bolt down the stairs to the street and get them back on track in less than a minute, due to the fact that Grandma had all the speed of a glacier. Her memory impairment caused Grandma to dither uncertainly at times, and instinctively Casey would then take the lead. It was a win/win, each working within their strengths.

The daily walk was important for Grandma's health and helped to keep her blood-sugar levels under control. At the same time, it allowed Casey to take care of her "business."

As their walks became an established routine, people along the route began to protectively watch out for them. Even the corner church made arrangements with my sister when they heard the tale from the furniture store next door. Because it was safer for the two, they allowed Casey to use the grassy area for her "business" as long as it was cleaned up every day or so. In that little city block of people, Grandma and Casey were as safe as if they were within the arms of their family. She became Grandma to them all.

Grandma had led a life of lonely solitude after Grandpa, her spouse of nearly fifty years, passed, but now she was enjoying a time of community with new friends and supporters.

Occasionally, Grandma would try to overrule Casey's imprinted path, even as Casey would try to steer her back on course. If Cheryl wasn't fast enough, one of Grandma's shop friends would hurry to Grandma and get her headed back in the right direction. It seemed everybody on the block watched out for them as they went about their daily travels.

Often they would initiate a conversation with Grandma to break up their day, if things were slow. Grandma would sink down onto the ever-present benches and rest while they talked. In the winter, some took her inside for a warm cup of coffee.

When it was too cold, icy or wet, my sister would take over Casey's walks, but Grandma sometimes insisted on going along. She'd pop up from her chair, with her purse in one hand and her shoes in the other, and off they'd go. Clutching my sister's arm, Grandma would wave to her "fan club" as they smiled and waved back from the shelter of their businesses.

Instead of dwelling upon the two companions' limitations, my sister had given Grandma a small portion of her world and freedom back while Casey fulfilled her purpose as a friend and servant to man.

— Laurel L. Shannon —

15

Humans

Properly trained, a man can be dog's best friend.
~Corey Ford

Humans have no sense of smell.
Also, they don't hear that well.
They have smooth skin, no fur, no scales,
And humans don't have any tails.
They have the most amazing claws,
And balance on their two hind paws.
They chatter on like chimpanzees,
As if they have a mouth disease.
And when they're happy underneath,
They curve their lips and show their teeth.
They're rude to everyone they meet,
Because humans don't know how to greet.
Wherever there is a good whiff,
They never even take a sniff.
They're dirty creatures on the whole.
They poop right in the water bowl,
Or treasure it in little bags,
Scooped up faster than a tail wags.
They store food in a special vault,
Locked with no key, no chain or bolt.
They leave the choicest parts alone —

They even throw away the bone.
They get around in moving crates,
That reek so much it nauseates.
But humans don't know how to ride.
They never put their heads outside.
They spend their time staring at screens.
They even talk to their machines.
You see how lonely they can be,
And why they need warm company.
And almost everywhere they go,
They like to play a game called throw,
With flying discs, or balls, or sticks.
They can be taught all kinds of tricks.
They respond well to licks and barks.
They like the beach, and trails and parks,
But won't go out unless compelled.
And somehow they have to be held,
Usually with some kind of tether,
Made from a chain or strip of leather,
To make sure that they don't get away.
It's sad to see a human stray.
They are not easy to maintain,
And yet love makes it worth the pain.
With the right training, in the end,
A human could be a best friend.

— Stuart Stromin —

16

Four-Pawed Caregiver

True devotion is motivated by love alone and
devoid of selfish entanglements.
~Rick Hocker

The cabinet door creaks as I descend the hallway stairs. No one is home except for me and my two dogs, but there is a strange noise. I stop on the bottom step and slowly peer around the wall into the kitchen. And then I see them. My rescue Boxer mix, Chance, pulls the bag of pig ears out from under the sink where I hide them — not very well. He tears open the bag and pulls out an ear.

It looks as if he's helping himself, but he carries the ear over to our blind and deaf English Spaniel, Patti, who sniffs the floor searching for the ear. Chance moves it up closer until Patti latches onto the ear. She tries to chew it but can't. It slips out of her mouth, and she slumps in defeat. Her ability to chew, much diminished with age, keeps her from enjoying the treat. Not willing to give up, Chance pulls back the ear, chews on it to soften it, and presents it again to Patti, who accepts it enthusiastically. A tear wells up in my eye as I watch. How incredibly kind of Chance, especially considering Patti's treatment of him.

In the beginning, only Patti existed in our household. She was a purebred English Spaniel, a gorgeous creature, but she would bite — randomly and without warning.

Thankfully, we lived fairly far from other people and had a fenced-in yard. The word *diva* doesn't begin to describe Patti's entitled attitude.

So, imagine how she felt, after seven years of being the only pet with a crew of five human servants, when a new dog entered the picture.

Oddly, she accepted the tiny pup as her own and carried him by the nape of the neck until he became too heavy. Then, sibling rivalry reared its ugly head. Chance, as a bouncy, friendly puppy, snagged more than his share of attention. Patti responded by bullying the pup and eating his food. Anytime someone offered Chance a treat, Patti would steal it. Despite this mean-girl approach, Chance adored Patti. He shadowed her every move. When we moved to an eighty-acre farm, the two would often leave in the morning — only to return for dinner.

When Patti got dementia, she sometimes couldn't find her way home even when she was just yards away. I'd instruct Chance to bring her home. Without any training, he'd gently guide her to the steps and use his own larger body as a barrier to prevent her from falling down the steps. By this time, I realized their adventures were no longer led by Patti, who'd lost her ability to navigate the woods and farmland. It was Chance who was herding the older dog through their old haunts.

In most situations, this is where the younger dog seizes the role of alpha dog as the older dog's abilities fade — not so with Chance. In the past, when they ate a lamb-and-rice dry dog food that the vet recommended, Patti would only eat the lamb pellets, leaving the rice pellets. Then, she'd go over to Chance's bowl and eat his lamb pellets. We tried to discourage this behavior by feeding them in different rooms, but Patti usually found a way. Now, I assumed that Chance would actually eat his meal undisturbed. Nevertheless, he would eat the rice pellets but leave the lamb pellets for Patti, pushing the dish across the floor and into the next room for her.

His behavior baffled me. Would I be that generous to someone who constantly stole my food and treats? Would I be that understanding of a person who took the best napping place and growled at me if I even tried to use the favored spot where the sunbeam always hit? Nope. Chance could teach me a great deal about being kind.

As Patti continued to lose her hearing, eyesight, and any sense of where she was, Chance became her keeper, often pulling pillows and throws from the couch to create a comfy bed on the floor. He even snuggled close, allowing Patti to use his body as a pillow. As the roles changed, he went from follower to caregiver, watching over his old friend.

Cesar Millan, the dog whisperer, once mentioned that dogs teach us empathy. Chance sure did.

—MK Scott—

17

You Can't Fool Me

*Your visions will become clear only when
you can look into your own heart.*
~Carl Jung

ur elderly German Shepherd was not pleased when we came home with a kitten. "Why would you do this to me?" his eyes pleaded as the tiny ball of fluffy energy scrambled up his back and batted at his ears.

The kitten adored her new big brother. She followed him everywhere, occasionally jumping up and clasping his tail for a ride until he shook her off. When he settled down on his bed for a nap, she was right there, using him as a jungle gym, begging him to play with her.

The old gentleman acted like he was above her. He would ignore all her antics until it finally got to be too much. Without ever looking at her, his large paw would whip out and pin her squirming underneath. While the kitten fought vainly for freedom, he would lazily look around the room as if he hadn't trapped a feisty feline.

"Kitten?" his nonchalant look would say if he caught our eye. "What kitten? I haven't seen a kitten." This was his attitude most of the time, as if denying her existence would make her disappear.

If she was noisy or naughty, he would look at us in disgust. "I tried to tell you this was a bad idea. Do something to make it stop." He became a master of the long-suffering sigh.

I guess you can't give an old dog a new friend, we decided. *Ah, well, at least he tolerates her.*

When the kitten was six months old, we took her to the vet to be spayed. The dog was unhappy to see us walk out the door carrying the cat. He loved adventures and riding in the car. Why was the kitten going somewhere while he stayed home? This was not the natural order of things.

The kitten had to stay at the vet's overnight. In the morning, we decided to let the still-grumpy dog ride along to pick her up. When we got back into the car with our groggy kitten, the dog was overjoyed. He was beside himself with relief to see her. All traces of Mr. Cool were gone. His beloved baby sister was back, and he couldn't be more pleased. We had to restrain him from smothering her in kisses.

Back home, he insisted we put the kitten on his bed where he curled up next to her and stood guard until she was back to her feisty, annoying self. Once she was healed, he tried to return to his previous aloofness, but we knew the truth.

You *can* give an old dog a new friend.

— Mary DeVries —

18

A Brother from Another Mother

You can't buy happiness, but you can rescue it.
~Author Unknown

t had hit over a hundred degrees here in Southern California, so I decided Mollie the Beagle and I needed to go to the air-conditioned pet store to cool off. She could use a new toy, and I could pick up some dog food.

We have been through a lot together — some illnesses, my husband's death — but happy times, too. Mollie is my pal, and even though her roots are getting gray just like mine, she has some good years left. An only child, she pretty much runs the house and lets me live there. Mollie has her side of the bed, and I have mine.

So, when I started considering a feline addition to the family, I wasn't sure if Mollie would agree. Outside, she chases cats off our property, no matter how much I object. She has become my protector and companion. Would she let another member into our pack?

"Hey Mollie, let's go look at the rescue-adoption cages. Wouldn't a cat be nice? You need some company."

Mollie followed on her leash, unaware where I was taking her. We got to the glassed-in wall of cats, and a strange thing happened. Mollie didn't bark, whine or get excited but went over to a cubby on the bottom row. A beautiful gray-and-white fur ball walked up and pushed its nose against the glass. Mollie put her nose against his with only the cold pane between them. She sat there mesmerized as if in a trance. Could this be? Was this love at first sight?

I went to the checkout counter and asked a few questions. The cat was a male and he was roughly eighteen months old. Perfect! He was found living on the streets and eating garbage, which accounted for his thin frame. I asked when Mollie and I could adopt him.

"Come back Saturday with these papers filled out," the cashier said, handing me a questionnaire. "We sponsor Helen Sanders CatPAWS rescue, but the woman who handles everything won't be here until then."

"Thanks. Well Mollie, looks like you're getting a brother from another mother," I said.

Mollie seemed pleased, and although I was skeptical, I couldn't wait. Would Mollie feel so smitten when she found out he was moving in and staying?

Saturday rolled around, and with more tidbits, food, litter and toys than I'd need for ten cats, I took our new addition home.

Brodie turned out to be a real pistol. His name had been Mr. Magoo before I changed it, and I could see why. He had a goofy personality.

I followed the instructions I found on Google for introducing new cats to the family. Everything went smoothly, but Brodie was a very active guy. He'd run up and down the hall at a hundred miles an hour and slam into the walls. He loved to play with silver pipe cleaners twisted in a loop, jumping over six feet to catch them. He didn't want to be petted except when he said so. To do otherwise would get you a bite on the hand. He attacked my ankles when I walked down the hall, and he loved to run up, nip me and take off. He was a real hit-and-run artist.

I worried about how Mollie was taking to this spastic cat running all over the furniture and commandeering her doggie bed. Life on the streets had made him wary of any affection. Although they were able to be in the same room together without incident, they stayed clear of interaction. Brodie seemed spooked when Mollie barked, and she gave him a wide berth.

I was worried. Brodie wasn't the lovable guy I had first anticipated. I think Mollie was skeptical that he would ever be a worthy pack member.

One morning about three months later, while I was having my coffee, Mollie tried to play with Brodie. With her butt in the air in the typical doggie-play stance, she approached him and started to gently nudge him and whine. Brodie seemed to like this and put this head down to rub her. Then, all of a sudden, she started getting rougher, which got her a clean swipe on the nose that made her yip and head for my bed.

I was sad. Wasn't my little family going to work out after all? Was this the start of the end? I couldn't give up Brodie now. Who would put up with his antics? They would definitely send him to the shelter or worse! I loved him, and this was his furever home.

Upset, I left at noon and went to do errands. I was afraid when I came home that I would find some fur or bloodshed, but I had to see if they could work it out. I didn't think Mollie would hurt Brodie, but he was a feisty guy.

I prayed, "Dear God, please let my kiddos get along. I can't abandon one of your creatures."

When I arrived home about an hour later, they were cuddled together, yawning on Mollie's doggie bed. Mollie looked up as if to say, "What's up, Mom?" I started to cry; my little family had reached a truce.

It's been six years now, and Mollie has accepted Brodie as a crazy pack member. They continue to find their own compromises and are working it out. Brodie has calmed down, but his exuberance shines through. He chatters and makes crazy noises as he does yoga every morning. He's become quite a hit on my Facebook page doing his downward dog, which puts Mollie to shame. Brodie sleeps cuddled between Mollie and me. Brodie has learned that no one is going to hurt him. He loves kisses and lets me pet him all I want. I caught Mollie and him nuzzling each other last week.

Mollie knew what she was doing the day she chose Brodie. We needed a little spice in our lives, and we got a red-hot pepper.

— Sallie A. Rodman —

19

Doxie Love

*Acquiring a dog may be the only time
a person gets to choose a relative.*
~Author Unknown

The news articles were heartbreaking. The pictures were worse. Animal-control officers removed seventy-one miniature Dachshunds from a home in Fall River, Massachusetts, where they had been neglected by their breeder to the point of abuse.

The most disconcerting part was that we were familiar with the breeder. Her home was where we had picked up our Dachshund Sadie five and a half years earlier. Sadie was born in Texas, but she had been shipped to Fall River to find a home. This should have been an alarm, but oddly it wasn't. We went through such an extensive adoption process that we joked it would have been easier to adopt a kid than it was to adopt Sadie.

Something had obviously gone terribly wrong in the years since. After several long discussions about whether to adopt one of the rescued dogs, my husband Steve and I decided we would try. Even though seventy-one Dachshunds seemed like a lot of dogs to re-home, the massive news coverage meant that people literally lined up on the day the dogs became available.

A snowstorm kept us away, and all the dogs were adopted in two days. I decided it wasn't meant to be, but I did register with a Dachshund rescue website. A few weeks later, a woman from the rescue group contacted me.

Two of the seventy-one adopted dogs were being returned and needed homes. They thought of us because we had already been pre-approved. We knew the breed well, love them, and have a quiet house. Plus, I work at home, so I had time to take care of a needy dog.

As soon as I saw the photo of Cooper, with his serious, little, old-man face, I knew he was going to be ours. I sent Steve an e-mail with his photo and the question, "Do you have enough love in your heart for this little guy?"

He did. Things happened quickly after that. I had already put in an application with the rescue group, but the contact person I spoke to said it would be better for the dog if the current owner and I did a private adoption because it would be much faster.

They put me in touch with a woman who lives in a northern part of our state. We talked on the telephone for two hours, and I learned a lot about Cooper from that conversation, including the fact that giving him up was incredibly difficult for her and her daughter.

The MSPCA had determined that Cooper was about two years old based on the condition of his teeth. He was most likely younger because all the rescued dogs had bad teeth due to the neglect.

Cooper had spent his entire life living in a crate with other dogs. He wasn't socialized to interact with humans. When he was rescued, his fur was caked with excrement. Despite many baths, the white part of his fur remained stained for months. Because he was never allowed out of his crate, his muscle development was very weak. At seven pounds, ten ounces, he appeared quite frail compared to our robust, twelve-pound Sadie.

The first person to adopt Cooper was very invested in saving him, but it just wasn't meant to be. It was a house with a lot of children, and Cooper was so intimidated by all the commotion that he never left his crate. His first adoptive mother explained that she didn't rescue him from a life in a crate just to have him live in a crate at her house. She and her thirteen-year-old daughter drove Cooper to our house during a snowstorm on Valentine's Day.

Sadie was thrilled with her new little brother, but Cooper was less enthusiastic. He refused to leave his crate, even for food and water.

On his second day with us, Sadie sat outside his crate trying to entice him to come out. When he ignored her, she climbed into the crate with him and snuggled by his side. He seemed happy to have the canine company, but he was still wary of us. The only way I could get Cooper to eat was feeding him by hand. I started worrying he was never going to be normal.

Our vet wasn't reassuring. He said that Cooper might be a broken dog and would probably always need the security of his crate so he could retreat whenever he felt threatened. He suggested moving Cooper's food and water bowls to the space next to his crate.

When we got home from the veterinarian, Sadie was so happy to see Cooper that she ran in circles around the living room. Then she ran over to her toy box and tipped it over to spill out all the toys. She grabbed a ball and tossed it in the air as if to show Cooper how to play.

Over the next few months, Sadie taught Cooper how to be a dog. I'm pretty sure she potty-trained him simply by example. He became her devoted follower. They cuddled together all day, and she was never out of his sight for long. He also slowly became more social with the humans in his house. He accepted me after just a day or two, but Steve had to work hard at it for months.

It was a slow but rewarding process. The longer he was with us, the more comfortable he became with us and our extended family. He still only lets me, Steve, my mother and one very gentle granddaughter pet him, but he has grown to tolerate everyone else without much more than a few protest barks when they arrive.

A few years later, Sadie slipped a disc in her spine and was paralyzed. After an expensive back surgery, she needed to be crated for six to eight weeks. This was torture for us all because Sadie had always been very active. But Cooper knew what to do.

Every day, Cooper rested outside her crate to keep her company. He never left her side as she slowly got better. The back surgery gave us eighteen more months with Sadie, but then she got cancer. She was in pain, so we had to say goodbye. We all grieved our beloved Sadie, but Cooper became despondent. He was so depressed that he spent most of his days hiding under the colorful afghan my grandmother crocheted for me. When visitors stopped by, he barely peeked his nose out.

After a few weeks of discussion, Steve and I decided he needed a new sister. We worried about whether he just specifically loved Sadie and if he would accept a new dog into our house. We found a new miniature Dachshund puppy we named Honey and sent up a prayer.

It was love at first sight. Cooper viewed Honey the same way that Sadie viewed Cooper: as a gift. Now, he happily lets her boss him around, and they snuggle together day and night.

— Laurie Higgins —

20

A Little Nudge Goes a Long Way

The dog was created specially for children.
He is the God of frolic.
~Henry Ward, The Most Famous Man in America

The look on my new neighbor's face quickly turned from elated to horrified as my children ran out of the house to meet her. I had just been telling Sandy about my children, Emma and Tucker. Emma, age seven, was to start second grade in the fall. Tucker, age four, was to enter preschool. Sandy, in turn, was telling me about her four children: Jane, nine; Joe, six; Christopher, three; and Kim, eighteen months. She seemed so pleased to have kids move into the neighborhood.

That was, until the door flung open and out ran Emma, Tucker and… Sam.

Sam was our six-year-old Labrador Retriever. He was a gorgeous, shiny black dog with a white stripe down his chest. He had soft brown eyes and a tail that wagged so hard it caused a slight breeze if you stood nearby. We had taken him in three years earlier as a foster, but he quickly became my third child and surrogate nanny to the kids. He had a sweet disposition and a playful demeanor. Sam loved to hang with the kids, serving as both playmate and protector.

Unbeknownst to me, Sandy was deathly afraid of dogs. She began to back up as he approached and let out a frightened gasp. I had never met anyone who didn't like dogs or experienced such an all-encompassing fear. I felt terrible.

As I saw her reaction, I quickly grabbed Sam by the collar and made him sit.

"He really is harmless," I said, trying to reassure her. Sandy looked at me, trying to stay composed, but I could see my assurances were unconvincing.

"I have to get the kids ready to go to their grandmother," she said as she backed away from me, graciously trying to remove herself from the situation.

As she turned to seek refuge in her house, her door swung open, and out ran a little, sandy-haired boy named Joe.

"A puppy!" he shouted. "A puppy!"

Emma and Tucker both beamed as they realized they had a new neighbor. Then, out ran Jane holding Kim, with Christopher quickly following behind.

I held Sam tightly as Sandy grabbed the younger boy. "Don't go near it!" she screamed as she grabbed Christopher.

I held Sam tighter and told the kids to all stay back.

"I'm so sorry, Sandy. But seriously, Sam is a good boy. He has never hurt anyone. He has been with us since Tucker was a toddler."

That did little to comfort her. The kids were circled around their mom, closely watching Sam. "Can we pet him?" Joe asked.

Sandy looked nervous but saw the desperation in her child's face.

"Okay, Joe, but be careful."

Emma showed Joe the proper way to slowly approach a dog with his hand facing down. Sam's tail was wagging at full speed as he accepted Joe's affection. With that, Jane too wanted to feel Sam's soft fur. She handed Kim to Sandy and put her hand out slowly. Sam quickly licked her hand, which elicited a loud giggle. The kids were won over, but I could tell it would take some time before Sandy would be a convert.

From that time forward, we were careful not to let Sam cross the street to our neighbors without me accompanying him. Emma and Tucker loved playing outside and always had Sam by their side in our yard. He served as guard, and if anyone approached the children, he would let out a warning bark for me to take notice.

One day, the kids were across the street playing. It warmed my heart to see all six kids outside together. Then I noticed the eighteen-month-old walking away from the rest, heading toward a little hill. There was a car approaching, and I let out a scream. "Watch the baby! She is going to fall down the hill into the street!"

With that, Sam stormed out the door. He ran across the street at a lightning-fast clip right toward the baby. I thought he was going to run straight into her. With his speed and strength, he could topple her and cause great harm.

But, instead, he ran up the hill, stopping just short of ramming into her. He gently nudged her back toward the house and away from the approaching car.

As the siblings ran toward her and Sam, I felt I could breathe again. Sam was a hero, but the kids were too involved in play to realize the gravity of the situation. The kids all cheered that Sam had come to play.

Then I saw Jane's face as she realized what had just happened and how lucky we all were that the baby didn't fall into the street. I went over and gave her a big hug.

I put Sam back on his leash and told them that Sam was whining to go out and play, but that he was in trouble with me as he didn't wait for me first. As one of the kids, he also needed to follow the rules and ask for permission. And, just like the neighbor kids, he had to have a buddy with him when going outside. "We must always watch after one another," I told them. "Especially the little ones."

With that, Sandy came out with snacks for the kids, unaware of what had just transpired. Jane and I shared a smile as she bent down and gave Sam a tight hug like he had never experienced.

Within the year, Sam made friends with all the neighbors on our short, little cul-de-sac. Within two years, almost every family on our street had a dog or two — except Sandy, who did eventually get a cat!

— Jeanne Blandford —

21

Rescued by the Dog

When I needed a hand, I found your paw.
~Author Unknown

With my rumpled pajamas sticking to my skin, I scuffed down the hall to the kitchen. Halfway there, I stopped as though my slippers had adhered to the carpet. I was stuck. Mired, immobilized, unable to free myself. If it hadn't been for my dog, I might have stayed that way for days. Maybe I would have remained cemented in place past all hope of saving me.

And here's the thing: It could happen again.

Good thing I have Molly, the bristle-faced bird dog. She'd come into my life when she was five, tick-infested and hungry, rescued from the neglect of an owner who'd used her as a pawn in a bitter divorce. Adopting her was one of those great strokes of luck that life sometimes grants us.

I certainly needed her on this particular day. It was a beautiful, sunny March day but I wasn't feeling it. Outside it was glorious. But inside me it was winter. I'd received two pieces of news. One was a writing assignment. It was an exciting opportunity, but it needed a fast turnaround. The other was a beloved family member's diagnosis, dire and frightening.

I was caught between the polarities, hopelessly tangled in my thoughts. One situation required fast action, while the other offered no action I could take that would change it. Meanwhile, I slumped against the wall, still in my sweaty jammies, unable to decide whether to get dressed or eat a banana. The clock ticked toward noon.

Molly, observing me from her position in a pool of sunlight on the carpet, knew that an intervention was called for. She'd seen me like this before, too tangled in my own thoughts to move.

At such times, I compound the problem by exhorting myself to achieve something significant. Write the novel! Find the cure! Climb the mountain! My inertia, I become convinced, can only be redeemed through heroic response — as though it makes sense to expect big things from myself when I'm at my lowest ebb.

Rousing herself from her cozy sunspot, Molly fetched her leash and brought it to me. Self-paralyzed as I was, I didn't see how a walk would fix anything. "I can't be wasting time. I should get something done," I told her.

Molly dropped the leash at my feet and gave me a pointed look. Did I mention she's a pointer?

Her gambit worked; she'd shamed me into action. Since I was clearly useless for anything else, I got dressed, grabbed her leash, and off we went on her favorite walk through the hills. At first, I grimly stomped along. But within minutes the fresh air, dappled sunlight, and comforting chatter of the creek began to work their magic. We spotted a pair of gray burros, fuzzy in the remnants of their winter coats, grazing in a meadow in contented company with a mule deer. Farther on, three sleek horses were turned out where they could munch happily on the lush grass amid the oaks and bay trees. Rivulets and freshets coursed down the hillsides, temporary waterways that would disappear in summer but now played their quiet music as though for eternity.

My steps felt lighter. My head did, too. By the time we stopped to admire a splendid gray squirrel lofting itself up a tree in which a resting turkey vulture also perched — a shaft of sunlight gleaming on its scarlet head — I felt as renewed as if I had molted.

Molly, too old and wise to chase squirrels, looked at me with an expression that clearly said, "You're welcome. Can we go home now?" When she's not acting as my live-in therapist, Molly devotes herself to con artistry and napping. She was clearly ready for the latter.

"You were right," I admitted. I took her home, gave her a dog cookie, and sat down to write. My internal season burst into springtime, and the words flowed. I was freed, and all it had taken was a walk and my dog.

This wasn't the first time she's gotten me unstuck. And, as I said, it may not be the last. I'd like to think that before I reach another self-created impasse, I'll remember to consult Molly. But, in case I don't, I keep the leash where she can reach it.

—Jan M. Flynn—

Step Outside Your Comfort Zone

22

A Dog and a Cookie

You can usually tell that a man is good
if he has a dog who loves him.
~W. Bruce Cameron, A Dog's Journey

When I was seventeen, I had a Border Collie mix by the name of Trixie. She was an awesome dog and loved me dearly but distrusted anyone else. She had been abused by men when she was younger, so anytime a man came around, she would emit a low growl and slink off to watch his every move from a safe distance. And, as he would leave, Trix would nip at his heels to hurry him away.

She simply hated men.

One afternoon, I was sitting on my porch reading a book with Trixie by my side when a young man who went to my high school walked by. He stopped and looked at me. He looked at Trixie, and he asked, "May I come in?"

I was not really interested in this guy, and I wanted to finish my book, so I said, "Sure. If you can get past my dog, you can come in." Knowing full well that this was not going to happen, I continued reading.

He lifted the latch on the gate and opened it to enter. I braced myself for the growl and the flurry that was coming. He walked in and closed the gate. Trixie remained oddly still. I peeked over the top of my book. The young man strode confidently toward me. I placed my book to the side, knowing that I was going to have to make a grab for Trixie at any moment to prevent bodily injury to this foolhardy boy.

I glanced down at my dog... and her tail was wagging! She got up and approached the young man. She licked his hand.

He asked, "May I sit down?" In wide-eyed, stunned silence, I nodded.

He said, "This is a very nice dog that you have here," and he petted her without hesitation.

I don't remember what else we talked about that evening because I couldn't for the life of me understand what had gotten into this dog of mine. She sat with us the entire time staring adoringly at him, tail wagging.

Six years later, this young man and I got married. Trixie was the bridesmaid at our wedding. My brother walked me down the aisle. While we waited for my bridal music to play, my brother whispered to me, "Who'd have ever thought this would have started with a dog and a cookie?" I asked him what in the world he was talking about.

And he told me this story.

This smitten young suitor (my future husband) had asked my brother how he could get on my good side to ask me on a date. My brother informed him that if he could make friends with my dog, then he might have a chance. So, every day, without my knowledge, he would stroll by our fence. When Trixie charged to the gate, barking and snarling to scare him away, he would drop her a piece of a peanut-butter cookie, talk to her lovingly, and keep on walking. Apparently, this went on for about six months, every day, until the day he asked if he could come in and sit on the porch with me.

Of course, she let him in because, although I was her first love, food was her second!

We have been married for thirty-six years. Thank you, Trix.

— Dorenda Crager Watson —

23

Dog Teach Dog

Whoever said you can't buy happiness
forgot little puppies.
~Gene Hill

Our Pomeranian-Terrier mix puppy, Dio, had to get up to ten pounds before I could teach him how to go up and down the stairs. When he was first born, he was a two-pound wad of fur. He was so small that we celebrated his growth by the ounce. He walked like a windup toy on four stubby legs. One of my friends once described him as looking like a tiny loaf of bread. If you cracked him open, there would be butter in the middle. Not to mention, he was top-heavy. Anytime he tried to waddle down the three brick stairs on our front porch, he would end up doing a handstand with his teensy tail waving in the air.

Naturally, since he could not take the three stairs out front, there was no way he could manage the seventeen steps between the two floors of our house. It was up to me to carry him until he was comfortable running upstairs on his own. Then, it was my job to retrieve him when he decided he wanted to come down again and perched at the top of the stairs, whining pitifully for my attention.

Once his little legs were long enough to keep his chubby belly from scraping every stair, I decided it was time for him to learn to go downstairs on his own. He hated every second of the process — except for the treats I gave him at the bottom of each step. He liked those.

I tried several methods, but the most effective method was simply to hold his front paws and gently place them on the next step down. He would stand spread-eagled like that for ages, too horrified by the idea of taking the stairs to move. So, even though it felt like cheating, I would gently help his back legs down. Then, I gave him a treat, a head pat, and a second to catch his breath. Once he stopped shivering, I would help him down to the next step the same way.

By the time we got to the bottom, he would run off, upset that I had made him face his fear. Like any worried mom, I wondered if I had pushed him too far outside his comfort zone. I figured the best thing to do was give him some space for a little while. Later, we could do another lesson down the stairs, and maybe I would start lower down the staircase.

I busied myself with folding the clothes that were piling up on my bed, which was in view of the staircase. My husband joined me, and we chatted about the best way to train Dio. Neither of us paid much attention to our surroundings until I noticed the familiar patter of paws on our creaky, wooden stairs. I stopped folding, mid-towel, and turned toward the stairs, expecting to see Dio run up them to lie on the couch per usual. Instead, I watched him go halfway up the stairs, stop, turn around, and then run back down the stairs on his own.

"He's practicing!" I laughed, elbowing my husband so he could watch. Sure enough, Dio ran up partway and then down again a few times before he noticed I was watching and waddled off again.

After that day, he became an expert at taking the stairs. It was good for him; it gave him the independence to go and lie on the couch and come back down for food or water whenever he pleased. That was great, but the best was yet to come.

Two years later, my brother bought a beautiful Husky puppy named Plato. Plato had one earthy brown eye, and one watery blue one. Just like Dio, he was a puffball. And, just like Dio, he was petrified of going down the stairs. My brother brought him over one day, asking for help in training him. I agreed, and we started the process just the same as before. If Dio hated learning the stairs, then Plato loathed even the sight of them. I was not sure we would ever get him down those stairs of his own volition, but as a Husky he would be too big to carry forever.

Just as we were about to call off the lesson for the day and take Plato home to think about what he had learned, Dio came to the rescue. Poor Plato stood on a stair in the middle of the staircase, whining nervously. My brother was perched on the stair above him, encouraging him with head pats. I was sitting to Plato's right, protecting him in case he stumbled and tempting him down the next stair with a treat.

Noticing his friend's distress, Dio hopped off the couch and met Plato where he was. He greeted Plato sweetly and then slowly started making his way down each step. Plato was encouraged and followed him step by step until they were both at the bottom. I will not say that Plato took the stairs confidently ever after, but when he needed emotional support, Dio was always there for him. That was the day when my dog became a dog trainer.

—Abigail Krueger—

One Very Special Guide Dog

Not all those who wander are lost.
~J.R.R. Tolkien

"**D**o you mind if I join you?" I asked the three women seated at the cafeteria table. As a new employee, I felt awkward approaching them, but there were no other seats available. I introduced myself, which was followed by an uncomfortable silence. I was finishing dessert when one woman finally spoke.

"I hate going home tonight," she said, "because we have to put our dog down."

I chimed in, "Oh, no! Is your dog ill?"

She replied in a pragmatic tone, "No, she's fine, just not a fit for our family. No one wants her, so it's best we put her down." Coming from a family whose home could be a petting zoo, I was shocked to think that people could be so heartless.

Haunted by this dog's fate, I asked my new co-worker a few questions. She shared that the dog's name was Lady. She was a German Shepherd and had trained for a year and a half as a guide dog for the blind. Unfortunately, Lady failed her final test because she demanded too many hugs after completing her tasks.

I begged the woman to give me a little time to reach out to my mom as we would consider taking her. With my flair for dramatic storytelling and my mom's compassionate heart, I knew Lady would have a home with us.

After work, I drove to pick up Lady. An old woman greeted me at the door, leading me to the kitchen. There sat this beautiful but very thin dog, crouched in the corner licking and scratching her right paw. "She did that to herself," the woman said defensively as she pointed to the injured paw. She continued, "That dog is hopeless!" The woman then took a broom and nudged the dog to stand. Lady whimpered as I clipped her leash to her collar and led her outside. There were no goodbyes from this family, just a sense of relief that Lady was no longer their problem.

I sat on the sidewalk with her and introduced myself. For me, it was love at first sight. She had perfect markings, a delicate, beautiful face, but the saddest eyes. "Lady," I said, "I'm taking you to your new home with my family who will always love you. Please give us a chance." With a little whispered prayer to St. Francis, I helped Lady into my car, and our new journey began.

As I pulled into our driveway, my mom was waiting with open arms and a buffet of delicious dog treats. We led Lady to our family room where my mom had placed a huge billowy comforter on the floor just for her. When my mom heard about the old woman with the broom, orders were issued to hide every broom in the house. Days passed while my mom made many more generous moves to Lady, but she remained distant. Lady retreated to our pantry, continued to lick and scratch her paw, and only went outside to take care of her business. This challenge between my mom and Lady went on for a few frustrating weeks.

Then one day, something miraculous happened. My mom ordered everyone out of the kitchen. Locking the doors, she sat on the pantry floor, talking one-on-one with that dog. Hours passed, but by the end of the day Lady's paw was bandaged, and both she and my mom walked out of the kitchen side by side. When I asked my mom how this miracle took place, she smiled. "Oh, just a little girl-talk about acceptance!" Giving a hug to Lady, she added, "I told her that even humans have to accept different walks in life, and sometimes those walks take us on the best paths." With a laugh, she continued, "Of course, I said it in dog language so she could understand!"

It was as though Lady did understand my mom's words of acceptance. That moment defined Lady's destined path, not just as a guide dog but now as the nanny dog of our home. We had a combination playmate and protector who shared our secrets, laughs, tears and hugs.

Her favorite place in the house was the landing almost at the top of the stairs. It gave her a perfect view of who was coming and going. Every night at 2:00 A.M., Lady religiously made her rounds, checking to see that we were all tucked in. Only then would she rest.

In her twelfth year, Lady could no longer climb the stairs. Each of us took turns helping her to the landing on the steps so she could still see her family coming and going. Sadly, we had to make the difficult decision to let her go.

Years passed, and I found myself in the middle of a messy divorce and a deep depression, trying to understand why my husband no longer loved me. I felt like a failure moving back to my mother's home. It was not the path I had expected.

One day, while sitting in my mom's kitchen, she shared an album filled with photos of Lady with our family. It captured years of beautiful memories. My mom reminded me of the day that Lady accepted her new path in life, which was not the one she expected. Yet, that new path was ultimately best for her. I understood it was time for me to accept my new direction in life, too, through the loving lesson of one very special guide dog.

— Lainie Belcastro —

Sunny's World

Scratch a dog, and you'll find a permanent job.
~Franklin P. Jones

"**C**an we get a dog?" This question is so ubiquitous that it is a cliché of parenthood. Some parents who had dogs as children, and actually like dogs, indulge their children with this perceived rite of passage, perpetuating the myth that children with dogs have happy childhoods. I have two children and three stepchildren, so of course I heard it. Of course, I indulged them — the stepchildren, that is. I had put my own children off for years and successfully turned them into cat people. But blending families when the children involved were ages eleven, twelve, fourteen, fifteen, and sixteen was already a step toward insanity. I had to throw a dog into the mix. (And another cat, but that is another story.)

My new husband is one of those people who actually likes dogs, so he was clamoring for a canine as much as the kids. In a moment of clarity, I asked for six months so that we could get used to each other before we thought about a dog. They agreed. On the last day of the sixth month, my stepson Jack bravely brought it up: "It has been six months that we've all been together, and I think it is going great. It is the best thing that has ever happened!" I was stunned, but before I was able to register my happiness, he dropped the other shoe. "So, we can talk about the dog, right?" Smart kid.

My husband had not mentioned dogs for six months, as promised, but had been researching and plotting. After that six-month mark, I was barraged with adorable videos of Golden Retriever dogs with their loving cat siblings — a constant video stream of reassurance that this would be okay.

Within a month, we were driving to a farm four hours away to pick up our very own Golden Retriever puppy.

Honestly, I had read the books, but being confronted with a living puppy was so different. The worst part was that I was the only one who was nervous about messing this up! Everyone else just played with her while I worried about things like where she should sleep, whether she should be crated, and all the other "new mom" concerns.

Sunny didn't die within that first month, which I thought was partially miraculous and partially because of my attentiveness. She got bigger, and I calmed down. We found a little routine, and she actually learned to poop and pee outside for the most part. However, anytime a guest would arrive at our house, or even one of our family members, she would jump and yip and let loose. "Happiness wee-wee" is what my husband called it. It was not cute. I would take her for a walk in the neighborhood, and if she saw another dog, she would take the leash in her mouth as though she were walking herself.

The defiance of that dog! When a ceramic bowl fell off the counter and broke into a million shards and slivers, I never imagined that Sunny would rush over and lap it up like it was kibble. She did. I completely freaked out. I had kept this dumb dog alive this long, and now she was killing herself. Nothing happened, which almost made it worse! There were never any consequences here. I was living in some nonsensical alternate universe where dogs rule. I wanted to take my three cats and return to the normal world.

Sunny had a terrible habit of licking the dishes in the dishwasher while I loaded it. It disgusted me. My husband thought it was cute. With seven people in the house cooking and eating, this was an almost constant occurrence. In spite of my barking and growling, the sound of that dishwasher door swinging down was like a dinner bell to her. She ignored me.

One Sunday after church, I was loading the top shelf, and she was licking the bottom, so I rattled the top shelf to scare her off. Scare her off, I did. She abruptly backed up, but her collar caught on the rack. That shook the bottom rack, which frightened her more. She tried to escape it, but the rack was a part of her at that point.

She took off with the entire rack full of dishes, running for her life through the house with dishes breaking in her wake. I was screaming. I only realized this when I saw the faces of our two youngest boys, fearfully coming down the stairs and around the corner. Later, they said they thought I was being murdered.

Finally, Sunny freed herself of both the rack and the contents of her bowels in the living room. The entire first floor resembled the aftermath of war — debris and excrement. I cleaned it up and then tended to my dog. It took a lot of petting and consolation to lower her heart rate. My consolation came with the thought that she would surely never go near the dishwasher again. Ha! That would be in the sane and sensible universe, but not in Sunny's world. She was back there after our next meal. I just watched her lick our dishes.

— Kristine Schuler —

26

Kayaking with Dogs

Marriage lets you annoy one special person
for the rest of your life.
~Author Unknown

This is the story of two people with two very different versions of events. Now, as a writer, I do try to represent the truth of a situation as much as possible. However, I must admit, a person's perspective is a thing.

Take, for example, a recent outing that my husband Adam and I had. The night before, we'd gone to sleep with the idea that we would take out our kayaks in the morning. We'd bought Adam a larger used one since the one he had turned out to be a little too close to the weight limit, if you know what I mean. I ended up keeping his little blue one and was anxious to hit the water and test it out.

So, that morning, I picked out all my fishing/water-sports gear and walked out expecting to see him ready to go. Instead, he was there in his man cave/garage, enjoying his second cup of coffee while lounging in his robe.

"So, I'm ready to go just as soon as I walk Archer," I said.

"Go?" he asked.

"Remember? Kayaking?" I prodded.

"Um, well, I…"

"If you don't want to go, it's okay. But I'm going to go. I really want to try it out." As our Terrier mix Archer and I walked, I figured I'd kayak by myself, even if it was a little chilly. However, by the time I got back, both kayaks were loaded and I had to rush to get Archer's life vest. Since he is all of fifteen pounds and already a proven paddleboard dog, I knew he'd be up for it.

"What about my Rosie?" Adam asked.

I looked at our sixty-pound Great Pyrenees/German Shepherd "puppy." She looked up at us with her most pathetic eyes, her tail wagging hopefully.

"Take her," I said. "She has to learn, and we're just testing things out today anyway. We can come right back."

The four of us arrived at the boat dock and started to load up. Adam looked at his kayak and then back at his dog. "Where do I put her?"

"I think there's room in the back," I said, gesturing to an empty spot that was probably meant for a nice, square cooler that doesn't wiggle.

He encouraged her to sit on the spot. The nose of the kayak tipped up to the sky, and she immediately jumped off. "That's not going to work," he said.

"Maybe between your legs in the front?" I offered.

"I shouldn't have brought her," he grumbled.

I attempted to make supportive noises as I thought of the great pictures I was going to get by the time this was all over.

Soon, we were off. Rosie did great, then she didn't, then she did, and then she saw birds, which she loves to chase, and nearly tipped them both over. Things were said on the big kayak that cannot be repeated in a family-oriented publication. Numerous times.

In the meantime, Archer and I floated along on the little blue kayak with his paws on the hull and nose in the wind, looking like a proud sailor in his orange life vest. The most dangerous moment we had was when I was laughing so hard at my husband and his enormous, wiggling passenger that I nearly tipped us over.

Eventually, Adam did get Rosie to jump off close to shore, and she was so happy to be on solid ground that she bounded off. Since she was still tied to him and his kayak, it looked like he had a 450 HP outboard strapped on the back.

As far as Adam is concerned, his side of the story is that I forced him to take his giant dog, making him feel guilty for even considering leaving her behind. Therefore, I put him in an impossible kayak-with-a-giant-dog-between-your-legs scenario that he barely survived.

Tomato, tomahto, I say. But, to be honest, I do have some killer pictures of the entire experience. So, who's to say what's true?

—Winter D. Prosapio—

27

Crossing the Bridge

Everyone thinks they have the best dog.
And none of them are wrong.
~W.R. Pursche, The Canine Commandments

Spot trotted ahead of us on Creek Road with his tail raised and wagging like a metronome. That cloudy summer day, he joined my husband Spence, daughter Ellen, and me halfway to the bridge across Deer Creek. I'd lured Ellen, on break from her epidemiology doctoral studies, out for a walk with the chance of meeting our neighborhood friendly Beagle.

Spot sniffed chicory, crown vetch, and tree trunks on both sides of the road. Every forty yards or so, he craned his head. If we'd veered onto a side road, he would circle back, gallop past, and run in front of us again. Suddenly he howled and tore off into the underbrush.

Ellen twirled. "Where'd he go? Should we wait?"

"Keep walking," I said. "He'll come back."

Spot belonged to Dick Hill, a farmer who lived on Route 173. But Spot considered the whole rural western Pennsylvania township his home. He slept on one woman's doorstep, ate another's outdoor cat food, and walked with us. Spence and I first met Spot a half-mile up the hill from his farm. He'd poked the back of my knee with his nose. Pickups, lumber trucks, and semis whooshed past way too close. Since the Beagle joined our walks frequently, Spence and I had switched to back roads.

Now we heard Spot's baying through the woods. Another quarter-mile down the road, he trotted past us again — paws pumping, tongue dangling.

Spot detoured after another scent before we stepped onto the serrated steel-bar grating of the bridge where we planned to turn around.

Resting my elbows on the blue railing, I gazed at Deer Creek. Swifts swooped after bugs. Water gurgled. The fragrance of fresh-cut hay drifted from a farm on Jacobs Road across the bridge.

Spot approached the grating, sat at the edge, and whimpered.

"He's afraid to walk on the bridge," Ellen said.

Spence tilted his head toward her. "If he's smart, he won't."

The first time I'd seen the grating, I stopped at the edge, too. Though my size-eight shoes couldn't possibly fall through, the water rushing below made me hesitate. After watching Spence stroll across the bridge, I reached for his hand and inched across the grating over an underlying I-beam.

Spot didn't have size-eight shoes. He stretched a front paw, a smidge wider than the holes, and touched the steel bar. He whipped his paw back to solid ground and ran down the embankment.

The tip of his tail wagged above the swaying marsh grasses, then he pranced through a crop of bird's-foot trefoil. Fifty yards upstream, he splashed across the rocky creek bed, climbed the opposite bank, and trudged through thick underbrush. Grinning and thumping his tail, Spot sat at the edge of the grating on the other side of the bridge, waiting for us.

"We're not going that way, Spot." I felt like a grouch after all his effort. "It's time to go home."

Spot stared into my eyes and yipped. He dashed up Jacobs Road and rounded the corner.

"He'll be back." Spence patted my shoulder.

I hoped so. Spot was more than two miles from his farm and on the other side of a bridge he wouldn't cross. I thought about our first meeting with Dick Hill in his front yard. He'd shaken his index finger at me and said I shouldn't touch Spot because then he would follow me.

Dick was right. And now I felt responsible.

When we didn't follow Spot onto Jacobs Road, he returned, barked a sentence, and ran off.

"Spot!" I called in vain. He didn't come.

We walked off the bridge and headed home. After a few steps, I turned to check. Spot was whimpering on the other side of the bridge.

"I'll carry him." Spence strode across the bridge, and Spot disappeared up Jacobs Road a third time. When Spence joined Ellen and me, Spot returned to the edge of the grating. "If I go back to get him," Spence threw his arms in the air, "he'll think we're coming and charge up the road."

That's the problem with a dog that follows from the front. I bit my thumbnail. "Doesn't he remember how he got there?"

Ellen jammed her fists against her hips. "He got distracted."

Beagles are single-minded, and Spot wanted us to continue the walk.

Spence crossed the bridge.

Spot charged up Jacobs Road.

Spence leaned against the railing and crossed his feet.

Spot sat at the bend in the road.

"We can't leave him." I twisted my wedding ring. "How will he get home?"

"He won't starve." Spence walked off the bridge. "He'll con someone into feeding him."

"But he wouldn't be in this fix if we hadn't walked to the bridge." I bit the inside of my cheek.

"Come on, Mom." Ellen linked her arm through mine and marched up Creek Road. "Time for tough love."

All three of us glanced over our shoulders.

Spot crouched and put a paw on the steel-bar grating. He stretched a second paw and sank low. Creeping, he appeared to slide on his belly. He didn't stop to sniff.

"Good boy!" I clapped.

He crept straight across the center of the bridge.

"Brave puppy." Ellen pumped her fist.

When he'd crawled halfway, gravel crunched and dust rose on Jacobs Road. A full-size pickup with an extended cab rolled down the hill, turned, and headed for the bridge.

Could the driver see Spot?

Wide, deep-tread tires rolled onto the grating.

I needed to stop the pickup, but the scream stuck in my throat. My arms froze against my sides. Gritting my teeth, I forced myself to step toward the bridge.

Ellen already had. She waved her hands above her head, then pointed at Spot.

The pickup stopped three feet from the Beagle. The four of us watched him finish the trek. Back on the road, Spot scooted to the berm, and the pickup accelerated past.

"Thanks," Spence shouted, exchanging country waves with the driver.

Spot dashed ahead, lifting my spirits and leaving me with his secrets for being a true friend: Give without conditions. Bridge impossible obstacles. Lead by following.

—Janet Wells—

28

Twice Saved

The average dog has one request
to all humankind. Love me.
~Helen Exley

L iving in Mexico, I struggled with the language. The kids in our neighborhood all knew me as "The American Lady." One day, as I was working outside in the small garden, two little boys ran up to my gate. "Lady, lady, blah blah blah." That's what I understood, but their agitation and pointing down the street made me want to find out what was so important. I walked down the street with them.

At the corner, I noticed a pile of garbage with a small dog on top. Around the puppy's neck was a collar and attached was a leash with a chewed end. The poor little animal smelled awful. I didn't know how long she'd been there, but I figured she needed water.

I ran home to get water and a little food. Ted asked what was up, and I explained what I had found. He returned with me, carrying a cat cage. I put down the water and a small cup with the food. The puppy looked at the food but didn't make any effort to eat or drink. Ted said we needed to get her to the vet as soon as possible. We put the puppy into the cage and immediately drove to the vet. As we were shown into the exam room, I took her out of the cage and put her on the metal table. The puppy looked up at me and then, with all her strength, pulled herself over to me and placed her head on my stomach. That was it. This was *my* puppy.

The vet didn't sugarcoat his ability to save this little animal. First, he said, he had to get liquids into her, and then remove the biggest of the thousand ticks that were sucking the life out of her. If she could make it through the night, maybe she had a chance but no guarantees.

We left a deposit with the vet and promised to return the next day.

At home, we had a rescued Miniature Poodle, Muneca (which means "doll" in Spanish) and a found kitten, Muddy, who had grown into a lovely cat. We didn't know how they would take to a new pet. The other thing that bothered me was the puppy was probably four months old, and we were in our late seventies. I don't think old people should adopt young animals. I had seen too many cases of trying to find homes if the owners passed away. But all that reasoning flew out the window when that puppy laid her head on my stomach. She had chosen me, and I didn't have a chance.

The next morning, we returned to find the vet feeding roast chicken to a starving puppy. With the IV tube still in her leg and about 500 fewer ticks, she was eating the meat as fast as the vet could feed her. The vet still wanted to undo the IV and check her out after she digested the food. If all went well, we could pick her up at 2:00 in the afternoon.

When we did pick her up, we were told that she had a skin infection, which was why she smelled so bad. We were to give her antibiotics, and when she was stronger, we could give her a bath in maybe a week. At home, I slowly removed over 500 ticks. She had ticks on ticks, all drinking her blood. Day by day, she got stronger. When I went out and returned, I would ask, "Where's Stinky?" The name stuck, and today, ten years later, she is still Stinky (in name only).

Our cat Muddy decided that the forlorn little puppy was her baby. During the day, she watched Stinky get stronger, but as we got ready for bed, Muddy would grab Stinky by the head and hold her still as she began licking her from head to tail.

When we returned to the States three years later, the pets came with us. On the Fourth of July, as we were walking our two dogs, nineteen-pound Stinky was attacked by two dogs who must have weighed eighty pounds each—an American Bulldog and a Boxer mix. They had managed to get out of their fenced-in yard. They ripped her throat open as they tried to tear her to pieces. With the help of some neighbors, we were able to rush her to the vet. Animal Control went and picked up the ferocious beasts that had hurt her.

Slowly, Stinky healed. Meanwhile, the dogs' owners disclaimed responsibility and refused to pay the $2,452 vet bill. I didn't have that kind of money to throw around either. However, after Stinky was hurt I had switched on the TV to distract myself and had come across the solution to my problem: *Judge Judy*. If my case was accepted and the defendants came on the show with me, the show would cover the vet bill.

I submitted my story to the show via the Internet and within a day or two they called. I asked the wife in the couple if they would go on the show instead of trying to pay me back over time and she said yes. So it was just a matter of waiting to hear whether we were definitely going on the show.

In the meantime, Stinky healed again, her second time coming back from disaster. When we finally got an appearance date, my husband and I drove from Sacramento to Pasadena, three hundred and eighty-five miles, stopping only to walk the dogs. The show put us up at a nice hotel and paid all our travel expenses. The next morning, I brushed Stinky and it was off to the show with her and my husband. I hoped I wouldn't freeze in front of the audience and the millions of viewers.

Stinky had no problem with her TV debut as she promptly went to sleep when we went up front to testify. I figured if she could go through everything that she did, and now be in a strange place with so many people, and lights and noise, I could certainly face the judge and tell our story. I did, and justice prevailed.

Stinky looked so cute on TV, even though she is one of those shaggy dogs who always looks like her hair was styled in a blender. She can be brushed and groomed, but she still looks as if she needs combing within two minutes. One lady in Mexico who owned a small grocery store at the end of the street had told us, "If I had known how cute she would turn out, we would have saved her." Her loss is my gain.

—Maria Ruiz—

Editor's note: You can watch Maria and Stinky's *Judge Judy* appearance by Googling "Judge Judy Ruiz vs DeHerrera Dog Attack" or going to https://www.youtube.com/watch?v=kUSrdGp8dtM.

29

Vanilla Bean

*Before you get a dog, you can't quite imagine
what living with one might be like; afterward,
you can't imagine living any other way.*
~Caroline Knapp

n February 2019, we moved from California to our new home
in Arkansas. We were excited about this new chapter in our
lives — being near our granddaughter, living in a new area,
experiencing a new culture, becoming homeowners, meeting
new friends, and having new adventures in this beautiful state.

About a year later, COVID hit, and the world as we knew it
completely changed. As a result, we, like many others, were forced to
stay at home. We thought about getting a dog to occupy our time and
encourage us to get out and get some exercise, but we just couldn't
decide if we were ready to add another responsibility and commitment
to all the changes we were undergoing.

We were new to living in a place where yards weren't fenced in.
Within a couple of months, a little dog started coming around our
house. She had a collar that simply said, "Vanilla Bean." We asked
our next-door neighbors about her, and they said she belonged to the
family down the street, but she really was a "neighborhood dog" and
everyone called her "Bean" for short.

She loved to wander around and visit the neighbors — and, of
course, get a treat from each one. As the months went by, she started
spending a lot of time coming down to our house. She would scratch

on the door to be let in and we would gladly oblige! This went on day after day. She'd come in, have a snack, and take a nap. We fell in love with her.

One day, her owners came looking for her. We searched the house but couldn't find her anywhere. The owner said, "Did you look under your bed?" Lo and behold, there she was, snoring away. The neighbor said she was more than welcome to stay with us as long as we wanted because they had three other dogs, a couple of cats, and a goat! They explained that "Bean" probably liked the personal attention she was getting from us and our granddaughter.

So, there it started… One night turned into two, which turned into a week. We happily went out and purchased all the necessities: a bed, bowls, toys, treats and food. We had "joint custody" of a dog. The owners would come get her every few weeks for a visit, take her to get her shots, etc., and then let her come back.

About a year of this went by, and the neighbors decided to move about ten miles away. We were devastated. What would happen to "our" Vanilla Bean?

Our worries were laid to rest when, right before the move, they came and asked if we would like to keep Vanilla Bean while they got settled and built their new home. Of course, our answer was YES! In the beginning, they came every month and picked her up for a few days and then would bring her back to us. The time that we have her has become longer between visits from her original family, but we are so thankful to them for letting us have shared custody of this wonderful dog.

Recently, Bean wasn't feeling well, and I called the other family to find out what vet they used for her. Not only did they tell me, but Bean's other "mom" met me at the vet and paid for the appointment. Little Bean had a UTI, and she's all better now.

Sitting here finishing this up, I realize that Bean was not only a godsend for us but for a whole neighborhood, and she has brought together many people in a very special way.

— Kendall Lee —

30

The Dog Walker

Ever wonder where you'd end up if you took your dog
for a walk and never once pulled back on the leash?
~Robert Brault

There was a chill in the air, and a light fog was lifting from Galveston Bay as my dad walked along. It was 5:00 A.M.—the first morning of my dad's new routine for his heart exercises. He hated every minute of it. The doctor had ordered an hour's walk every day. But what my dad longed for was a hot cup of coffee and the morning news.

As he approached the woods at the end of the street, three large dogs came running toward him from the last house. One was a German Shepherd, one was a Pit Bull, and the third was an indefinable mix. Dad stopped dead in his tracks, wondering if he was in danger. But the dogs just seemed to want to play. Relieved, he petted them and then continued on his walk. The dogs followed closely behind.

"Go home!" he commanded, to no avail. The four of them entered the woods and walked along the path that followed the bay for some miles. Dad's new walking partners seemed to delight in the adventure. They chased the seagulls, cornered a possum, and spotted a coiled rattlesnake lurking in some leaves near a tree. Dad yelled at the dogs to get back, and then they continued on their journey.

An hour passed, and they emerged from the woods. The three dogs stopped at the last house on the right, and Dad continued up the street. He had to admit it: The walk had not been that bad. His companions were a lively lot, and he had had little time to feel sorry for himself.

The following morning at 5:00, he headed out for his daily walk. Waiting for him at the end of the street were three frisky dogs, ready for their walk. He gave a whistle, and three woofs greeted him.

Once again, they traversed the path that ran along the bay near the edge of the woods. And the same thing happened on the next day and the next. Soon, weeks and months passed, and somehow two years slipped by. Dad's companions were faithfully waiting for him every day, and the four of them struck out along the path. Now, there were days when Dad extended his walks to an hour and a half. He looked healthier than he had in years, and his spirits had noticeably improved. In all this time, Dad had never seen the owner of the dogs.

One day upon leaving the woods, the dogs rushed toward a man standing in his driveway in the last house on the right. He was fixing a flat tire. He looked up in surprise as my dad and his three dogs approached. Dad introduced himself and told the man that his three dogs had been following him for two years every morning.

The man was flabbergasted. "Every morning when I leave for work, they are never here," he said. "It's been a mystery that we haven't solved. On the weekends, here they are!" Fortunately, the man had a good sense of humor. He said that he was pleased that someone was exercising them as he had no time with his busy work schedule.

So, for the next several years, as the fog slowly curled up from the bay, fourteen legs raced along the path near the edge of the woods, five mornings a week.

— Judy Kellersberger —

Be Open-Minded

31

The Little Ones

*My fashion philosophy is, if you're not
covered in dog hair, your life is empty.*
~Elayne Boosler

Promptly at 7:45 A.M., fifteen minutes before my alarm is set to go off, a compact body covered in wiry black curls squirms against my chest and tries to take over more than half the pillow. Sometimes, I just put my arm around him and pretend I'm still asleep. Other times, I curse softly and tell him to shove over, that it's not time to get up yet. It doesn't matter what I do — he's staying put for another fifteen minutes, at which time he'll start to bark as the alarm goes off and I get out of bed.

"Good boy," I mutter as I stumble off to the bathroom. "Good dog."

Even though he doesn't understand the concept of weekends and follows this behavior on Saturday and Sunday, I know I'm lucky. Feed him, walk him and rub his belly in that special spot. Whenever I need him, he's there, looking at me adoringly, ready to cuddle. Anytime, night or day. Not a bad deal. Better than most of the men I've dated.

If you think my behavior is strange, you obviously don't live in a liberal enclave like Park Slope, Brooklyn, where local zoning regulations seem to require that at least ninety percent of the residents have either babies or dogs. Many have both. Many can't tell the difference.

Walk through Prospect Park any morning, and you'll hear voices calling:

"Zoë, stop fighting. Learn to share your toys, or you're getting a time-out!"

"Jean-Claude, drop that. You know not to take treats from strangers. You have allergies."

Think you're hearing some yuppie parents socializing their kids? Look closely. That lady with a pocketful of vegan goodies isn't talking to a toddler. Those treats are for a Goldendoodle.

This is a kingdom where yoga moms deftly maneuver their progeny in double- and triple-wide strollers, where co-op boards might as well ask for proof of fertility before accepting applicants, and lactating women (a few skillfully manipulating one twin at each breast) picket bars that dare ask them to cover up. It's also an area with more doggy boutiques than baby-clothing outlets, and it's a toss-up as to which group is more stylishly dressed. (Personally, I believe four little red booties are much cuter than two.)

I got my dog three months before my only child went off to college. There was no doubt the doggy would be spoiled. He's a thirty-five-pound Kerry Blue Terrier, a ball of black fluff named Ivan. Ivan the Terrier.

I've tried to shield my son from the embarrassment of knowing that Ivan is more socially accomplished than he was as a youngster. I don't mention how humiliated I was when my human darling was rejected by our first-choice nursery school or boast that Ivan sailed through his interviews with Ivy League doggie-daycare facilities. My dog now wears a bright orange bandanna as he romps in the area of the park restricted to canines. (Despite a neighborhood aversion to conformity that discourages school uniforms, doggy uniforms are acceptable, in deference to the fact that it's a lot easier to spot a particular child than to tell pugs apart.)

If I want to enjoy some time at a humans-only resort, I arrange for Ivan to be chauffeured to a canine mountain resort where he can romp on fifteen acres of bucolic, fenced-in property. There's a lifeguarded lake in the summer and snowy winter trails groomed with paw-friendly salt.

When it's time to leave for puppy camp, each dog and its human companion take their monogrammed luggage to designated city street corners, like vacationers waiting for the Hampton Jitney. The properly tagged carry-alls contain special food with feeding instructions tucked inside. To combat my separation anxiety, I visit the facility's Facebook site and check daily videos that show Ivan exploring the idyllic farmland with his new pals.

Curious about the cost of my dog's upkeep? All I'm saying is that it's more than I paid for chemistry tutoring for my kid, but less than his college tuition.

Unlike parents of teenage humans, neighborhood doggy parents can rest assured that there'll be no unwanted repercussions from unchaperoned socializing. While not all dogs have pedigrees (mixed breeds and shelter pups are valued in a neighborhood that stresses diversity), most quality social and educational institutions require medical documentation to insure that the participants won't reproduce.

There is an urban legend (which I totally believe) about a local man who threatened a civil-rights suit on behalf of his intact Rottweiler, who was barred from a prestigious puppy school. The man threatened to march up and down in front of the kennel with a sign that accused the institution of practicing ethnic cleansing. (I've always found it odd how even the most liberated man will clutch his groin and wince at the mention of getting his dog fixed.)

The conflict was settled when the Rottweiler's human parents amicably divorced. The husband and the Rottweiler moved to the suburbs, and the wife adopted an adorable neutered Pomeranian that's welcomed everywhere. She's been heard admitting that, in retrospect, she'd have been wiser to worry about her husband's philandering than fixating on fixing the dog.

Since Ivan refuses to learn that the park and surrounding sidewalk are not just one big salad bar, I watch his diet carefully. For years, I resisted social pressure to buy only organic food for my family, but today I regularly patronize the health-food store to stock up on natural canine treats. I've learned that my dog will eat anything but supermarket dog food, so I get a regular UPS delivery of high-nutrition, organic, veterinarian-approved kibble.

On his last birthday, I mixed a half-pound of ground sirloin into Ivan's dog food. It did my heart good to see how enthusiastically he lapped it up. But my enjoyment was short-lived. As soon as we went for a walk, Ivan leapt into a pile of filthy snow to retrieve a moldy pizza crust and scarf it down with equal delight.

Over the years, Ivan has eaten the inner soles of my shoes, a cell phone, Dior eyeglass frames, half a box of Godiva chocolates (supposed to result in instant death for dogs), a tube of cortisone cream, chicken bones covered in dirt, and just plain dirt.

He's chewed up so much paper — magazines, newspapers, and other printed material — that I accept "the dog ate my homework" as a valid excuse from my students.

Ivan does have a right to at least one of the publications he devours. A few years ago, to show my marketing class how businesses use magazine subscriptions to create their mailing lists, I put my subscription to *The Economist*, a high-class publication, in my dog's name. Each month, Ivan Ende received *The Economist*, and pretty soon he began to get some pretty classy junk mail: offers of platinum credit cards, expensive vacations and sports cars.

One day, there was a letter for Ivan from the Republican National Committee. I opened the envelope and, on thick, creamy stationery, was a message that started out: "Dear Fellow Republican" and asked for a campaign contribution. Enclosed was an embossed silver card that read: Official Member of the Republican Party — Ivan Ende.

I live in a neighborhood so heavily Democratic that when someone posted a pro-Trump sign in their window, it warranted a story in *The New York Times*. We're proud liberals, loudly supportive of all races, religions and sexual proclivities. Well, almost all.

I hid the card, fearful that neighbors might discover I'd reached a level of kinky behavior that could lead to eviction by the block association. Forget about whips and chains and dressing like a French maid — I'm sleeping with a Republican.

— Jean Ende —

32

Brandy

*Any glimpse into the life of an animal quickens
our own and makes it so much the larger
and better in every way.*
~John Muir

"You brought a Pit Bull that's bleeding home on Christmas Eve?" I asked in a tone as sarcastic as they come. "She's not coming into my house."

My mother and mother-in-law looked at each other and said, "That dog better not hurt my granddaughter."

My husband was completely outnumbered but didn't fight us on it. He was happy to have the dog, and from what he described, our cold garage was an upgrade from where she came from. Apparently, he knew someone who had an uncle who had this female Pit Bull. She wasn't spayed, hence the bleeding she was doing when he brought her home, and she had been neglected, tied to a tree and underfed. Her owners had to get rid of her because they were moving to a place that wouldn't allow bully breeds, so my husband took her, sure that she would be euthanized if they surrendered her to a shelter.

I'm not against animals. In fact, if he would have brought an entire litter of kittens home, I would have thought it was the best Christmas gift ever. My work in emergency medicine led me to form the opinion that no dog is trustworthy around children. I had seen plenty of "the dog never bit anyone before" cases that I didn't want repeated with my two-year-old.

I made it clear that this was *his* dog, and I wanted nothing to do with her. My husband adapted an area in the barn for her that included a room with warm bedding and an opening she could go through to a chain-link enclosure facing the house. He fed her in the morning before he left for work and took her out in the evening when he came home. She was a pleasant dog, and she could run. Whenever my husband let her out, she would rip and tear around the yard, never leaving the property. She was very well-behaved. Still, she was a dog, and I wasn't taking chances with my child.

Brandy endured the limits I imposed on her, giving me no reason to dislike her. In fact, I found her to be endearing. As the seasons passed, I started to feel bad for her being stuck outside all the time. She was proving to be a kind and gentle soul. My daughter started toddling down to the fence and handing sticks to Brandy. Brandy gently took the sticks from her and proceeded to make toothpicks out of them. Day after day, I would notice Brandy in her little enclosure, alone, watching the house. The guilt was eating at me.

My daughter grew a little older and capable of understanding what was expected of her around the dog. So, when my husband went on one of his annual trips to the mountains, I decided to see what would happen if I let Brandy inside our house.

She had been patiently waiting to live with us and was a perfect house guest, even becoming buddies with one of the cats. The oldest cat didn't like her and would swat and hiss if she got too close. Although Brandy could have made short work of the cat, she never did. She was obedient and never showed even a glimmer of aggression. With my husband out of town, I felt much safer with her in the house, so in the house she stayed. I immediately noticed a kind of lightness in the way she moved, different from the days spent moping outside in her pen watching the house.

We made up for lost time with treats, soft beds, and warmth. Once she made the transition into our house, she went from being my husband's dog to a member of our family. We took her camping and found her to be great at traveling. We got her spayed and up to date with all her preventative care. She never caused a single moment's worth of trouble, inside or outside our house. As she became a senior dog, I realized that I didn't want to be without a Pit Bull. Finding a little brindle through a rescue, we took Brandy to meet her. Our old, white-muzzled girl played with the puppy as if she were one herself, making it clear that there would be no problems bringing the young one home. Brandy welcomed the scrappy little thing right into our home and showed her the ropes.

Pit Bulls get such bad publicity, but my experience has been anything but negative. The bullies I've known are friendly, fun-loving, entertaining, silly, loyal, obedient dogs. If you would have told me that someday I would have a Pit Bull (or two), I would have argued with you. But Brandy's patient, gentle spirit showed me one tail wag at a time that you can't judge a book by its cover — or a dog by its reputation. Brandy reminds me how much better off we are when we stop stereotyping not only dog breeds, but also people. I almost missed out on a wonderful opportunity because of my fears, but by opening my mind and my heart, I was able to give her a chance and learn the truth about her. I'm so thankful for Brandy and the way she touched our lives, and the lessons she taught me.

— Heidi Kling-Newnam —

33

A Promise Kept

One of the most enduring friendships in history —
dogs and their people, people and their dogs.
~Terry Kay

e loved our neighbors' dog, Sheba, as though she were our own. They'd adopted her from the pound less than a year after we'd adopted our dog, Dax, and the two grew up together as the best of friends. Any time the Williamses went out of town, we had the honor of watching Sheba in our home. She fit in like part of the family, and her comfort here was obvious.

Over the years, we made a point of telling them that if they ever needed a new home for Sheba, we'd take her. We were joking but serious. We knew they had no intention of ever giving her up, but we meant every word of that promise.

A day came when the Williamses had to move. Greg had been laid off and was forced to leave the area for a job in his field. It also meant that he and his son had to move from their house into an apartment. They searched earnestly for a place that would allow dogs of Sheba's size, to no avail. They were forced to sign a lease for a pet-free residence. Of course, as soon as he knew Sheba wouldn't be able to go with them, Greg gave us the first option to take her.

But things had changed drastically for us. Our Dax had passed away, as had a second dog we'd adopted during that time. Their deaths had been very hard on me, and Sheba was twelve — elderly for her breed. Just the thought of going through another loss like that within the next few years was too much for me.

Also, our new young dog wasn't keen on sharing her domain. She'd tolerate Sheba for short periods, but we'd have to make major adjustments for long-term cohabitation. Not to mention, our new cat was terrified of Sheba.

We told Greg we would need to think about it, and in the meantime he began asking around among other friends and family members to find a home for her. It burdened me deeply. I felt as though we'd gone back on a promise to a dear friend, but I just was not at peace with the idea of taking Sheba in permanently.

Then, Greg learned the apartment complex he was moving to allowed big dogs after all. There was excitement all around!

The day Greg and his son moved in, everything seemed fine while they loaded furniture into their new place and unpacked. They were even pleasantly surprised to find out that the old girl could manage the stairs to the second floor. But when they went to shop and have lunch, Sheba howled. Nonstop. The neighbors complained, and the apartment manager told Greg he had to find a new home for Sheba or move out — the very next day.

Greg called me and laid out his dilemma.

"Bring her over," I said. There was no way we were going to let Sheba be taken away. Still, my stomach churned as I waited for her to arrive. Our situation had not changed. I racked my brain for an answer and finally decided I would make one post — one — on the forum for my homeschool group, reaching out for someone who might take Sheba. I knew the chance was slimmer than slim, especially for a dog her age, and began the process of psyching myself up for Sheba to stay with us.

In the post, I gave as much information about Sheba as I could, emphasizing her age. I wanted anyone considering her to know exactly what they were stepping into. Then I waited.

Surprise nearly bowled me over when a fellow homeschooler e-mailed me the very next day asking to come see Sheba. She and her husband had been looking for the right dog for their family, which included a six-year-old special-needs son. I wrote back, specifically making sure she understood about Sheba's age.

"We've had big dogs before," Belinda said. "We know what that age means. We understand exactly what we're getting into."

The next day, Belinda, her husband, and their son came to our house to visit Sheba. I knew the moment they walked in the door that Sheba would be going home with them. She greeted them as though she'd always known them. Their son hit it off with her immediately. But what really got me was the boy's dad — the look of love at first sight on his face couldn't be missed.

Within twenty minutes, they were heading out the door with Sheba and all her belongings. She followed them without question and jumped right into their car. They let me reach in and give her a hug — one I wished didn't have to end — and then I found myself waving at the departing car as tears streamed down my cheeks.

Had I made the right decision?

Yes. I knew in my heart I had. It was confirmed many times over the following months as Belinda sent me pictures of her husband, their son, and Sheba playing together, snuggling on the couch, and opening presents on Christmas morning. And when I saw them at homeschool events, Belinda's son, with eyes bright and smile wide, always had stories to tell me about his adventures with her.

The guilt I felt over not taking Sheba vanished. She wasn't meant for us, not permanently. She was meant for Belinda's family, and she would never have made it there without us as the connection. We'd played our part by being her temporary refuge, ensuring she reached her forever home. Our promise was kept even if it wasn't in the way we'd expected.

— Kat Heckenbach —

34

A Perfect Little Mess

Our perfect companions never
have fewer than four feet.
~Colette

When I was five years old, I was obsessed with the idea of having a puppy. I wanted a playful, lovable companion who would sleep by my side and brighten every day. I wanted this more than anything, and one summer day, it seemed the universe was on my side.

My family and I were at the park, and a man with several adorable Poodles was advertising puppies for sale. Apparently, two of his older dogs had just welcomed a new litter into the world, but he did not have the space to accommodate all of them. Naturally, my younger brother and I begged to go see them. We promised to complete every chore, train the puppy ourselves, and be the best big siblings we could be to the newest member of our household. After some convincing, my father hesitantly agreed.

That night, we ventured to the man's home to see the litter, but only two puppies were left. There was a beautiful, fluffy white male, and a shivering, scrawny, champagne-colored female. According to the breeder, she had been the runt of the litter, and she was rejected by her mother shortly after being born. She was also sent to two other homes prior and returned both times. No one wanted her because she was neurologically impaired, deaf, and almost completely blind.

To my brother and me, she was perfect.

Much to my parents' surprise and dismay, we immediately fell in love with the tiny female. The fact that she had been rejected by two other homes only motivated us further. We wanted to be her forever family. So, we brought her home and called her Ching Ching. This is what the breeder had named her. We had no idea why, but the name stuck.

Ching Ching was certainly not the puppy I had always dreamed of. She constantly shivered, refused to be held or cuddled, and would scream for hours on end for no apparent reason. Her blindness made it difficult to take her on walks, and her additional deafness made it next to impossible to teach her the kinds of tricks other dogs could learn. On top of that, her neurological disabilities prevented her from forming bonds with other dogs and, at times, caused her to distance herself from my family and me.

Regardless, Ching Ching taught me unconditional love and acceptance. Even as a child, I couldn't bear the thought of a little soul like her without a home. On numerous occasions, my parents offered to take her back and get me a "better" dog. I always refused. I didn't want a different dog, and I didn't want my little friend to be lonely ever again. Despite her challenges, I knew she deserved love.

So, Ching Ching was here to stay. Over time, my parents couldn't help but become as attached to her as I already was. My brother and I crafted creative ways to play with her that accommodated her disabilities. For example, although she could not see or hear, her sense of smell was superb. So, we used heavily scented treats to play tug-of-war, hide-and-seek, and several other games to try and stimulate her mentally.

During family movie nights, Ching Ching would nestle herself beside the couch and watch the colors on the screen. Bright flashes and shadows would hold her attention long enough for us to snap a photo or two of her in all her adorable glory.

On chilly winter days, my mother would clothe her in a pink, puffy coat that read "Princess." She seemed to love this coat more than anything and perked up every time it was offered to her.

Though we never taught her tricks, Ching Ching learned some on her own. She learned how to climb stairs without falling (with supervision, of course). She learned how to drink water without tipping the bowl. She learned the scents and schedules of every family member, so she could greet us all in her own little way. That way usually involved quite a bit of scream-barking, but it was heartfelt nonetheless.

As she grew, we took her to a variety of different veterinarians and groomers. All of them told us the same thing: Why do you even bother with this dog? Why not just have her put down? My family simply couldn't process why so many saw our little Poodle as nothing more than an inconvenience. She wasn't like other dogs, but she was our dog, and she was special to us.

We eventually found groomers and veterinarians who could appreciate Ching Ching with all her differences. In fact, most of them came to love her just as much as we did. It took a great deal of patience to keep Ching Ching calm in such stressful settings, but it was possible with enough care.

Ching Ching stayed with us through many different stages of life. She was my childhood best friend and saw me grow through elementary, middle, and high school. Although she could not offer traditional cuddles and tail wags, she showed me love in her own way. Whenever I felt sad, I would sit on the floor, and she would come up to me and give me rapid-fire sniffs. Occasionally, she'd allow me to pet her once or twice.

Despite every doctor, groomer, and breeder that claimed Ching Ching should have been euthanized in her puppyhood, she lived to be about sixteen years old. Even in her golden years, she was full of energy and life. She didn't let her disabilities stop her from exploring and enjoying the world around her. She didn't let them hinder her ability to be loving and loyal to her family. Her final moments were spent in the arms of my mother, surrounded by a cloud of love, beside her favorite blankets and puppyhood toys.

I loved Ching Ching with all my heart. My entire family did. We are all so grateful for the time we got to spend with her and even more grateful that we met her breeder in the park on that long-ago Saturday afternoon. She taught me so many wonderful things. She taught me the importance of patience, compassion, and kindness. She taught me that everyone deserves love, no matter how different they are.

Ching Ching was not the picture-perfect puppy I dreamed of as a little girl. However, she was the puppy I needed. She was a scraggly, shaky, panicked little mess, but she was *my* scraggly, shaky, panicked little mess.

— Brittany Marasciulo-Rivera —

35

The Little Dog Who Chose Me

A dog is a bond between strangers.
~*John Steinbeck,* Travels with Charley:
In Search of America

A sad little dog with soulful brown eyes ran into my yard and begged to be picked up. From the innocent look of him, I doubted that he was vicious. Not with an old man's face like his, etched with sorrow and a slight glimmer of hope.

It turned out that a friend of my neighbor's gave her the scruffy little dog. My neighbor didn't want him and boy did he know it. Every day, he snuck out of her yard and roamed the neighborhood looking for love. He found me on his first foray. Even though he was adorable, I knew I couldn't take him because I was pretty sure that my indoor cat would never tolerate a dog. I felt so bad for him. He had been owned by an older lady who was put into a nursing home. She asked a friend to find a good home for him. The man dumped him with my reluctant neighbor.

Noticing how often he visited me, my neighbor asked me twice to take him, and twice I declined. I couldn't see how it would work with the cat. Nevertheless, the little dog kept coming around. When he saw me, he would run toward me like a scene out of the movie *10*. And, whether I was ready or not, he would leap up to me from several feet away, confident that I would catch him. The moment I did, he would shower me with unrelenting doggie kisses. Slowly he began working his way into my heart.

As time passed, I noticed his fur becoming matted and full of stickers. Fleas raced all over his little body, causing him to constantly scratch. Though he was a mess, his sweetness never diminished. One day, he walked lethargically into my back yard, looked up at me with eyes that begged for help, and lay down on my porch. I put out a large bowl of water that he slurped down until not a drop remained. I gave him a big helping of cat food. He ate it like a starving animal, which I realized he was when I picked him up. I could feel his ribs protruding through his fur. I got out a cat comb and tried to comb out the mats, but it was useless; they were too thick. I used scissors to cut off what I could until he protested. I laid him down in a cat bed I brought out of the house. He fell asleep and stayed all day and night.

A week later, my sister came to visit and brought grooming tools she uses on her own dogs. The first day, we applied flea medicine. The second day, when we observed only dead fleas, we set him on a tall table outdoors and proceeded to shave him. Then, we used blunt-end scissors to trim his face and feet. A remarkable little being emerged. When we began, we thought we were cleaning up an older dog with dull brown, black, and dark-gray fur. But, when we finished, we discovered a young dog with white-and-silver fur. Next, we bathed him with baby shampoo and made a second discovery. Once clean, his fur glistened like sparkles on water when the sun's rays hit it just right. Plus, he tolerated bathing with surprising aplomb.

I knew he was now our new family member, and I had to talk to my neighbor and tell her that I was keeping him. I put on his new collar and leash and walked him over to her house. She took one look at him and said, "Wow, you did that?" I nodded. "So, I guess that means you're gonna take him?" I nodded again. She told me that his name when she got him was Mitch, which she promptly changed to Boo-Boo. I didn't like that name at all, implying he was a mistake. He was such a kindhearted little guy that my husband suggested we call him Mensch, a Yiddish word for someone good. Even though the word pertains to people, it fit him perfectly. Besides, he was used to being called Mitch and Mensch sounds similar, so I thought he might adjust to the new name faster. He did right away.

I took him to the vet where he got a clean bill of health and his shots. They examined his teeth and told me he was two years old. He was a Schnorkie — half Miniature Schnauzer and half Yorkie (Yorkshire Terrier). Though technically he was an adult, he was a puppy in every silly way. It became quite evident that his puppyhood was cut short when he was separated from his first owner.

After the vet, we visited a big pet store where I put him in a shopping cart and let him help me pick out some really good dog food. I'm not sure what he ate before. All I knew was that with proper food and grooming his fur shone like the hair in a shampoo commercial.

Eventually, he moved into the house, and the cat adjusted, with the caveat that she was the alpha. I don't know how she conveyed that to him, but he got the message. From the moment they met, she terrified him — and not just because she outweighed him. If she lay across a threshold of a room he was in, he'd whine for someone to move the cat so he could get out. He wouldn't cross her.

He's been with us for two years now and takes his job as "the dog" seriously. He has learned a few commands, still politely succumbs to his baths, notices when the afternoon light wanes and tells me it's time for his walk, assumes he is the guardian of the house, barking if a stranger walks by the front yard, and knows that when we say "bedtime," he obediently gets into his bed for the night.

People tell me it's projection if I say that he smiles a lot. Not so. I have never seen a dog grin as much as Mensch. He's happy all the time. Where once there was sadness, now an unmistakable radiance emanates from his eyes. He doesn't walk; he prances, his tail standing high and waving like a flag. And, of course, there are the sweet kisses he plants each time I get within range. When I look at him, I smile too and feel my heart race a little faster — in a good way. Though his wistful days of searching for a forever home are long over, he still gazes at me with soulful brown eyes, and I still melt. I knew that I had to save this little dog. He deserved a better life, and everything in my being told me that I was the one to do it. Although I have no doubt that he chose me, deep down I chose him, too.

—Jeffree Wyn Itrich—

36

Answered Prayer

We never know how God will answer our prayers,
but we can expect that He will get us involved
in His plan for the answer.
~Corrie ten Boom

am not a dog person. That sentence makes me giggle as I sit here with my sixty-pound English Springer Spaniel, Barkley, cuddled up beside me on the couch. One floppy ear covers the Delete and Backspace keys on my keyboard.

Two of my three children begged for a dog at various stages of their preschool and early elementary years, but they gave up when they learned that I am more stubborn than they are. They received a "No" from this mama every single time they brought it up. Not a "Maybe." Not a "Someday." Not a "Let me talk to your dad." A hard "N.O."

Then, we hit some bumps in the road. Breast cancer struck when I was forty. We had a falling-out with some people we loved, which changed the trajectory of our lives. And we crashed head-on into the teen years when I was smacked with the reality of how little time I had left with these three boys I thought would stay small forever.

So, I started praying this prayer:

Lord, life is hard sometimes. Our family has walked through some tough stuff. Please show me how to love my boys well and make the most of the time I have left with them. Amen.

After I started praying that prayer, a picture of a dog started popping into my head. I ignored it, mind you, because getting a dog was not an option. But it wouldn't go away. I found myself wishing God was leading me toward a Disney Cruise, but it became very clear that it wasn't a vacation but a furry little four-legged creature he had in mind.

Yowzers.

It took a while to wrap my head around it, but I finally submitted, and we found an English Springer Spaniel puppy looking for a home. He was stinking adorable, but I had some anxiety thinking about all the work that lay ahead of me. I mean, I've potty-trained three humans, but I wasn't sure if I was up to the task of potty-training a non-human. I was committed to that little puppy, but I still wondered, "Is this huge undertaking going to be worth it?"

We surprised the boys with Barkley on a September Saturday morning. Shock and awe is probably the best way to describe their reaction. They all three loved Barkley from the start, but I was surprised to find that my oldest son, Carter, the one who had never once in his life asked for a puppy, seemed to connect immediately with the little guy — more than his brothers, who had worked to wear me down for years.

About twenty-four hours after Barkley came into our life, Carter's girlfriend of almost a year broke up with him. It was his first teenage break-up, and it was painful, both for him and for the mama who had to stand on the sidelines and watch. But with a broken heart and puffy eyes, he cuddled that puppy. The little fluff ball became his comfort.

It's been a few years since Barkley rocked our world. And though he likes to eat shoes, remote controls and books, he has changed our family for the better. He's been around for a couple of broken hearts, he's been a pal to play with to alleviate boredom, and he's served as a personal space heater for every member of our family.

I don't know what the future holds, and Barkley may be the only dog that we ever invite into our family, but he has been a gift to us. An unexpected, fur-covered gift.

— Kim Harms —

37

Small But Mighty

*Sometimes, the bravest and most important
thing you can do is just show up.*
~Brené Brown

She was little more than half the size of the others. The tips of her black satin ears jiggled as she trotted over to greet us on big, scruffy paws. She sat down beside us, tail wagging, and didn't budge when the other pups ran off to play.

"I guess that settles it," I chuckled as the boys scratched her behind the ears.

"Now you won't be the only girl in the house, Mom," they teased.

My husband Erik and I had promised the kids a Labrador puppy. But with four rambunctious boys at home, I was on the lookout for a dog who wouldn't add to our boisterous mix.

I'd seen the ad at the local hardware store. "Thirteen puppies in all," Sally, the owner, said when I called. "There're only three left."

"Are any of the puppies especially calm?" I asked.

Sally laughed when I explained.

"There's one puppy that just might be what you're looking for," she said. "The runt of the litter is very sweet-tempered."

She sounded perfect. "We'll be there tomorrow to take a look."

The boys whooped and hollered as I copied down directions and hung up the phone.

Early the next morning, still discussing names, we wound our way through the mountains to meet our family's new best friend.

We learned about our puppy's pedigree as we prepared to leave. She came from a long line of champions with equally long fancy names we couldn't remember, much less pronounce.

"You can't be serious," the boys groaned under their breath as they piled back into the van. "We'd never give our puppy a name like that."

I had to agree. Our boys had simple names: Ike, Sam, Ben, and Dom. And on days when my maternal gas tank was empty and I needed a new set of plugs, I could barely keep them straight!

"A sweet little dog needs a sweet-sounding name," I hinted, stroking her velveteen nose. "She looks like a Rosy to me...."

"Rosy," the boys repeated softly.

Our little puppy cocked her head.

"She likes it," they cheered and set about making Rosy comfortable for the long drive home.

They offered her a chew toy and lifted her up so she could see out the window. They took turns cuddling her and offered her a snack. But something was wrong. Rosy wouldn't stop crying.

Desperate, they offered a suggestion. "Put in some music, Mom."

I dug an easy-listening CD from the bottom of the cluttered glove box and popped it into the player. Rosy relaxed and then fell asleep as the elevator music played. She was my kind of dog.

Though small in stature, Rosy grew strong and healthy beneath her shiny black coat. And, just as I'd hoped, she was a calming addition to our houseful of rowdy boys. But sometimes a mother's wishes are different from her sons'.

"It's like she doesn't know how to play," Sam commented one day after school.

"Dogs have different personalities, just like people," I said. "Besides, she's still very young."

"But her legs aren't very long, and one eye is smaller than the other," Ike added, trying to make sense of why Rosy was different from other Labs he'd met.

I looked across the room to where Rosy sat nestled between the boys. The last golden rays of autumn sunshine beamed on her face. Sure enough, one eye was misshapen. Not only that, it didn't glint in the afternoon light. I drew in a breath. Rosy, our pedigree puppy with a name as short as her four little legs, was blind in one eye.

The mood in the room grew somber.

"It's not fair," Ben cried.

"Sometimes, life isn't fair, even for little dogs, but we love and care for them anyway."

Sam cradled Rosy in his arms and rubbed her squishy tummy.

The lesson was bittersweet. "Remember, Rosy was the runt of a big litter. It's a miracle she even survived." Sometimes, sadness and hope go hand in hand.

Still, the boys looked heartbroken. Dom blinked back tears. "We don't have to give her back, do we, Mom?"

"Of course not," I assured him.

The room grew silent as they passed Rosy between them and ruffled her fur.

"Looks can be deceiving," I reminded them. "Rosy may've gotten stuck with the leftovers, but who knows what she'll be capable of once she grows up."

Their moods brightened. Grins replaced sniffles.

Rosy thrived and grew into her oversized paws. In spite of her blind eye and short legs, she learned to fetch, navigate woodland trails, and wade in the river near our home. Every day, like clockwork, she met the boys when they got off the school bus. But when the weather warmed enough to go swimming in our big above-ground pool, I laid down the law: "Rosy's not allowed in the pool."

"But Mom," the boys whined, "she's a water dog."

"We can't risk it. She must learn the pool's off-limits," I insisted. "Rosy can't touch the bottom, and she can't climb out. If she jumps in and we're not there to help, Rosy will drown."

From that day on, we all did our best to keep Rosy safe and out of the pool. We took her on long walks and let her play in the sprinkler. She was never left alone outside and stayed indoors when friends stopped by for a swim. Weeks went by without incident. Then, the unthinkable happened.

Something was amiss. "Where's Rosy?" I asked as we cleared plates from the dinner table.

"Rosy! Rosy!" the boys yelled.

She didn't come.

Concern turned to worry and then panic.

"Quick. Out front!" Erik made a beeline for the door.

The front yard was eerily quiet. Then we heard it… just a little splash.

We ran to the deck and peered into the pool, afraid of what we might see.

There in the water, nose barely above the surface, Rosy, our spare-parts dog, paddled around swimming laps.

We urged her to the side of the pool.

Swish. She obeyed.

Bracing against the deck, we reached down and pulled her to safety. Rosy sprawled out in a puddle, panting and exhausted.

After that scare, a change in strategy was in order. The very next morning, the boys took Rosy into the pool and taught her to climb the ladder. The child-size rungs proved the perfect fit for her short legs.

To their delight, Rosy thanked the boys with a few tricks of her own. She played water tag and swam laps underwater, blowing streams of bubbles from her big, black nose. She dove and, twirling downward like a legged dolphin, fetched toys from the bottom of the deep end of the pool.

For the next thirteen summers, Rosy did what came naturally and amazed those she met with her aquatic feats. She reminded everyone that limitations need not keep us from doing what we love. Rosy truly was a miracle.

— Mary T. Post —

38

Take Two

*You have to take risks. We will only understand
the miracle of life fully when we allow
the unexpected to happen.*
~Paulo Coelho

Although we didn't know it at the time, the forlorn, foul-smelling dog we reluctantly brought home from the shelter had already been adopted and returned three times. The volunteer, who could have sold rusted-out used cars for a living, told us the 120-pound mongrel was "overdue on his rent," meaning that he was going to be destroyed if no one adopted him that day!

Looking like the schmucks we were, we signed the papers and opened the back door of our tiny car. He happily jumped in.

"Well, we can give him a bath," I said uncertainly, as the foul odor wafted up to the front seat.

Even though he was part Rottweiler and Shepherd and several other unrecognized breeds, he had looked shy and pitiful in his cage at the shelter. But now he looked scary and ill-tempered, and he punctuated that by barking unexpectedly every so often all the way home.

But I had trained a few dogs before, so I was optimistic that the three of us would adapt to each other.

At the shelter, they said he answered to "Duke," but he didn't seem to know that. When we looked at the adoption papers, it turned out he had also been named "King" and "Harley" by two other recent owners, but he showed no recollection of either of those titles. My husband named him Hambone.

Our new roommate spent the evening examining his new digs. He seemed pretty mellow. I showed him where the bathroom was several times (in the back yard), but he didn't seem interested, so I went to bed.

He woke me up a short time later by putting his front feet on the bed and barking sharply. Okay, this was scary. I got up, and he led me through the house. I tried to take him outside, but he wasn't going. After an unsettling half-hour, I went back to bed.

He woke me again. This time, he seemed to want me to follow him, so I did. He had chosen the hallway for his bathroom, which he had already used, and apparently he wanted me to clean it up. This was good and bad. I realized the hall was the closest thing to resembling his cage. The good thing was he seemed as disgusted as I was. After I took him outside once more, he got the idea and was happy to relieve himself outdoors. He wasn't a bad dog, and he was pretty good at communicating.

The next day, we went shopping to buy him some toys and a bed. It was a warm day in Reno, Nevada, so we had left the windows open a few inches. When we came home, Hambone was lying leisurely in the front yard. He was delighted to see us, completely oblivious to the fact that we would be less than happy that he had jumped through the screen in the living room. Apparently, he had pushed the window up, using his nose to give him better access. Clever indeed.

Perhaps he had gotten hot in the house, I explained to my husband. When we left the next day to replace the screen, I closed all the windows and turned on the air conditioner.

When we came home hardly an hour later and opened the door, the first thing we saw was woodwork — shards of wood covering the entire entryway. Plaster dust was everywhere. Not only had the entire doorframe been ripped off, but part of the wall next to the door was gone as well. And there, covered in white dust, his tail wagging and oh-so-happy-to-see-us, was Hambone.

My husband said his first thought was that someone had broken in and attempted to tear off the door from the inside, although that didn't make sense. It looked as if someone had taken an ax to the wall. It didn't seem possible that a dog had been able to do that much damage. But it was possible, and he had done it. We were even more sure when he got diarrhea, and the paint he had eaten stained our new carpet.

Truthfully, we both wanted to return him to the pound, even though he did smell better and hadn't been too much of a nuisance. But he seemed to like us, even if we weren't sure about him.

After thinking it over, I took pity on him. He had already had so many owners. But my husband wasn't convinced.

"Maybe we could leave him in the back yard when we leave," I pleaded.

"What? And watch him tear down the fence?" my husband replied.

"We could tie him up."

"I am not going to be responsible when that dog hangs himself," my husband said.

"But they will put him down if we take him back," I reasoned.

My husband's silence told me that might not bother him as much as it did me.

I called the Humane Society and asked what would become of poor Hambone if we brought him back.

"It seems like you like him," the clerk said. "He must have anxiety attacks when you are gone."

I agreed with that. He was so happy when we came back that he nearly knocked us down.

"Why don't you get a second dog to keep him company?" she asked. I said I would think it over, but it wasn't me who needed to think about it. It took a day or two before I was able to convince my husband.

I went back to the rescue facility alone, not convinced our marriage would survive another howling, barking, mangy, has-been mutt who had been cooped up in a pen too long. I walked up and down the narrow halls with dogs lunging at me, desperate to be released.

I came to the end of the hall where a Beagle sat quietly, the exact opposite of the other dogs. She was composed, not moving, with her head erect, polite and alert. When I turned around, she finally spoke once, very ladylike, as if to say, "Hey, don't ignore me. I am on my best behavior."

She didn't move while I inspected her except to tilt her head a bit in my direction. This was just what I needed. Well, to be clear, she was just what Hambone needed: calm, well-trained and good-natured.

Yes, I had found my companion dog. Sadie was happy to meet Hambone, who promptly brought her a few of his toys and left them at her feet. He never opened a window or tore up a doorframe again.

—Linda L. Meilink—

39

The Greatest Gift

No animal I know of can consistently be more of a
friend and companion than a dog.
~Stanley Leinwoll, The Book of Pets

utumn shades of red and burnt orange flashed on either side of us, and pine limbs waved in the cool breeze as we drove along the dirt road. We'd been traveling for almost two hours, and I knew from my printed directions that we were getting close. "Slow down," I said to my husband as I watched for a sign. Ahead, a rural mailbox with ANIMAL RESCUE painted in bright letters came into view.

The gravel driveway that led to the old stone farmhouse was long and straight with none of the curves that would have provided a semblance of charm. Our car inched over bumps and hollows while barks announced our arrival. The owner of the shelter made her way to us while we parked.

"Right on time," she said as we stepped from our vehicle. "Follow me inside. I'll get the dog you inquired about."

A vision of the Golden Retriever we'd selected from one of the photos on the shelter's website had been stuck in my head for days — deep yellow fur, six years of age, friendly, abandoned. We sat on the worn and scratched leather couch and waited.

Clicks from toenails on the wooden floor sounded from behind. In seconds, the Retriever was at our feet, his tail wagging like crazy.

"He's shedding at the moment," the rescue owner said as puffs of fur flew into the air and settled on our clothes. "All he needs is some oil added to his food."

I began to read the list of questions I'd prepared, but the owner stopped me with a raised hand. She had only a small amount of information on the dog's history.

"I feel that I should tell you that this dog has never been on a leash of any kind and has not had any training… so that's something you may want to consider."

I looked at my husband with disappointment.

"But we can try a collar and short leash on him outside to see how he responds."

As soon as we stepped onto the wide, fenced lawn, I noticed a pickup headed toward the house. Dust spewed from its back tires.

"This must be the couple I spoke with yesterday," the rescue owner said. "They're dropping off their dog. It won't take long."

I tried to focus on the Retriever, now playing with several other dogs, but my eyes were drawn to the young man and woman as they came out of the pickup along with a Border Collie. The young man walked with a noticeable limp. He motioned to the dog. "Go and play, buddy," he said, throwing a ball across the lawn. The Border Collie ran after it, soon joined by the other dogs.

A pang went through my chest as the young man came closer. His eyes were red and damp. I turned my attention to the shelter's owner. She smiled kindly as the couple told her their story about why they had to give up their dog.

"My wife and I just had a baby. It's been difficult. I was in an accident," the young man said. He bent over to give his dog a pat on the head when he returned with the ball. "I'm going to miss you." There was a catch in his voice.

I couldn't move. It suddenly felt as though I was at a funeral. The young man described to the shelter's owner how much the Border Collie loved to run and fetch. She acknowledged his statement with a cheerfulness that contrasted with the pain in his words. It was obvious she'd listened to sad stories before.

The young man threw the ball again. Then he started to sob.

Instinctively, I stepped nearer to him. He wiped his eyes with fingertips and shifted his weight as if he was having difficulty standing on the uneven gravel.

"The dogs seem happy here," I said, hoping to make the situation easier for him. "I heard you say that you were in an accident."

For the first time, he gazed directly into my eyes, now damp as well. "Yeah. A construction accident."

His wife spoke for the first time. "One of his legs was crushed."

Calmly, I replied, "I've worked in a hospital for years. It's incredible what modern medicine can do these days. I see miracles happen all the time." I felt the gaze of the shelter's owner on me. I had no idea if she was still smiling.

The young man said he had enjoyed his job and desperately wanted it back. So far, it wasn't possible.

"Life can be so unfair," I said, the words coming out clichéd but true.

"Life isn't fair," he said.

"But you're a new dad. And that's the greatest gift life can offer, right?"

He nodded once and smiled faintly before he threw the ball one last time. The Border Collie ran after it while the young man limped back to the pickup with his wife close by. When the Border Collie returned with the ball, he stood next to me and watched them drive away.

It's been ten years since that happened. And even though I think I helped in some small way, in my dreams I get a total do-over. I hand a note to the young man inscribed with my phone number and instruct him to call me whenever he would like to hear about what a wonderful new home his Border Collie has with my family. I will forever wish I had done exactly that.

— Nancy Thorne —

Chapter
5

Find Your Purpose

40

The Bridge

Dogs are not our whole life,
but they make our lives whole.
~Roger A. Caras

"Lila will be a bridge." The trainer looked directly at me. Her eyes were smiling but serious.

I thought it was an intriguing metaphor (former English teacher here), but little did I realize how appropriate and true it would be, and how using that "bridge" would lead me to experiences and opportunities I could never have imagined.

Several months ago, when I first started planning an early retirement, it sounded like an exciting concept: staying up as late as I cared to, sleeping in when everyone else's alarms were beeping, and having all that extra free time. Yeah, all that extra free time to fill with... what, exactly?

One of the reasons I opted for an early retirement was so I could spend extra time with animals, my own four rescues as well as those at our local humane society. But I needed something more, something to get me up every morning.

Then, one Sunday morning, as I sat in the church pew waiting for the service to begin, I opened our church bulletin, and the word "dog" jumped out at me. Our church was welcoming Lila, an LCC (Lutheran Church Charities) K-9 Comfort Dog—the first in my home state. And handlers were needed. My pastor encouraged me to call the church office and have my name added to the list.

I placed the call early the next morning. No sleeping in that day! The list was already full. They already had enough handlers but thanked me for calling. My dogs had trained me well enough to know that persistence usually pays off—in their case, with extra attention or possibly treats. In my case, after presenting my list of reasons for inclusion, not to mention staying on the line indefinitely, I was added to the bottom of the list.

After traveling to the Chicago area for Comfort Dog training, Lila's calendar quickly filled up with regularly scheduled visits to senior residences, hospitals, assisted-living and memory-care homes, as well as presentations at schools, libraries, and community events. Most importantly, there were priority visits for unexpected, often tragic, events: sudden deaths, crime-victim support, natural and manmade disasters.

There were so many, but one stood out for me. A Labor Day party celebrating a local boy's birthday ended tragically when the twelve-year-old drowned in a hotel pool. The only other people in the pool area at the time had been his eight-year-old sister and another child.

And the following Tuesday was the first day of school.

We cleared our schedule and arranged to meet first with the boy's cousins and closest friends. Understandably, they were quiet and reserved, and somewhat reluctant to approach us. Before long, they joined us on the floor and began to stroke Lila's fur and ask questions about her. The stress they were under seemed to lessen as the minutes went by.

Throughout the afternoon, we met with small groups of students. One young lady told us that when she first came in, she was "mad at the world" over the inexplicable tragedy. But after spending some time down on the floor and talking things out, she told us, "I'm not mad anymore."

As the afternoon progressed, the dean of students brought the student's sister, who had been at the scene of the drowning. Earlier, she had spent most of the day in a private office, too sick with grief to join the rest. Once again, Lila worked her magic, bringing comfort to her hurting heart. As we prepared to leave, the dean and the cousins shared hugs with us, and every single one walked us to our car for a final goodbye.

A gentle dog... warming hearts in the midst of tragedy.

Another time I watched Lila perform a miracle in the back corner of a memory-care unit, where a lady sat motionless in her wheelchair. Carol was slumped over with her eyes closed. Her husband told me that she was aware but didn't care to respond. He also said that dogs had always been an important part of her life, but for many months now, Carol had retreated into "another world."

"Visit," I told Lila, and she rested her chin on Carol's knee. Her husband took Carol's seemingly lifeless hand in his and slowly stroked Lila's neck. Before too long, her hand started to tremble a little, and then she began to blink her eyes. When she looked down and saw Lila staring up at her, their eyes met. Lila and Carol visited for quite some time, silently connecting. Eventually, Lila and I moved on to other residents.

As we turned to leave, Carol's husband was wheeling her over in our direction, asking for "just a few more minutes." Carol, with her eyes wide open, had begun softly speaking. We couldn't really understand the words, but we could decipher "dog" in just about every sentence. When her husband stretched her hand out toward Lila, Carol began to pet her on her own, softly whispering. Staff members in the unit began to drift over and stare. A wordless dog had been able to reach out through the darkness with a ray of light.

Another day, we were just about to leave a hospital's I.C.U. when we noticed a man sitting alone in the family waiting area. He caught sight of Lila and me and smiled faintly, but I could tell he was distraught. His father had suffered a stroke, and he was apprehensive about his future. In his distress, the father had had a serious a-fib episode, and his son had run out of encouraging things to say to him. It seemed that both of them were ready to give up. As Lila approached the son, he bent over and deeply massaged her shoulders and laid his head against her neck. Soon, he started breathing more regularly, and we sat and talked with him for over twenty minutes. Did our visit solve any of his problems? I doubt it. Still... someone had led us into that waiting area, and Lila and I had been wise enough to follow that lead.

And it all started with a phone call.

By the grace of God, I was given the opportunity to meet, engage, and connect with hundreds of people. Yes, I could have gone out on my own and tried to reach these people. But would I have? No. Definitely not. I needed something, someone, to pave the way.

I needed a bridge.

I needed Lila.

—Joyce Styron Madsen—

41

He Ain't Heavy

What counts is not necessarily the size of the dog in the fight;
it's the size of the fight in the dog.
~Dwight D. Eisenhower

There was a time in our lives when two energetic Labrador Retrievers in the household seemed like a good idea. First, there was a small black Lab given to us in exchange for a bag of dog food. She came with the name Brandy. She wasn't cuddly; she was almost aloof. But she was gentle with children, which made her a good fit for our young daughters.

Not long after Brandy's arrival, my husband called from work to ask if he could bring home a puppy — another black Lab that needed a home. We named the friendly newcomer Alexander because we thought Brandy and Alexander had a nice ring to it.

The two dogs got along fine. Brandy tolerated Alex's playful puppy behavior even though he ended up being twice her size, at nearly 100 pounds.

In time, the dogs developed a bad habit of bolting if a gate happened to be left open. While Alex would always come back of his own accord when his stomach told him it was dinnertime, Brandy would stay on the lam for days. She often returned exhausted, caked with mud and who knows what else. We could only imagine where she had been and what she had experienced.

Brandy and Alex loved to swim. On one of their escapes during the summertime, I found them miles away from our house taking a dip in someone's backyard swimming pool.

The dogs especially loved swimming in a lake. One afternoon, my husband left in the fishing boat. As he sped off, both dogs decided to follow. They launched off the dock and began to paddle furiously in the boat's wake. My husband had no idea the dogs had followed him.

I called for the dogs repeatedly. After a while, Brandy turned around and headed back for shore. Alex, though, kept going. The lake wasn't deep in this back bay, but it was filled with wild rice and weeds. My mother-in-law joined me in calling for Alex, to no avail. He kept paddling and slapping the water with his big paws.

After a few more minutes, Alex began to look as if he were struggling. He was swimming in circles by then with his head strained forward, trying to make progress. Brandy arrived back on the bank and stretched out next to me, panting.

"I think Alex is in trouble," I said. "His legs must be tangled in weeds."

We didn't have another boat, and I didn't think I could swim that far out. My mind raced for a solution. Before I could come up with a plan, I heard a splash. Brandy had leaped off the dock and was swimming toward Alex.

We held our breath as Brandy seemed to ride lightly in the water, almost like an otter. My mother-in-law had her binoculars out, so we watched Brandy reach her buddy, who looked wild-eyed by then, as if he were panicked. As Brandy pulled up next to Alex, he put his paws around her back and shoulders. And then Alex held on for dear life while Brandy swam for shore.

"That little dog is saving that big dog's life," my mother-in-law shouted, temporarily forgetting their names.

I cheered on the valiant Brandy as she made slow but steady progress toward us. A line from a song came to mind, "He ain't heavy; he's my brother." Tears began to fill my eyes.

Finally, two exhausted dogs tumbled onto shore, gave a big shake, and collapsed in the sand. That night, the two friends enjoyed a larger-than-normal dinner, although Brandy's portion was just a smidge larger.

— Constance Van Hoven —

42

Ruff

*Fall in love with a dog, and in many ways you enter
a new orbit, a universe that features not just new
colors but new rituals, new rules, a new way of
experiencing attachment.*
~Caroline Knapp

When Ruff came into our lives, we immediately fell in love with her. She was an adorable puppy, a blend of Border Collie, Labrador, and a few others. She bonded with the five kids and quickly became their protector.

With boundless energy and enthusiasm, she frolicked with the kids as they played soccer in the field, attempting to steal the ball and run away with it — and succeeding more often than not. She loved chasing the boys when they rode their dirt bikes on trails through our evergreen forest.

Every weekday morning, Ruff would walk with the kids down the long, steep, gravel road to meet the school bus, returning home after they were safely aboard.

Ruff was not only devoted to the kids. She loved running behind the tractor, trying to catch flying dirt clods as my husband tilled the ground. A farm dog at heart, she didn't miss an opportunity to join me as I fed the chickens and gathered the freshly laid eggs every morning.

That sweet dog never met another animal she didn't love; she was protective of our cats and other pets, including a pot-bellied pig, a couple of horses, several ducks, a rabbit and a turkey.

Ruff also followed the kids up the road to visit Granny and Papa daily, and she loved running to greet my parents when they walked down to visit us. It didn't take Mom and Dad long to form a close bond with her. And, realizing they were family, Ruff dutifully took them under her wing.

When my father died unexpectedly, Ruff appeared to grieve his loss as much as we did. She didn't run to greet Mom with the same joyous enthusiasm as she did on those days when Dad had walked with her.

However, it wasn't long before Ruff sensed that Mom needed her more now than ever, and she made the trek up the gravel road every day to spend time with her. As the kids became more involved with school activities and didn't have as much time for her, Ruff spent more time with Mom, who cherished her companionship and the comfort of her protection.

Taking on the responsibility of caring for two households proved easy for Ruff. She split her time equally, and we didn't mind sharing her. Our home was where she ran and played with the other animals and the kids, while Mom's house was the perfect place to unwind and enjoy some quiet time.

As Ruff grew older and began to make the trek less frequently between the two houses, she chose to spend the majority of her time with Mom. We visited several times every day, so it was never as though we were far away. It warmed our hearts to see the two of them looking after each other.

Ruff had an amazing ability to know when and where she was needed the most, making the best of every moment throughout her fourteen years. She was our cherished friend and protector — a special blessing for not just one but two grateful families.

— Connie Kaseweter Pullen —

Axel

Empathy is seeing with the eyes of another,
listening with the ears of another,
and feeling with the heart of another.
~Alfred Adler

When I was a freshman in high school, I got my first dose of responsibility. It came in the form of a Rottweiler puppy who my aunt had bred.

One night, I was getting ready to take Axel outside when he started to act out of character. He was banging and scratching at the door like he was desperate to get out of the house.

"Okay, you little monster," I said with a chuckle as I opened the door. He flew out the door and across the street, which I thought was odd because he never left the property without my father or me.

"You need me to go get him?" my father asked.

"Nah, I got him," I said, walking out the door. "Axel!" I yelled walking down the driveway. I saw him come around the side of my neighbor's yard, circling and barking. "Axel, come home!" I called to him. He ran back across the street to me and started hitting me in the hand repeatedly with his snout, as if trying to get my attention. Then, he ran back across the street. I shook my head and followed him. My dog was in serious distress.

As I came around the side of the house, I finally saw why he was acting the way he had. Our elderly neighbor, who lived alone, had fallen down her front steps. She was lying on her side, her planter broken beside her. I called 911, and Axel and I sat next to her while we waited for the paramedics. When they came and got her on the stretcher, she asked them to stop for a moment.

"Thank you," she whispered, looking at me. "And you," she said, reaching over to pet Axel. "You are a good boy."

As I rubbed his back, I thought, *He is not a good boy. He is a great boy. He is not only my mischievous troublemaker, cuddle bug, and best friend, but he is the biggest blessing I have.* Sometimes, the sweetest things in life have four paws and teach us lessons we would never expect.

—N. Evans—

44

The Neighborhood Dog

Today, I choose to live with gratitude for the love that
fills my heart, the peace that rests within my spirit,
and the voice of hope that says all things are possible.
~Author Unknown

Zoey appeared in our lives one dreary January day while my boyfriend and I were watching TV. Scraggly and skinny, she peered through the living-room door with wild eyes. Our black Lab, Zander, was delighted to have a new doggie pal around.

Over the next few days, as we searched for her owner, we got to know Zoey. We learned she was afraid of loud noises. She shook in terror if we took her on a ride and often threw up in the car. She was skittish and hesitant to trust us.

With no leads in our search to find her owners, we decided to keep her, and she joined our fur family of three cats and Zander.

Zoey was about a year old and had not been spayed. Our first challenge was putting her through surgery and recovery while not losing the delicate trust we had gained in the few weeks since she'd come into our lives. It was a tricky battle. We live on two and a half acres in the country and do not have a fence. We had trained Zander to stay on the property, but Zoey knew no boundaries. She would run off daily and disappear for hours, returning home without her surgery cone. She licked and pulled her stitches, which added another element to the recovery because we had to care for the wound. I worried that Zoey thought the surgery was a punishment, and she would run off and not come back. But she stayed, and she healed while her trust in us grew.

She was a medium-sized dog and a DNA test revealed she was a mix of German Shepherd, Collie, and Chow. Over the next few months, Zoey reached a healthy weight, and her coat began to shine in the sun. We took long walks with her to the river on the logging land at the end of our road. She wasn't too fond of the water, but she happily chased sticks on the shore while Zander swam for them in the river. She became more relaxed and playful.

But despite our attempts at training her to stay on our property, she still had a penchant for running off and disappearing for long periods of time. Sometimes, we could hear her barking in the distance. She believed it was her job to protect, and she took the job seriously. And she had decided that her territory was very large — larger than I wanted it to be. But Zoey was willful and demanded her freedom. As I struggled with anger and pouted over why she didn't want to spend all her time with us, I realized she was teaching me a lesson. Zoey insisted on being herself, with her own set of rules. My attempts to control her would always be in vain. I could continue to fume about her absences, or I could recognize the lesson she was showing me: the gift of loving and allowing.

Over time, I learned that Zoey was purposeful about where she went and who she visited. She developed an extremely close bond with my neighbor, Linda, and spent a lot of time there. Linda lived alone, had recently lost both her cats, and was struggling with myriad health problems. Zoey's presence was a comfort to her. Linda and I began to spend more time together as well, often calling each other or visiting to exchange stories about the dog we both adored. Zoey was a lovable, faithful companion to Linda, and they enjoyed seven years of sweet friendship before Linda moved away.

I thought Linda's departure would break Zoey's heart. I went to Linda's house to say goodbye as the movers packed her things. I swear I could see tears in Zoey's eyes. But she quickly found another neighbor with whom to share her love and companionship. Zoey started disappearing for two to three days at a time, usually on the weekends. We also noticed she was gaining a lot of weight. One day while walking Zander, my boyfriend couldn't believe his eyes when he saw a man in the distance walking Zoey. He said to the man, "Hey! That's my dog!"

The man replied, "I thought she was the neighborhood dog." They laughed and walked down the road together as they talked about Zoey. The man, Ron, was a Vietnam veteran who owned land behind our woods and lived there part-time, mostly on the weekends. He admitted that he'd been feeding Zoey table scraps because she looked so pitiful when she begged, which explained her recent weight gain.

As my boyfriend walked with Ron and the dogs, he learned what a joy and companion Zoey was to this man. When my boyfriend told me about Zoey's mysterious "other owner," I took it personally and felt betrayed. Why weren't we enough? Weren't we her family? But then I thought about how much Zoey had meant to these two neighbors and how interesting it was that Zoey sought them out. She knew where she was needed, and she shared her love openly. That was a beautiful gift. This was my second lesson from Zoey about love. Love is not conditional; love does not mean expecting something in return. She gave her love freely to those she deemed needed it, and I could love Zoey with that same kind of freedom.

When Zoey was eleven, Ron's wife passed away. Zoey began spending more and more time at his place, and over the past few years she has made Ron's property her home base. Instead of being angry this time, I understand she is doing her job: sharing love and bringing comfort to someone in need. She still returns to visit, and we welcome her with open arms. We cherish the moments she chooses to spend with us. She and Zander both have arthritis now and can't race around like they used to, but Zander is always happy to see her when she visits. We have gotten to know Ron better, too, and learned more about Zoey's beginning. The neighborhood rumor is that she originally belonged to a family that moved. When they left, Zoey refused to get in the car.

Zoey has been a challenging dog for me. She didn't fit my expectation that a dog should listen and obey. But her job has been to spread love and joy, and she has done that exceptionally well. Zoey taught me to love without imposing boundaries.

—Becca Hardwick—

45

The Sleep Ninja

*The bond with a true dog is as lasting
as the ties of this earth will ever be.*
~Konrad Lorenz

've had pets my whole life. I just love having a dog at my feet or a cat nearby.

So I turned to pets when I was going through one of the most difficult times in my life. In 2019, I was diagnosed with complex regional pain syndrome in my left foot. This chronic condition makes the affected limb extremely sensitive to touch. Every contact with my foot felt like extreme pain, which made sleeping difficult if not impossible. Even the feel of the sheet on my toes was excruciating. As I struggled with the condition, I wondered if a dog would help. I knew I felt better when I had a pet near me, so maybe a dog sleeping by my side would distract me from the pain.

At the time, I had a 100-pound Golden Retriever named Candie. Like all Goldens, Candie is a gentle giant. She is a good dog, but she was too big for my bed. She would take up too much space and probably bump into my bad foot. I thought that a smaller, lap-size dog might provide comfort while I slept, so I started to look around for the perfect dog.

I started at the local animal shelter, monitoring their website and Facebook posts for available dogs. It took a few months, but then there he was. They had a Jack Russell Terrier named Buster, and I just knew he was the dog for me.

I went to the shelter as soon as I could to check out Buster. The kind folks there told me that they were eager to get Buster out of the place. He was an old dog (at least eight) and had been in and out of many homes. No bad behavior, just a string of bad luck, and living at the shelter was really stressing him out. They wanted to be sure he got along with my Golden, which was the only requirement for adoption.

So, later that afternoon, I asked my kids if they would like to meet a new dog I was thinking of bringing home. They were skeptical at first (I do have a lot of pets), but they agreed to check him out. Off we went with Candie to meet Buster. It was love at first sight. My kids thought Buster was the cutest dog they had ever seen. He was a happy chap, all wagging tail and hellos. And Candie was more than interested in a new friend. We filled out the paperwork and brought Buster home.

Buster adjusted quickly and seemed happy at our house. My husband would often joke that I got a "used" dog, but it worked out well for everyone since Buster had a lot of previous experience as a family pet. Buster and Candie got along easily, and Buster was very entertained by our four cats.

At first, Buster slept in bed with me, and everything worked out like I imagined it would. If I focused my attention on the warm dog at my side, I could draw some attention away from the pain in my foot and relax. In fact, Buster was a super sleeper. My husband was working nights at the time, so Buster spent the night in bed with me and then slept most of the day in bed with my husband. My husband even came up with a nickname for Buster: The Sleep Ninja.

As time went on, I began noticing that my son Henry was really interested in Buster. The two of them were often sitting together on the couch, or I would find Buster lying in a sunbeam in Henry's room. Henry even began throwing the ball for Buster to chase outside. Henry suffers from some serious anxiety, so it seemed good to me that he was making a friend. And Buster sure seemed to be enjoying all the attention. He was the star of the house, earning lots of pets and treats. He was living his best life.

It didn't take long before Henry asked if Buster could sleep in his bed instead of mine. He had a point. How come I always got the dog, and he never did? I could hardly say no, but I was disappointed. Buster had helped my sleep so much, and I worried I wouldn't be able to sleep without him. But I knew that Henry also had trouble falling asleep. Many nights, his anxiety kept him awake until one or two in the morning. So Henry and I worked out a schedule. He would take Buster three nights a week, and I would take him for four.

It became clear right away that The Sleep Ninja was the perfect name for Buster. On the nights he had Buster by his side, Henry would fall asleep right away. There was just something about the warmth of Buster's comforting presence that helped Henry feel safe and secure. We went from Henry not being able to fall asleep for hours to him drifting off within a matter of minutes. Sleeping with Buster was a success. It was a Sleep Ninja miracle.

But, on the nights when Buster wasn't with Henry, Henry couldn't sleep at all. He asked for more and more nights with Buster. As a mother, I could see where this was going. Henry needed to sleep, and it looked like The Sleep Ninja was the solution we had been looking for. So, Buster switched to Henry's bed every night.

I'll be honest: I missed Buster. Over the months he had slept with me, my foot pain had become so much more tolerable. But, as a mother, I could hardly let this perfect opportunity pass. If The Sleep Ninja was the right fix for my son, then I had to let him go. Buster transitioned to every night in Henry's bed, and Henry hasn't had trouble sleeping since.

As Henry has grown older, Buster remains his best friend. The Sleep Ninja isn't just a bedtime companion. Now, he is a shoulder to cry on and a place to share secrets. As my son prepares to enter middle school, I can't imagine it any other way. Just like I did growing up, my son is learning to love and appreciate animals. Buster, The Sleep Ninja, was just what he needed.

As for me and my foot, well, now I have a reason to get another dog!

— Heather Jepsen —

Two Lonely Souls

Saving one dog will not change the world, but surely
for that one dog, the world will change forever.
~Karen Davison

He wasn't a puppy; he wasn't full-grown.
He had been adopted; he did have a home.
But Harley the dog was so sad and so lonely.
He wished, and he wished, "If only, if only…"

"My people were home more, if someone would pet me,
"If there was occasion for someone to let me…
"Go outside for a walk or maybe a car ride,
"Not stay in my kennel but sleep at their bedside."

But he'd be surprised that his people thought, too,
"Harley's so lonely, but what can we do?
"Our jobs are consuming, we're always away…
"It's not fair to Harley to leave things this way."

That's when they decided to take out an ad,
Tell all about Harley and why they were sad.
Explain all the reasons he needed a home,
Where time and attention would always be shown.

They hoped they'd find someone who'd read it and come,
Take one look at Harley and say, "He's the ONE!"
They met lots of people but still hadn't found,
The right place for Harley where love would abound.

Then who should they meet on a warm summer's day?
But a little, old lady wind could blow 'way!
They knew by her face, so loving and dear,
A match for their Harley was certainly here!

They planned the right time to go to her house,
To see where she lived, so they wouldn't have doubts.
The three made their way to her house on East Byrd.
They knocked on the door, and the lady emerged.

"Now, won't you come in. I'm Marion Thompson.
"I hope you're still open to Harley's adoption."
But while they were talking, Harley was sniffing,
So, what they discussed, Harley was missing.

Their talking got quiet, and something occurred,
That Harley could sense, though he didn't know words.
By the feel of the stroke, the goodbye that they said,
Harley knew he would stay with the lady instead.

The lady gave Harley his forever home,
That came with more love than he'd ever known.
She'd take him outside, say, "You're my good boy!"
It's moments like these that gave Harley such joy.

So loved and contented, this dog spent his days,
Right there by her side. Harley found lots of ways,
To guard and to guide her, to love and defend her.
I witnessed the ways that Harley would tend her.

He'd bark when the bell rang. He'd sleep at her feet,
And not move a muscle till morning would peak.
He'd gather her slippers and bring them with haste.
He'd park by the table and hope for a taste…

Of some little morsel that fell to the floor,
But he'd never bark or beg for some more.
He gave Mrs. Thompson his love without fail,
But as the years passed, the old lady grew frail.

Then she took a tumble, oh, no, broke her hip!
The ambulance came, and then she had a trip…
To fix her old hip with the surgeon's repair.
She worked hard in rehab and made friendships there.

But she missed her sweet Harley and being at home.
He missed her, too, and he felt all alone.
When finally together, he sensed what she needed.
He was more than her dog. That's why he succeeded…

At meeting her needs, he knew just what to do.
Like times when she'd drop things he'd fetch them, that's true.
I knew that her Harley just loved that old lady.
And she told him daily, "I love you like crazy!"

The bond that they shared with time never faded,
For this was a friendship that God orchestrated!
Two lonely souls that needed each other,
The dog known as Harley and Marion, my mother.

— Pat Severin —

47

Raising Miracles

Faithful friends are gifts from heaven:
Whoever finds one has found a treasure.
~Author Unknown

t the onset of a global pandemic, a dog's purpose might seem like a silly thing to worry about. Yet, in March 2020, as plans were made for working and schooling and grocery shopping online, I looked at the German Shepherd sprawling on the living room floor and I worried.

"Unprecedented" was the word of the season. Lost amidst the headline-grabbing closings and lockdowns (Disney World! Broadway! International travel!) was the unprecedented hiatus taken by The Seeing Eye, the oldest guide-dog organization in the world.

It wasn't just The Seeing Eye that was closing its doors. Every guide-dog school in the country paused operations for some period of time. This meant that they wouldn't be fulfilling their missions of giving independence to visually impaired people.

"What will happen to the dogs?" I asked my father, who was reading the e-mail about The Seeing Eye's suspension.

I, like many other twenty-somethings, had flown back to the nest to wait out the pandemic. Ours was a puppy-raising family. I'd been a volunteer raiser for The Seeing Eye since I was eleven years old. Twelve dogs later, we'd gotten used to the various puppy stages and personalities. Helping transform seven-week-old puppies to eighteen-month-old dogs was our specialty. I knew that The Seeing Eye pausing its operations meant that the hundreds of dogs completing their "formal" training at The Seeing Eye facility in Morristown, New Jersey, would be sitting idle.

My father scrolled to the end of the e-mail. "They're moving them out. Urgent call for anyone who can take a dog."

That's how the all-out blitz started: with an e-mail. There was so much uncertainty in March 2020. So many things we couldn't control, like the spread of the virus or when we'd be able to see each other in person again. But other than stocking up on toilet paper and downloading Zoom for the first time, it seemed like there weren't a lot of practical, tangible things to do. Until that e-mail.

There were three hundred dogs to be moved out of The Seeing Eye. Three hundred two-year-old Labradors, Golden Retrievers, and German Shepherds that needed to find a home before The Seeing Eye locked down. Our group, covering two counties in South Jersey, had seven families raising seven dogs. The response? Unanimous. Every single family would welcome an additional dog into their home.

My social-media feeds that first couple of weeks of the pandemic were soon flooded — not with COVID graphs and directives to wash the hands but with "welcome home, puppy" stories. Raisers broke out an extra dog bed. Trainers took home a charge or two. Even The Seeing Eye board members made space for a furry houseguest.

Puppy raisers have a difficult job. We get a seven-week-old fluff ball, teach it how to be a good dog and a good citizen, and take it for hundreds of walks and dozens of outings. We love these dogs deeply. And then we give them up.

The Seeing Eye has a unique model, even among service-dog organizations, discouraging contact between the puppy raisers and the visually impaired handler. This means that when we say goodbye to our pups, somewhere around a year and a half old — when we hug them in the driveway next to a Seeing Eye-emblazoned van — it's a real goodbye. It's the last time we get to touch "our" dogs.

I have personally given up thirteen dogs. Parting is indeed such sweet sorrow.

The elation that raisers felt that week was soul-deep. Raisers who took in their own former puppy experienced a kind of dream come true. Imagine thinking you'd never hold your dog again. And then imagine that during one of the worst months of your life, at the very beginning of lockdowns, that dog was suddenly snoring in your living room.

Emotions were near the surface that season. I wept over every reunion. Heck, I even cried over the ones that weren't reunions. Some families welcomed dogs they'd never met before — strange animals with new quirks and personalities, fetching sticks in spring-bloomed back yards.

As for my family, we had that sprawling German Shepherd in our living room, a mostly-black-coated male named Rockford. He had been due to return to The Seeing Eye in April 2020, to be swapped out for a new puppy, a seven-week-old chocolate Labrador. Rockford's return was delayed, of course. He and that new Labrador became our family's quarantine fosters.

In my living room, and in living rooms across the tri-state area, slept puppies born into a pandemic and puppies that were not where they were supposed to be.

The feelings that spring were complicated; we were facing the unknown. I was hopeful that all the pups in Rockford's tumultuous 2020 class would have a chance to get into formal training and become the service dogs they were meant to be. I reflected on a comment that puppy raisers often receive from well-meaning members of the public: "Look at that poor puppy! He shouldn't have to work!"

We train these dogs to give humans independence. In exchange for that service, puppy raisers, trainers and handlers love the dogs to pieces. My family has a new puppy every year. We love them, teach them, watch them grow… and then they are supposed to move on.

Rockford would be a great buddy for the foreseeable future. He was one of the happiest, cuddliest Shepherds I'd ever met. But as hard as it is to give up our dogs, I knew I'd be even more devastated if Rockford never got the chance to change someone's life. Being a guide dog was a job he was born to do.

This virus derailed a lot of lives. Rockford's presence in our living room, snuggling next to our thirteenth guide-dog puppy, was a study in displacement, but also testament to the extraordinary effort undertaken to keep people and animals safe. In the chaos and destruction of that first pandemic spring, hundreds of families opened their homes.

Two years later, I'm fortunate to know how this story ends. Rockford has finished his training and is waiting to be matched with the visually impaired individual whose life he is destined to change forever. Even that tiny puppy we got in April 2020 is back at The Seeing Eye, ready for his own training. One pandemic, two years, and three puppies later, a new German Shepherd is asleep on my feet.

As one of The Seeing Eye club mottos goes: Some people wait for miracles. We raise them one at a time.

— Katie Avagliano —

48

Growls and Broken Crayons

*It is amazing how much love and laughter they bring
into our lives and even how much closer we become
with each other because of them.*
~John Grogan

sat down next to Sam, the first-grade boy I was assigned to mentor through a program at my church. I was supposed to become a trusted adult in Sam's life by spending an hour a week bonding with him, but so far it wasn't going well.

It was the third time I'd come to see him, and Sam still hadn't uttered a word or even made eye contact. His teacher had shared a little bit about his home life and warned that it might take time for him to let his guard down with me.

"Every adult in his life has failed him," she said. "Earning his trust won't be easy."

I nodded solemnly, but in my head, I thought, *Kids always like me. Sam will, too.*

During our first visit, Sam had stared at his well-worn sneakers for the entire hour. I asked him some questions, but he never even glanced my way. On my way home, I'd stopped at Walmart to buy a few games, hoping that if he didn't want to talk to me, he might at least play a round of *Sorry*.

The prior week, I'd set up the game board and tried to hand

him the dice. Without a word, he'd swiped his arm across the table, knocking everything to the floor. Then he stared at his shoes while I picked up the pieces.

Today, I left the board game in my bag and pulled out a coloring book and crayons. "Last week, I noticed that you were wearing a Pokémon shirt," I said quietly. I pushed the Pokémon coloring book toward him, hoping it wouldn't end up on the floor.

It didn't. But every crayon in the brand-new box did. Many of them got broken in half, too.

That night at dinner, I expressed my frustration to my husband, Eric. "I'm going to e-mail Sam's teacher on Monday and tell her I'm not coming back," I said. "Sam clearly doesn't want a mentor, or if he does, he wants someone other than me."

"I understand how you feel, honey," Eric said. "It's sad that a six-year-old boy would already be that distrustful of adults."

I nodded, feeling a lump in my throat. "His story is heartbreaking, and I guess most people in his shoes wouldn't trust easily."

"But it's harder than you thought it would be." Eric reached for my hand and accidentally knocked his fork onto the floor. When he bent to pick it up, we heard growling come from under the table.

It was Peyton, our new rescue Terrier mix, lying by my feet. In the month we'd had her, she'd been friendly with my daughters and younger son and stuck to me like glue, but she was terrified of Eric and our older sons. She growled when she felt threatened. She'd never snapped at anyone, but her fear aggression broke my heart because it was evidence of her painful past.

Just like throwing board games and breaking crayons. This realization changed everything.

That night, I snuggled Peyton close. "I need your help with Sam," I said. "I think it will help you, too."

On Friday morning, I asked Sam if he liked dogs. He didn't answer. No surprise there.

I found a photo of Piper, our Pomeranian/Poodle mix, who loved everyone and feared nothing. I held the phone where Sam couldn't help but see it. "This is my dog, Piper," I said. I explained that we'd had Piper since she was a tiny puppy, so I knew pretty much everything that had ever happened to her. "She's always had our family to love her, and she loves all of us."

Sam didn't respond.

I scrolled to a photo of Peyton and put the phone back within Sam's gaze. "This is Peyton," I said. "She's a grown-up dog, but we just got her." I explained about her fear of men. "We think someone was mean to Peyton before we got her. Now she's afraid because she thinks we might be mean to her, too. We never would do that, but she hasn't learned to trust us yet."

The phone went dark, and I held my breath, praying Sam would speak.

"More pictures," he said, so quietly I barely heard.

For the next hour, Sam and I scrolled through dog photos on my phone. When I was leaving, he said, "More pictures next time."

My heart soared. Piper and Peyton had accomplished something I couldn't do on my own. They'd gotten Sam to talk.

When I got home, I grabbed the dog treats and my phone. "Okay, girls, it's time to be cute," I said. I videotaped Piper and Peyton fetching balls and playing tug-of-war. When my youngest son, Nathan, lay on the floor, both dogs jumped on him and licked his face. I captured every giggle on video.

On Friday, when Sam watched the video of Nathan with the dogs, he said, "I thought the fuzzy dog was afraid of boys."

"Not boys. Just men."

"Because men were mean to her?"

"We think so. She growls at men. Not because she's mean or bad but because she's scared. Sometimes, when animals are afraid, they do things that might seem mean because they're trying to protect themselves." After a pause, I said, "People do that, too."

Sam started another video, but when I was leaving, he said, "Sorry I broke the crayons."

I made it to my car before I cried.

That night, I was sitting on the couch with both dogs asleep on my lap. Eric walked in, carrying a bowl of popcorn. Peyton woke up and growled.

I murmured in her ear, trying to calm her. Eric sighed and sat on the far end of the couch. Piper ran over to him to beg for popcorn. Eric gave her a piece and then tossed one toward Peyton. She gobbled it up.

"Don't toss the next piece so close to her," I said. "And don't look at her when you throw it."

Eric did as I suggested. Cautiously, Peyton crept across the couch to get her share of the popcorn. I taped it, knowing that Sam would enjoy watching Peyton's progress with Eric.

When the popcorn was gone, Peyton quickly returned to my lap. When Eric scooted a bit closer, her eyes were wide, but she didn't growl.

"You're safe here," I murmured, scratching behind her ears.

Eric squeezed my hand. "Peyton and I will get there, and so will you and Sam. We'll just keep loving them until they learn to love us back."

Earning the trust of someone with a painful past isn't easy. It takes time and patience. Whether it's a sweet rescue dog or a little boy who's endured more than any kid should, we must understand that undesirable behavior is often caused by fear, not rebellion.

I snuggled Peyton closer. "You hear that, sweet girl? You and Sam are going to get there, and we're not going to stop trying until you do."

She licked my hand, and I felt hopeful that her fear — and Sam's — would fade someday. And, in its place, they'd both enjoy relationships filled with love and trust.

— Diane Stark —

49

Perfectly Imperfect

Dogs have a way of finding the people who need them,
filling an emptiness we don't even know we have.
~Thom Jones

We were in our first apartment. Everything had been set up and unpacked. It was the beginning of our new life together as a couple.

My husband came home one day and surprised me with a little white ball of fur. He had a black nose and two dark eyes.

It took a while to come up with his name. We toyed with Snowball and Fluffy. Nothing stuck. Finally, a neighbor of mine said, "He is so pure white. How about Whitey?" Whitey, it was!

Two years later, the first of our three kids arrived. Whitey was getting less time with us so we got him a female companion — another Maltese. Heidi was smaller than Whitey yet largely in charge. They were a great pair. They were always cuddled up sleeping or staring out the window together.

As time passed, we discovered Heidi was expecting puppies. We did not think she would have more than one or two since it was her first litter, but she had five! One of them had a shiny pink birthmark on its head where white, fluffy hair should have been.

We called him Pinky. As families came by to choose puppies from the litter, he was left behind. Soon, two puppies were left: a female with a perfect fur coat and our Pinky. Pinky had been passed over each time for the other fluffy puppies, although Heidi loved him and treated him just like the rest of the litter. We grew to really love Pinky, expecting that he was going to stay with us forever.

One Saturday, the phone rang, and it was a woman inquiring about the remaining puppies. We had a pleasant conversation, and she said she wanted to get her six-year-old daughter a puppy. I let her know that since there were only two puppies left, we had just the one truly available. I told her that we had decided that the last puppy would be staying with us. I explained that his name was Pinky, and he had a large pink birthmark on his head, so the other families never chose him.

As I described Pinky, the woman got excited to know we had a puppy that was different. She asked if she could come over that afternoon to see him. She was more interested in Pinky than the perfect female. She explained that her young daughter was born with a birth defect. She wanted her daughter to have a dog like Pinky so she would see that Pinky was just as lovable, beautiful, and perfect as she was. I began to cry on the other end of the phone.

The woman came alone and met Pinky, and she fell immediately in love with him. She said, "This is the perfect dog!" As the woman drove away with Pinky my husband and I had tears in our eyes. We would have a hole in our hearts, but knowing that he was bringing so much joy to a little girl — who needed him more than we did — made us feel incredible!

What started as a way to keep our own dog from being lonely turned into the beginning of a love story between a little girl and her dog. I never heard if he kept the name Pinky, but he will always be Pinky in our hearts.

— Blanche Carroll —

Find Your Inner Strength

50

Our 9/11 Angel

Angels have no philosophy but love.
~Adeline Cullen Ray

A month into our marriage, my new husband and I traveled an hour east of Raleigh, North Carolina to check out a breeder's ad for Boston Terrier puppies. We zeroed in on a scruffy male all by himself in a separate pen. "Li'l Rocky," the owner told us in a thick Southern accent, "is a misfit. At six months old, he don't meet the breed standards since he weighs over thirty pounds. Also, his nose ain't the preferred Boston nose. It's long instead of stubby, and it's out of proportion with his body." As he droned on about the shortcomings of this dog, I studied his short legs, stout torso, and protruding eyes, and fell in love with this underdog on the spot.

"Let's bring him home with us," I whispered to Brian. Brian nodded and then called out, "We'll take the six-month-old Boston!"

On the ride back to our home, we pondered a name change. "Well, we live on Gabriel's Bend Drive. We could call him Gabriel," Brian suggested.

"There's also an angel named Gabriel in the Bible," I added, as I stroked his fur. "He looks like a little angel."

When we arrived home, Li'l Rocky-turned-Gabriel looked delighted at the pastoral two acres he had at his disposal. And we delighted in our new addition to the family.

After my husband finished his short-term work stint in Raleigh, we moved back to New York City with Gabriel in tow on July 6, 2001. He went from doing "zoomies" in two acres of grass to doing zoomies in our 800-square-foot apartment in the Financial District. At first, I worried about Gaby's adjustment to this major change of environment. However, Gaby seemed no worse for wear, and he especially took to our 300-square-foot terrace on the twenty-fourth floor, which was my favorite spot as well. As I sipped my coffee and gazed at the Twin Towers, just six blocks away, Gabriel would lie on his side on the red-brick floor and sun himself. After a while, we were out more than we were in, causing Brian to laugh and declare, "Let's just keep the balcony door open all the time. The constant door opening and closing is driving me crazy!"

"We're off for a walk! Be back in forty-five!" I yelled to Brian as I closed the door behind me. I loved that my recently christened city dog had adapted so easily to his new "back yard." I'd walk him to nearby Battery Park, which lies at the southern tip of the island of Manhattan. This twenty-five-acre park abuts the New York Harbor, and as we walked by the water's edge, we'd look out at the Statue of Liberty and watch boats sail up and down the glistening Hudson River. Then we'd make our way up and over to the World Trade Center to walk around in the Austin J. Tobin Plaza. "Gabriel, treat-ee!" Our building's concierge, Flo, would entice Gabriel with a biscuit in her hand as we walked through the lobby after our walks. As he munched on the treat, I smiled. *Dang, I don't think I could love this apartment building any more than I do!*

Two months after we moved to NYC, my husband rushed into our bedroom. "Get up! Get up!" Brian yelled as he shook my arm. "Someone's bombed the World Trade Center!" We rushed to our terrace and stared in shock and horror at the black smoke and destruction caused by the first plane. Out of nowhere, the second plane came roaring overhead and struck the South Tower just 500 feet above us. The impact hurled us backward into our living room and knocked us unconscious.

"Do you want your shoes?" I groggily heard Brian call out. His voice sounded as if he were in a tunnel. "No, let's get out of here!"

Brian immediately grabbed our whimpering Gabriel and threw him over his shoulder before we evacuated the building. Barefoot and still wearing pajamas, we sought safety in nearby Battery Park. But the nightmare continued. The towers soon fell, covering us with dust and debris. Heavy smoke surrounded us in a deadly cloud. We ran around in a toxic snow globe, trying in vain to find pockets of clean air in which to breathe. Gabriel's lungs were working overtime as he tried to keep up with us.

Exhausted, we stopped for a break by a brick wall. Gaby was panting heavily with his mouth open and his tongue hanging out. The poor thing was shaking in fear. Brian, trying to save his breath, nodded wordlessly as he petted him, unable to do much more. Gaby began licking his fur, and as a knee-jerk response I blurted out, "Stop!" as I pushed his head to the side. I understood it was his instinct to clean himself, but I worried about what he was ingesting.

After enduring three hours trapped in a dust-and-smoke windstorm, we managed to board a boat that was sent to evacuate us off the island of Manhattan. After sailing across the Hudson and disembarking in Jersey City, we made our way to a hotel. When we walked into the lobby, the receptionist asked us, "May I help you?" She looked at us uneasily, as if she didn't trust her eyes. All three of us were caked with several layers of yellow dust. Gabriel's fur was so permeated that you couldn't tell what breed he was, much less his color. As soon as we were handed the key, we ran to our room.

Scooping Gabriel up, I called out, "I'm off to wash us both off!" as I dashed to the tub. I directed the showerhead to spray a strong stream on his coat as I wanted all the gunk washed away before I lathered him up. The water trail it made to the drain looked like I'd thrown a large bowl of yellow oatmeal into the tub. I was utterly astonished at the amount of stuff that had been caked on him. I rubbed and rubbed his fur for a full fifteen minutes before the water began running clear. The same was true for me as I scrubbed myself down.

As I washed, I began to notice something off about Gabriel's demeanor. Normally, he liked to be washed, and he'd shake and snort to show that he was enjoying himself. But now he stood still with his head down, not lifting it up to even clear his nose to breathe. He seemed to be in a state of shock. I felt so bad about what he'd been through, and we couldn't even explain it to him. As I dried him off with a towel, I noticed how red his bulging eyes were. He kept rubbing them with his paws, clearly in pain.

At 8:00 P.M., Brian offered, "I'll call down for some burgers for room service."

"That sounds good," I murmured, my eyes glued to the TV as President Bush addressed the nation.

When the burgers arrived, Brian pulled out a beef patty. "Here, sweetie," he said as he set it in front of Gabriel. He just sniffed it, took a few bites and then looked at us, disinterested. Brian and I glanced at each other in surprise, since Gabriel would normally wolf it down. Not long after, Gaby threw up the bits of hamburger.

After two more days of throwing up everything he ate and generally looking miserable, we were able to take him to a veterinarian. A few hours later, the vet called us into a small room. "The dust Gabriel licked contained ground-up glass that he ingested. Because of this, he sustained cuts to his esophagus."

The vet adjusted his glasses and continued in a flat yet sympathetic tone.

"Terriers are prone to experiencing esophageal issues, and his has been damaged during this ordeal. They are also are predisposed to having brachycephalic syndrome, another condition affecting short-nosed dogs. It leads to severe respiratory distress."

I had read in the newspaper that the dust was made up of bad stuff: powdered concrete, asbestos, jet fuel, ground-up glass, wood particles, pulverized electrical equipment, and human remains. Animals, and particularly Gabriel, are low to the ground, so they couldn't help breathing in this toxic dust in a more direct way than humans did. I recalled memories of Gabriel running around in the dust, tongue hanging out, and licking it off his fur.

"Lastly," the vet continued, "Gaby has large eyes, which makes it easy to sustain cuts on them. Probably these cuts came from glass particles in the dust. We need to attend to that as well."

As the vet rattled off the list of ailments, Brian and I stiffened. We didn't know what to expect, but I for one didn't expect so many medical issues. I wondered if the vet was implying that Gabriel might not make it, but I was too afraid to ask.

"Let's not approach surgery at this point," the vet advised. "Keep a close eye on Gaby, and we'll revisit that idea in a week if he hasn't improved." He prescribed two weeks of antibiotics, along with other medications to treat the esophageal inflammation and pain. We were to chart his breathing to see if he made progress and apply ointment to his eyes daily. We collected Gaby, as well as our $517 vet bill, and Brian carried him back to our friends' apartment, where we'd been staying. For the rest of the week, we gave him the prescribed medication. It made him lethargic, but we hoped that resting would allow him to recover more quickly. Another layer of trauma had been added to our already full plate.

On the day of the attacks, the mayor had ordered a complete evacuation of the neighborhoods surrounding the attack zone, including ours. When we were finally able to move back into our apartment on September twenty-third, we were met at the door by Gus, an employee of our building. "Brian and Christina! How have you two been?"

"We've been all over the place, Gus," Brian answered, giving him a hug. "How the heck are you? What did you do after 9/11?"

"Three of us have been here around the clock, sleeping in the lobby to keep out anybody who shouldn't be here. Each day now, we've been looking in on every apartment on every floor. We go up and down the stairs in the dark, checking on pets and watching for looters." As I listened to Gus, I was reminded of an article I'd recently read about pets that had spent several days in apartments alone. Sadly, some pets were left alone because their owners had died. Other pets simply had to wait for the owners to be allowed back in their apartments. It made me so thankful for the building employees who checked in on those pets and made sure they were being taken care of.

Gabriel slowly got better. His energy returned, and he regained the six pounds he had lost since the attacks. Other animals I knew weren't so lucky; the two Golden Retrievers who lived on our floor died within weeks of 9/11. When we spoke with friends at the dog park, we'd hear the latest news of pets lost due to 9/11. It made us shiver every time.

As the years went by, Gabriel seemed to make a full recovery. He was happy and well-cared for, and we continued to adore our little angel, taking him everywhere we went.

However, in 2009, Gabriel seemed depressed and slow-moving. His energy noticeably lessened. He ate less until he refused to eat at all. While Brian was out of town, I took him to the vet. "I'm sorry to say this," the vet said with a sad look in his eye, "but Gabriel has a rare stomach cancer. It's impeding his ability to ingest food and use the bathroom, which is why he quit eating. There's not much we can do at this point." Gabriel was dying. As the vet proceeded to tell me what was happening to Gabriel's body, my mind wandered to September 11, remembering Gabriel covered with dust and debris. In the years since, I had read that researchers who studied the dust toxins had identified over 2,500 contaminants, which in humans have been tied to almost seventy different forms of cancer. It made sense that this 9/11 debris would be toxic for dogs, as well.

I left Gabriel at the vet and took a taxi back home. I cried so hard during the ride that it startled the driver. "Miss, please, what's wrong? Miss, please, don't cry," he repeated in a thick Middle Eastern accent while constantly checking on me in his rearview mirror. When Brian arrived home, he dove onto the bed, crying inconsolably after I told him the vet's news. Gabriel had been with us during the worst time in our lives, and losing him was almost like another addition to the loss of that day. We survived as a team, and we were bonded forever through the experience. We couldn't wrap our brains around his loss.

Gabriel died in May 2009. We believe without question that he died of 9/11 causes. But just as we were grateful to have survived, we were blessed to have had Gabriel for the years that we did.

— Christina Ray Stanton —

51

Rosa the Wonder Dog

A dog is the only thing on earth that loves
you more than he loves himself.
~Josh Billings

cicles hung clear and cold from the porch roof, but Rosa The Wonder Dog needed her walk. I sighed deeply and put on my heavy down jacket, snapped on her leash, and started out the door. As my feet crunched into the snow, I realized I'd left my hiking boots in the house and had worn my everyday walking shoes, but it didn't seem to matter much. We'd walk our regular route along Blue Grass Lane, with a turn onto White Oak and then back up our lane again.

The song of the creek beckoned though, so we decided to go just a bit farther, past my friend Martha's big white house and across the bridge. The sun shone brightly on the snow, delighting us with silvery sparkles. As we got to a snowy field, I threw a stick for my black Lab mix to catch, and she caught it and buried it in the snow instead of bringing it back to me. I laughed at her antics and snapped the leash back on her collar.

As we crossed the narrow bridge over the creek, two huge yellow dogs seemed to emerge from nowhere. They ran down the hill barking fiercely, baring their huge teeth. I screamed and dropped Rosa's leash. I slipped as I turned, and the ice on the bridge proved too much for my slick-soled shoes. I lay sprawled on my belly, face down on the bridge.

I heard the dogs snarling as they got closer and were almost on top of me. I thought Rosa had surely run away from them, but as I lifted myself to all fours and then to my feet, I saw her. She had run around me to stand between those two angry, snarling dogs and me. She stood there silently, staring them down. She did not bark. She also did not move. To get to me, those two mean yellow dogs would have to go through her.

They thought better of it, huge and mean as they were. They turned tail and ran together back up that hill.

As I got to my feet I picked up the leash, and Rosa and I hurried home as fast as we could in case those yellow dogs changed their minds. Never, in my whole life, has anyone of any species put themselves directly into the path of such anger and meanness the way that Rosa did that day.

I do not eat much red meat, but that night I went to the grocery store and bought a steak for Rosa, my protector and hero.

—Kiesa Kay—

52

Lessons from Grover

*A dog will teach you unconditional love. If you can
have that in your life, things won't be too bad.*
~Robert Wagner

He was just a mutt — half golden Lab, half something else. Even his name wasn't fancy: Grover. It was always a bit unclear how he came to be ours. He belonged to the neighbor across the pasture, who probably tried to use him for herding cattle, but somehow he ended up at our house. I think he loved us because his story was much like ours. You see, we were also mutts — displaced from the big city into the country where we just didn't fit.

Grover came to us back in the decades when there were no such things as leash laws. He roamed the countryside with his furry friends, always returning home to his yellow doghouse. It never occurred to him to be an inside dog. He was a free spirit. The only thing that would bring him inside was a thunderstorm. During a thunderstorm, he would push open the doors and dart upstairs and hide under a bed.

He would bound along with us as we walked across the road to church and wait patiently for us to return for lunch. As a furry protector, he would also accompany my mother on her morning walks. One dark morning on one of those walks, tragedy struck. In the early morning darkness, Grover was hit by a car.

We awoke to find Grover lying in our back yard, my mother crying, and my father bent over him splinting an obviously broken leg. The fur on the leg was gone, replaced only by bleeding muscle and exposed tissue. During the day, our friends gathered to see the poor dog and offer comfort. There were whispers. There was only one thing to do. It was only logical. The dog would never again have use of his leg, and we had no money to take him for medical care. I'm not even sure there was an animal hospital within fifty miles of our home.

Grover's saving grace was that our family knew what it was like to be broken, unwanted, and thought to be useless — and we were not about to discard our faithful friend. After a few days of round-the-clock care and medicine donated by a friend, Grover began to walk unsteadily. Three of his legs worked perfectly, but he never regained use of the broken one. Eventually, all that was left from the accident was a lifeless leg and a patch of skin that never grew hair again.

Grover lived for years after the accident. We weren't quite sure of his exact age, but he was probably nearing the twenty-year mark when he passed away. My parents called while I was out of town to relay the news that Grover had collapsed during a thunderstorm and never awoke. My dad buried him under a large tree with a small wooden cross marking his grave.

Grover, a simple country dog, was probably one of life's greatest teachers. He taught us that pedigree meant nothing, and heart meant everything. And even more importantly he taught us to go where you are loved — even if you have to cross the pasture to get to the place where people will take care of you.

He also taught us to run free, and that your best friends are never to be chosen by the color of their fur or their gender. We would often see him cuddled up next to our other dog, their black and yellow coats intermingling. One time my mother ordered him to go and find our lost girl dog. He arrived soon after with her trailing behind him.

In hindsight, I believe the most important thing Grover taught us was that scars and brokenness on the outside do not have to determine your value or the life you live. After he healed, people would ask what had happened, and we would relay the story of how our little mutt survived. "He doesn't even act like it hurts," people would comment. If it did, he never let on. A bum leg wasn't going to stop him from living life. He didn't care if people thought he was beautiful; he had a place to sleep, food to eat, and a family that loved him. Many would say that he was a very lucky dog. I would say that we were the lucky ones.

— Corrie Lopez —

53

Chicken Soup for the Soul

The Little Hero

True heroism is remarkably sober, very undramatic.
It is not the urge to surpass all others at whatever cost,
but the urge to serve others at whatever cost.
~Arthur Ashe

y husband had a multitude of dogs growing up. A shining example was a little brown-and-black Terrier mix named Freebie. Rescued from a Texas pound, this little dog had a big attitude and a protective streak the size of the state she lived in.

Freebie loved "her" kids more than anything and would protect them no matter what. Once, a large snake entered the yard where the boys were playing. Freebie made sure Wes and his little brother Will didn't go anywhere near it. Then that little dog bravely fought the snake until my mother-in-law, Sherri, came running to kill it.

But, by far, Freebie's most heroic moment was the fateful night she stopped a home invasion.

A few weeks earlier, Wes had caught a boy selling drugs on the school bus and turned him in. The boy was punished and vowed revenge, swearing that he'd make Wes pay. Sherri made sure to drive Wes and Will to school from then on and took other precautions. But one day when Wes's father, a Coast Guard officer, was out on duty, Sherri heard someone trying to break down her front door. She called 911 but the police were twenty minutes away.

"He's going to break down the door. I have to do something," Sherri told the 911 operator. She looked at her two dogs, one of which was a large, intimidating-looking (though ancient) Akita named Bubba, and the other was Freebie. Knowing the intruder was going to come in anyway, she came up with a crazy plan: Knock down the intruder by slamming the door that opened outward into him and then scare him away with Bubba.

"Don't do it," the operator warned her, but the intruder had already nearly gotten through the lock, so Sherri couldn't afford to listen. She quickly opened the door, slamming it into the intruder, and heard him fall down the steps.

"Get him, Bubba!" she called to her Akita, who just looked at her like she was crazy. Freebie, however, sprang into action. Barking like a mad dog at the hellion who dared to threaten her family, she charged out the door before Sherri could close it.

Sherri gasped, terrified her little dog would get killed. "The wrong dog went out!" she told the operator.

"What do you mean 'the wrong dog went out'?"

"My Terrier went out instead of the Akita!"

The situation was explained, and after a little while, the cops arrived. The intruder was long gone, and instead they found a triumphant Terrier proudly running around the yard with something in her mouth. One of the cops tried to catch her and get it, but Freebie evaded him. However, once my mother-in-law came out and called her, Freebie ran over and proudly dropped the object at her feet. It was the sole of an expensive shoe, with the Nike logo still showing.

Brave little Freebie had driven off the intruder, biting at his ankles and tearing off the sole of his shoe, doing her duty and not only protecting her family but delivering some evidence for the police. And while it's unknown if the culprit was ever caught, he was taught a valuable (and humiliating) lesson: Never mess with a little dog with a Texas-sized spirit.

—Jamie Lomax—

54

Luna Belle

You can be in the storm, but don't let
the storm get in you.
~Joel Osteen

y husband and I bought a farm during the COVID-19 shutdown. We both love dogs, so less than three months after moving in we started looking for the perfect dog to add to our family. We wanted an adult dog that was trained. We preferred medium size, but we were not too fussy on the breed.

Luna Belle was the third dog we met, and we knew she was perfect for our home. We received Luna from a rescue that had saved her from a kill shelter somewhere in the southeastern U.S. She appears to be a hound mix. She was estimated to be about five years old, and she is impeccably trained. She does not push partially open doors, and she gently takes treats from the hand of our two-year-old grandson. She naps during her baths at the groomers and has no objection to having her paws touched for a nail trim. She will lie down in our chicken coop and watch "her" flock. She has never lunged at the birds, but she does chase raccoons and stray cats off our land.

When we received Luna, she would occasionally drag her right rear foot. We suspected she might have either a hip problem or that she was older than the rescue originally thought.

The last time we took Luna Belle to the groomer, her hind legs slipped out from under her on their vinyl flooring, and she would not get up. The groomer was sure something was wrong with her, but we were certain the slippery flooring combined with the memory that they had cut her nail to the quick the last time she was there was causing her to refuse her spa day. We took her home and hired a traveling groomer for her.

Not long after this failed appointment, I noticed she was starting to drag her left rear foot. Shortly after that, she was knuckling — walking on the top of — her right rear foot. We knew something was wrong. Through process of elimination, she was diagnosed with degenerative myelopathy, a relatively rare condition that is very similar in symptoms and progression to ALS in humans.

Like ALS, there is no treatment or cure for this condition. Dogs typically survive six months to three years from when they first start showing symptoms. Our beautiful, sweet girl was already past the six-month point when she was diagnosed.

She struggled with walking upstairs, and we often had to help her lift her right foot. She could not get into our truck for rides without our help. She always enjoyed going for walks around the border of our property and occasionally waded into our pond. She stopped this except to go as far as necessary to relieve herself. She even stopped wagging her tail. Our hearts broke for her a bit more every day, but we were so thankful she was not in pain.

Care can be provided to slow the progression of her disease. Exercise is great to maintain weight and muscle mass. Unfortunately, walking on the tops of her feet can cause injury and infections, so she wears braces on her hind legs to keep her feet from curling. The braces have an added benefit because she must lift her leg higher to walk so she no longer drags either foot. Not dragging her feet means she can walk up the stairs again. We also provide physical therapy. If she is lying around, we move her back legs to keep the muscles working. We've discussed the possibility of wheels if she is otherwise happy and healthy when she loses use of her hind legs.

We thought having another dog might help her. When we were presented with the opportunity to rescue a two-year-old white German Shepherd we jumped at the chance. His foster family brought him to our home after I explained Luna's inability to climb into vehicles. We had to make sure the dog we got was right for our family and farm but was also gentle with our disabled dog. The first night Bolt joined our family, Luna played with him. She pounced and wagged her tail. This brought tears of joy to our faces because we had never seen her play before. While boundary-training Bolt, Luna Belle joins in on the walks. Bolt probably walks ten times as many steps as Luna Belle, but she's out there doing it.

We have learned so much from Luna as she navigates this disease. She knows things are not right with her, but she is determined to walk and do the things she enjoys if we provide her with the tools to make it easier. She has taught us to accept the help that is offered. We have learned the value of a supportive friend as we watch her trudge along behind Bolt on their walks. We have learned trust, as Luna trusts us to do what is best for her and trusts Bolt to be gentle and not knock her over.

We know the time to say goodbye to her will come sooner than we hoped. It always does. But we will be thankful for the unconditional love and the lessons she has taught us along this journey.

— Aviva Jacobs —

55

Role Model

I have found that when you are deeply troubled,
there are things you get from the silent, devoted
companionship of a dog that you can get
from no other source.
~Doris Day

Gunner wasn't yet two years old when I got the call from the emergency veterinarian to come in with my kids to say our goodbyes. After undergoing multiple surgeries, the first of which revealed a stomach full of cancer, the vet didn't think he was going to make it through another night. But how was I supposed to let go of the dog who was helping to hold me together?

I wouldn't say my marriage was on solid ground when we welcomed Gunner into our family, but the word "divorce" hadn't yet become a fixture in my vocabulary. Maybe on some level, we thought a puppy would fill in the gaps of love and affection that were missing from our marriage. Maybe we thought a new family member would teach us how to be happy again. Or maybe we just needed a distraction from each other and our marital problems. Whatever the reason, my then husband and I decided to get a puppy. I had no idea of the extent I would come to depend on my bond with this sweet black Labrador Retriever.

I fell in love with Gunner's affectionate personality. He never missed a chance for a belly rub and seemed to instinctively know when a human was in need of canine cuddles. That's why he was the perfect companion to have as I endured one of the most challenging times of my life: divorce.

At first, Gunner maintained the same custody schedule as the kids, bopping from my apartment during the week to stay with my ex-husband on the weekends at the house we used to share. But after Gunner went into a routine surgery and came out of it on the verge of death, I took full custody to nurse him back to health.

After the first veterinarian discovered cancer, closing Gunner back up with the belief she had removed it all during surgery, she advised me to transfer him to an emergency vet overnight. I drove him across town with tears streaming down my face, pulling into the parking lot of another veterinarian, where employees were waiting for my arrival with a stretcher.

I left Gunner in the ICU overnight while I went home wondering if he would make it through the night and how I could possibly live without him.

Gunner survived the night, but by the time I called the vet in the morning, he was still bleeding internally. The emergency vet opened him back up for another surgery.

When the vet called with the update that Gunner had to spend a second night in the ICU, she delicately told me his prognosis wasn't good. Losing hope, I said goodbye. As I looked down at his lifeless body, I kissed his head, thanked him for being the most loyal companion a girl could ever hope for, and begged him not to leave me. I sobbed as I watched my children say their goodbyes to the only pet they remembered having. Then I watched Gunner being carried off on a stretcher, not knowing if I'd ever see this vibrant, happy dog alive again.

To my surprise, the next morning I got the call that Gunner was still alive. He required a day of observation, but I was allowed to visit him at lunchtime. When I got there, I was amazed to see that Gunner was not only up and around, but he was practically jogging outside in the sunshine.

Late that night, Gunner was back at home with me where he belonged. Worried that he would try to jump up on my bed with me, I blew up an air mattress and slept in the living room beside him.

Night after night, I set my alarm for early morning hours to adhere to his strict medication schedule, but I barely slept as I woke to his every twitch and drugged, dreamy moan.

For days, we both attempted to rest as much as possible. I constantly monitored him for irregular breathing, bleeding and changes in the color of his gums. I hand-fed him cooked chicken and rice, and kept charts of his medications. I found myself having regular one-sided conversations. I wanted Gunner to make sure he knew how much I loved and needed him, and how thankful I was that he was fighting to stay alive.

But those conversations were more than just pep talks for my sick dog. As Gunner stared back at me with his big brown eyes, those talks were like therapy sessions for me. I confided in him about everything from my struggles with life after my divorce, to managing a full-time job as a single mom, to my fears that I would never find another partner in life. I poured my heart out to him, and I felt he was answering back whenever he snuggled a little closer to me or licked my hand. In those days and then weeks when he required close attention, it felt as if we were recovering together.

Soon enough, Gunner was almost back to his old self. Other than the cone he had to wear around his head to prevent him from chewing his stitches, no one would ever be able to guess that a team of veterinarians had given him less than a 50/50 chance of survival. And when the stitches were removed and his cone was thrown in the trash, he was given a clean bill of health and I realized what a true fighter Gunner was.

I also realized that somewhere along that road of recovery that Gunner and I had traveled together, I found something I'd been looking for as I prepared for a new life after divorce. I found the true fighter in me, too.

— Heather Sweeney —

56

My New Best Friend

A person who has never owned a dog
missed a wonderful part of life.
~Bob Barker

When my son was three years old his action figures began to overtake our living room. My husband and I could not reach the couch without having a hard plastic figurine become embedded in our feet. It became increasingly evident that we'd either have to renovate our home or sell our son.

Since we'd grown quite attached to our little towhead, we opted to utilize our unfinished attic and build a master suite. It appeared that we'd found the optimum solution. We'd create an Austin Powers–worthy love shack on the second level. Our old bedroom would be converted into a playroom for our son's inanimate friends.

As you know, in every story there is always some form of conflict that the heroine needs to resolve. For me, that would be the moment that I began to have panic attacks over our son sleeping downstairs alone.

My concern didn't arise because we lived in a neighborhood prone to violence. Nor was he prone to sleepwalking or playing Texas hold 'em all night with his cigar smoking buddies. No, my anxiety arose from the sheer fact that I was a prime example of the neurotic first-time parent.

After two minutes of deep soul-searching I came up with a brilliant solution. We would get a pup, a big dog that would both adore us and mutilate anyone that dared to even ponder an evil thought our way. The dog would sleep downstairs with Luke.

We all became ecstatic about the thought of expanding our family. I immediately began to educate myself on various breeds. I researched the characteristics and quirks of every pedigree.

I must admit we had some heated debates on what type of dog to get, but eventually we all concluded a Boxer would fit us best. The breed was known to be loyal, smart, athletic, protective, and playful.

We checked the classifieds daily. I began to wonder when dogs had become such a commodity. When I was a kid there was always a neighbor down the street whose dog had a slew of puppies that they prayed that they could get rid of before they grew too large. Today dogs practically come with a resume and their cost could pay for a year of community college.

Finally, after interviewing dozens of little tail-chasers, we found our new baby. Forgive me if I sound like a doting mother but she was perfect. Her eyes were a soft brown that stared at you lovingly. She had a black mask. Her body was solid. She would play but she would also settle down and let you hold her. We named her Tyson. I know it's a boy's name but try arguing with a three-year-old; I'd learned to pick my battles carefully.

For the first few weeks Tyson was a dream dog. She housetrained immediately. She was a mild-mannered puppy who alternated between eating, sleeping and playing much like a newborn baby. But as she grew, I seriously began to wonder if she needed an exorcism.

She devoured our TV remote. She ambushed our tomato plants, running through the yard with them tightly gripped between her clenched jaws. She assaulted guests, crushing their vulnerable private parts.

I kept waiting for her to display some of the positive characteristics that were associated with her breed. Months passed. Tyson was what we educators would term "a challenge." She would tug on her leash and drag you down the street. She ignored me if I asked her to come to me. She did manic laps around the back yard, knocking over anyone unlucky enough to cross her path.

I'd almost given up on expecting her to turn into the loyal intelligent sidekick that I had anticipated. Until one memorable day when my angels must've heard my desperate pleas.

Our back yard had long been the focal point of our home. We had a large built-in pool adorned with tropical foliage. We ate dinner on our concrete patio on warm evenings. Our deck was prime for sunning. The lounge chairs whispered my name from the last day of school to somewhere around Labor Day.

It was a typical hot Jersey summer day. I was relaxing on a chaise lounge. My son was near me choreographing a huge battle with his army men. Tyson was sprinting back and forth around the yard. I leaned back into my chair and picked up my latest copy of *Cosmopolitan*.

Suddenly I heard the low drone of a bee. It flew past me. I returned to my reading. After years of living behind a reservoir I'd accepted the unwritten law of nature that most critters smaller than you would not challenge you unless they felt threatened.

Now remember I did say "most" living things wouldn't attack. Apparently on this day I had met up with the Osama Bin Laden of bees. The yellowjacket suddenly swooped underneath and stung me on my posterior. I bolted to my feet while swishing the little menace with my magazine.

A normal bee would sense danger and hit the highway; however, this was a steroid king. He swept towards me again. He bypassed my defense and stung me again. This time he took a bite out of my breast.

"Ouch, you little pecker," I cried out.

"Luke, hurry, run inside," I called out to my son. I figured that if one of us had to go down I would do the right thing as his mother. I would sacrifice myself and distract the insects to save him.

Luke took one look at the bees encircling me. A dozen bees had revealed themselves. They began entrapping me with the same silent intimidation as those birds in the Hitchcock classic.

Luke did what every intelligent macho man would've done. He ran to safety.

Tyson, who had settled down on the cool concrete patio, was observing everything. She watched with interest as I thrashed about with as much coordination as Elaine dancing on *Seinfeld*.

Finally, she took action. She ran alongside Luke escorting him to the house.

I could hear him urging her to get inside. He sounded like a dictator who had inhaled helium.

I had to survive. I began karate chopping the gang of buzzing predators. I was battling fiercely but the little bugs were winning. They started to fly faster and began attacking me like kamikaze pilots. Finally, as a last resort I leapt into the pool fully clothed.

"Ha, you beasts," I declared victoriously, coming up for a breath of air. "You can't get me in here."

I was so wrong. They came full force at my head. I dipped back under the water, but not before I took notice of Tyson. There she stood a few feet away at the edge of the pool.

Her eyes were lit up as if she were processing what was happening. I suddenly became concerned for her safety. I realized that I had actually become attached to my challenging little companion. "Run, Tyson," I tried to urge her. "Go by Luke."

But as usual she wouldn't listen to me. Instead, she began to bark in some animal language that the hostile bees seemed to comprehend.

The swarm flew towards her. She began snapping at them. She was chewing the fleet one by one. Her face began to swell from the venom but she was undaunted. She continued to devour the bees.

I tried to persuade Tyson to run away as I dipped my head in and out of the chlorine. but she would not leave me. My crazy little Ritalin-worthy dog knew what she was doing. She stood her ground, luring those bees to her and killing them one by one.

I climbed out of the pool and grasped her beautiful swollen head. She tried to French kiss me. I pushed her away. I was grateful, but a hug would be enough. I rushed her inside and immediately administered Benadryl to both of us. The swelling quickly went down.

I don't know what came over her that day. That dramatic incident placed a mutual bond of trust and loyalty between us. Tyson's behavior improved incredibly after that. In time she matured into the best dog I'd ever had.

We took long walks together, we cuddled together, and we always looked after one another.

For nine years my relationship with Tyson thrived. It grew to be the best possible connection that you could hope for with a best friend.

— Patricia Senkiw-Rudowsky —

57

The Old Dog

*The relationship between a military working dog and
a military dog handler is about as close as a man
and a dog can become.*
~Robert Crais

He was limping down the street on a hot July day with his tongue dangling from his mouth. In our community, people will approach a small dog to look for identification to contact the owner. Few will go up to a larger dog though, especially one that appears to be injured or sick. As the coordinator for our Neighborhood Watch "Lost/Found Pet Program," I'd advise those who find such pets to keep a distance and call animal control.

However, the two people who spotted the dog were the daughter and granddaughter of a woman across the street from where the dog was walking. They saw his distress and couldn't leave him, so they went up to him slowly and coaxed him into the back yard. The dog was hesitant, but a bowl of water lured him into the yard. After he finished the water, he lay on the grass. He looked tired, and his legs shook.

I went over to scan the dog for a microchip. Fortunately, he had one. Unfortunately, the information was outdated; we had no way to contact the owner. All I was able to get was that his name was Zephyr and he was fifteen years old. I noticed scars on top of his head, and my first thought was that he might have been abused. But he was friendly, though shy, and watched me carefully, trusting me not to hurt him. We locked eyes, and I quietly said, "You're an old guy, aren't you?"

The only options were to wait a few hours or to take him to the police station and, from there, to animal control. We decided to wait.

Two hours later, I received a phone call from a woman who was distraught. Her dog had gotten out of her back yard, and, as a new resident, she didn't think he'd know his way home. With the information she gave me, I knew it was the same dog. Within minutes, Zephyr was home.

Then, I learned that Zephyr wasn't an ordinary pet. He was a Belgian Malinois who had served time in Afghanistan as a bomb-sniffing dog. In his last mission, a bomb had exploded, killing his handler and leaving him blind in one eye, mostly deaf and injured from shrapnel. The military was going to put him down, but a rescue in New Mexico took him to be adopted once he'd healed.

A retired veteran saw his picture and knew Zephyr belonged with him. For the next few years, they'd walk two to three miles a day and become best friends. When the veteran died, his widow and Zephyr moved to a new community. Less than a month later, Zephyr went missing.

Because of his challenges and age, it is unlikely that Zephyr would have been adopted at the animal shelter. Even now, it looks as if his time is limited. But, because of the kindness of the New Mexico rescue, the couple who adopted the injured dog years ago, and the young woman and her daughter who approached him that hot day in July, Zephyr will live out the rest of his life in his own home.

After his years of service to his country, he wasn't ignored. This soldier wasn't left behind.

— Alison Shelton —

Chapter
7

Live in the Moment

58

Eat, Sleep, Fetch, Repeat

A dog can express more with his tail in seconds than his owner can express with his tongue in hours.
~Author Unknown

"So, what do you think?" I said, bending down to eye level with my dog. Sierra, my large Goldendoodle, was watching me with anticipation, waiting to hear the words that she hoped I would say. "Fetch first and then a walk? Or walk first and then fetch?"

Sierra decided on a walk first, made obvious by her dashing toward the cabinet that contained the leash. After the walk, she had just enough energy left for a few rounds of fetch before heading to her bed for a nap.

I'm sitting at my desk now, watching her sleep. Her ears twitch, and her legs move, running in a chase that will never result in a catch. It's a marvelous oddity to watch because she's chasing after something she can't have. But the moment she awakes and sees me, she is glowing with happiness. She has a new chase... one that involves being with me.

Essentially, she is a best friend with a constant positive attitude.

So, when was the last time I could say that about myself?

The moment I turn back to the project in front of me, her furry head is underneath my elbow, a ball in her mouth, asking for me to throw it by nudging my arm. A few throws and she's back to lying down, happily engaged in resting once more, the tennis ball placed next to her paws for future use.

I'm sensing a theme from her actions. The theme is contentment.

Sierra is content to sit and watch me — happy to just be in the room with me. When it's time to feed her, she's content with the same dog food in her dish every day. She's enthusiastic about having fresh water to drink. She greets me with joy every time I come home, even if I'm only gone for ten minutes. Her energy and happiness at my return are contagious. Who doesn't want a happy face to greet you at the door?

It dawns on me as I take a sip of my coffee and watch her sleep that I've got more to learn from her — way more than everything I've taught her.

How did this happen?

In my mind, I begin to scroll through her actions, and I realize every single one of them is something I could do to make my life better.

Her contentment could be my contentment.

So, what about when I don't feel like exercising? Maybe I should try exuding the same enthusiasm she has when I ask her "Wanna go for a walk?" If I act like it's the most wonderful thing, it becomes the most wonderful thing.

I want to be excited when I see someone, even if I just saw them, because she acts that way with me! And I love it.

I want to be happy for the food that I have because any food in my belly means I have much to be thankful for.

I want to be content with the bed I sleep in, the roof over my head, and the arms of the family that hug me.

Because my dog sure is.

To be in a happy state of mind all the time seems almost not doable. And yet, it's possible if I simply appreciate every little thing around me exactly the way my dog does.

Perhaps, all we ever needed to know — the secret to life, if you will — can be learned from our dogs.

Is this normal? Is this a good thing? Is it crazy to want to live a simple and wonderful life based on the attributes of my dog?

I get up from my desk and begin to rub her ears, paying particular attention to an area she always has difficulty scratching, running my hand over her thick, soft fur. It's been said that the simple things in life are best. That's what we have if we think they're truly the best. These thoughts can seem crazy in our world of constant accumulation and the need for new, more, and better.

But my sweet dog is happy, and she has a simple life. So, again, I ask myself, this time out loud to Sierra, "Am I crazy to want to live my life based on your attributes?"

I conclude I am not. I know without a doubt that I am a happier person when I'm with her. I love that she appreciates everything I do for her. And it's not a stretch to think I can be happy living a simple, appreciative life like she does.

Her joy is contagious. I can live my life the way my dog does.

— Heather Spiva —

59

Hawk Dance

The main difference between play and playfulness is
that play is an activity, while playfulness is an attitude.
~Miguel Sicart

Through the years, I never gave much thought to birds. Sure, as a kid on a farm, I played with the chickens and ducks and took pleasure in the early morning melodies of my mother's canary. Still, I'm a dog man, and for the longest time I never saw anything to bring me over to the bird's side of the bench.

Then came Ruby, a red-and-white Border Collie. She was the first dog to point me in the direction of birds, and it was in a most unusual way. Starting as a puppy, Ruby never walked anywhere when she could run. She quickly came to learn that while running was fun, it was even more fun if she had something to run against. Border Collies are competitive dogs, and Ruby wanted to compete. She started by chasing chipmunks and squirrels. My wife Genie and I quickly learned that this had nothing to do with a hunting instinct. After all, she was a herding dog. One time, Ruby overtook a squirrel, and the squirrel wound up in her mouth. The only thing we could figure was that, in the confusion, the squirrel must have mistakenly leapt into Ruby's mouth. Ruby wasted no time in spitting out the squirrel. So, no, Ruby didn't want to eat any of the animals she chased — she just wanted to see who was faster.

One day, we noticed that Ruby's habit shifted a bit: She started chasing geese. What made it truly interesting is that she had no interest in chasing the geese hobbling around near the river's bank like so many, pardon me, sitting ducks. No, she only chased flying geese, those already high in the air. In other words, those she had no chance of catching.

One day, Genie asked in an exasperated tone, "Why in the world does she chase something she has no earthly chance of catching?"

"Two reasons," I said. "The geese give her something to compare her speed against."

Genie smiled and said, "Okay, Professor. That's one thing. What's the other?"

"She loves hearing you laugh. And let's face it, you always laugh when she runs hell-bent-for-leather after a bunch of squawking geese."

When Genie heard that, her smile broke wide and turned into a laugh, and that's when Ruby made a beeline for her and pressed into her legs. Ruby had always reacted strongly to Genie's laughter but especially now. For the past few years, Genie had been battling cancer, and it had recently come back with a vengeance, spreading into other places, including her brain. Ruby knew that, just as she knew that laughter had become a rare thing of late.

One night, I took Ruby for a walk through the neighborhood. Though I would have liked for Genie to accompany us, she needed to conserve her strength. I'd also come to treasure these moments as an opportunity to talk through my worries with Ruby. Cancer takes away many things, like quiet moments of reflection. In Ruby, I had two things: someone devoted to Genie and someone who understood that sometimes it wasn't about how much you fought, but how much you laughed and loved.

That night, as the last golden rays of daylight turned to silvery twilight, we turned the corner to head home, and I saw something ahead that baffled me.

We'd had a hot, miserable summer that killed our lawn. A few days earlier, I'd had the yard aerated and seeded. When we set out on our walk, I turned on the oscillating sprinkler to soak in the seed.

From the top of the block, I saw the sprinkler spreading water in tall arcs. But something was standing next to the sprinkler. Something big. And it was moving. Not just moving but hopping, like a kid on a pogo stick.

Ruby had zeroed in on it, too.

As we got closer, I couldn't believe what I was seeing. There, in the yard next to the sprinkler, stood a giant hawk. With its wings fully extended, it was jumping through the refreshing water.

I whispered just loudly enough for Ruby to hear, "Friend of yours?"

Then the hawk spotted us. He froze, no doubt hoping we'd keep walking.

"Sorry. We live in this house," I said.

The hawk begrudgingly took flight.

I unsnapped Ruby's leash, and she went straight into the front yard and stood where the hawk had been next to the sprinkler. I joined her and we stood in the center of the yard under the tall arc of water.

Ruby and I were getting soaked. "I suppose I should turn off the sprinkler."

As I was about to take a step toward the faucet, a thought came to me. "No. Genie needs to experience this."

I turned my gaze to Ruby. "You're behind this, aren't you? I don't know how, but I know," I told her.

I took out my cell and called.

"Where are you?" Genie asked.

"Outside."

"Outside?"

"Front yard."

"Wait. You used your cell to call me... from the yard? You never use your cell." She let out a small laugh.

"Yeah. Ruby has something to show you. Come on out." Ruby pressed her now soaking body into me.

Genie came outside, but when she saw what we were doing, she stopped just outside the arc of water. She said, "I knew one day you'd go nuts like that dog of yours."

"Come on in," I said.

She hesitated like someone who stands at the lip of the pool before working up the courage to jump in.

I said, "This is a beautiful kind of nuts."

Genie stepped into the arc of water. Then she laughed.

As water pinged into us, I told her about the hawk.

That night, and with Ruby as our guide, Genie and I saw the joy in the world for the first time in quite a long time. No matter what had come or was yet to come, it wouldn't be the last time we'd taste joy. Ruby would help us see that.

— David Weiskircher —

60

Satisfied

They motivate us to play, be affectionate,
seek adventure and be loyal.
~Tom Hayden

The early morning air was clear and crisp, and the sun was coming up. There was a dusting of snow that made everything sparkle.

It was the perfect time for Titus's morning walk. He loves walking in fresh snow!

Titus has been in our family since he was seven weeks old. He is a delightful mixture of black Lab silliness and Cockapoo curiosity. He spent his first eight months sleeping in a wicker basket under my desk in my home office, nestled between a warming blanket and an oversized, stuffed pink bunny. Now, at age eleven, he has a new stuffed rabbit he keeps close by in his bed.

This morning, he danced anxiously, waiting for the leash to be attached to his collar. It was time to explore his favorite route — right at the driveway, down the sidewalk adjacent to the empty field, right at the corner, across the street, and into the neighborhood golf course.

It is a hilly course, allowing him some needed running space and me a cardio challenge.

We crossed the ninth hole and made our way up the slope to the backside of the course. We found pockets of deep snow in the shadows of the large pine trees. Titus investigated each pile, thrusting his head deep into the middle of each mound, and then extracting it just long enough to take a breath, look in my direction, and move to the next pile.

We crisscrossed the fairway. Areas of brown grass peeped through a snowy blanket of white. Our footprints created a border around the bare patches — shoe prints followed by paw prints, looking like stitchwork dividing the squares on a patchwork quilt.

Titus ran to chase a pair of Canada geese. I made my way up the last rise and, to my delight, found a beautiful blanket of pristine snow covering the far side of the hill. A thin film of ice had collected on the surface of the slope, making it a slick, crunchy combination.

As Titus crested the top of the hill, he saw the snow, ran directly toward the frozen sheet, and dove nose-first. His head popped up, tongue licking the frozen crystals off his muzzle. He jumped to his feet and again flung himself onto the blanket of white, wiggling and rolling, creating a doggy snow angel.

Standing at the edge of the slope, he took another plunge. This time, he caught his back foot on a patch of ice. He kicked to free himself and slid slowly down the hill with each kick. Once at the bottom, he jumped to his feet and stood motionless. I could tell he was thinking about what had just happened. His thoughts must have formed a plan because he ran to the top of the slope, fell onto his side, gave a push, and slowly slithered to the bottom again.

I spent the next fifteen minutes watching the scene repeat: run, fall, kick, and slide.

As I watched, I could not help but think that I want to be that present in the simple moments of my life. I want the courage to run with abandonment and thrust my mind and heart into new challenges, investigate the unknowns, and embrace my awkward quirks without apology. I want to live with a deep awareness of how blessed I am to live, breathe, and have a purpose in the world. And as I continued to watch, my breathing slowed, my heart calmed, and I felt a joyous satisfaction.

- After he finished, we returned home. Titus walked with a prance.

He looked back at me occasionally, tongue hanging from his mouth, ears perked up, and there was the faintest twinkle in his eyes.

He was joyously satisfied.

And so was I.

—Allison McCormick—

61

Dog of the Many Beds

What do dogs do on their day off?
Can't lie around — that's their job.
~George Carlin

When we adopted our dog, the shelter volunteer suggested that we have beds for our new family member in more than one location in the house. This would make her feel welcome with several special places that she could call her own. We took that advice to the extreme.

"Dog of the Many Beds" would be an appropriate nickname for our Piper. She has a bed in the living room, another in the den, a third in the basement, a fourth in our family room, and a fifth, her "official bed," in an extra bedroom that houses her crate (sixth bed?). Her official bed is the one she spends the night in. We guide her into that room at lights out, put the child gate across her doorway, and turn on the burglar alarm. We call that her "hibernation bed" since it is where she does her deep sleeping. The use of the other beds, however, is completely at her discretion.

It's become clear that Piper has particular preferences about where she rests during the day. If the family is out, she selects the bed in the living room, no doubt because it is the closest to the front door. Upon hearing the key in the lock, she gets up, shakes herself from head to tail, and quickly takes her spot as a welcomer. Her exuberant greeting adds a bit of joy and excitement to every homecoming.

When family members are at home, Piper generally divides her time among her various beds to follow the day's action. Her dual intention is to keep us company and to make sure she doesn't miss out on anything. Because I feed her, I am prioritized as the main person she keeps in her sights. She generally follows me around the house and settles into the nearest bed to wherever I am. Her commitment to staying close to me reaches a crescendo around dinnertime. She might look relaxed, but her eyes are intensely trained on me to catch the most subtle indication that I might make a move toward the kitchen and her food bowl. The slightest twitch on my part sends her running ahead of me to the refrigerator, toenails clicking on the tiles. She turns and looks at me quizzically, wondering why I am not faster.

At other times, Piper might settle in close to another family member. When I work on my computer in the basement, Piper will often choose not to follow me down the stairs. Rather, she will stay on the main floor with my daughter, who has been working mostly from home for the past two years due to the pandemic.

If her sharp ears discern the opening of a bag of snacks by some-one watching TV, Piper is off like a shot to the den. Frequently, she is rewarded with a small piece of a chip. Then she sits in her nearby bed on the lookout for any crumbs that might fall.

Of course, as might be predicted for a well-loved (and spoiled) pet, Piper is not restricted to her beds, despite her many choices. She is also a couch potato. If a family member is sitting on the sofa reading, she approaches with her puppy-dog pleading facial expression, sits at the feet of her target, and waits for an invitation onto the furniture, where she will get belly rubs.

Piper will occasionally crave some alone time, particularly as she has gotten older. In those cases, she heads for her hibernation bed where she remains until she gets curious about the world outside her room and comes back out to investigate.

Most of the time, however, she craves company, and so we always know where she is. One day I was looking for her in the house. "Did you let her in from the back yard?" I asked my daughter. She assured me she had. Then I noticed a blanket from the sofa in a pile on Piper's den bed. Investigating further, I discovered her in the middle, all covered up. Apparently, she had dragged the blanket to her bed and then encased herself. Not even the tip of her nose was showing! How she managed to make herself into a wrapped-up burrito was a mystery until I got to witness her process one day.

A blanket had fallen on the floor a few feet from her bed in the den. She gripped it with her teeth and, walking backward, dragged it to her bed. Once there, she used her head to toss the edge of the blanket up and then burrowed under it, turning herself around several times until she was all covered. With a sigh, she curled up, ready for a nap in the personal dark space she had created. Knowing now that she likes to be wrapped up, we have given each of her beds its own small blanket.

When she is in her burrito state, it is hard to tell which end is which. The remedy is to call her name. The flickering of her tail in response disrupts the smooth line of her blanket and lets us know if she is pointed east or west under it.

Although adept at bundling herself up, Piper has difficulty removing her blanket when she leaves her bed. Her curled tail prevents the blanket from getting fully off her back, and she winds up wandering through the house while dragging it with her. It doesn't seem to slow her down. She knows it will fall off eventually, and someone will return it to her bed to use the next time she feels the need to escape under its darkness.

Apparently, the multiple-beds suggestion offered when Piper first joined our family was good advice. She has clearly made this her home, where she is not only comfortable but resourceful as well. And we are endlessly entertained by her ingenuity.

— Lisa C. Castillo —

The Life of Riley

*Some of our greatest historical and artistic treasures
we place with curators in museums;
others we take for walks.*
~Roger Caras

hear it first: the quiet huffing, Riley's impatience growing. I open an eye to see his furry face beside the bed. He's been my alarm clock every day for the twelve years he's been with me. His cold, wet nose is pressed against the side of the bed. There's an apologetic look in his eyes, like he understands it's Saturday, and I don't want to get out of bed.

I know he won't give up, so I reluctantly throw my legs over the side of the bed. My feet hitting the floor sends his tail into overdrive, wagging back and forth, making swishing noises on the carpet. He's still in sit mode, trying his hardest to behave. "Let's go." It's all I have to say to send him flying down the hall and racing down the stairs. He stops at the bottom, turning to make sure I'm coming. As I reach the bottom step and try to push the sleep from my brain, I realize that the first snow of the season has fallen overnight.

Riley, a twelve-year-old Portuguese Water Dog, looks like a five-year-old on Christmas morning when he realizes that Santa has brought the goods. As I open the door to let him out, he looks at me one last time with pure gratitude in his eyes and darts out the door to his version of heaven. I move to the coffeemaker, my salvation. Taking my steaming mug to the window, I watch as he jumps and rolls in the pure-white, fluffy snow with absolute joy.

Knowing his backyard romp won't satisfy him for long, I head back upstairs to throw on some warm clothes — and grab my boots and hat and his leash. Riley doesn't need his leash, but it makes me feel like a responsible parent. I step out into the cold morning air, and he falls in stride beside me. We walk the same route to the park every day like it's a ritual. I take in the silence that comes with the snowfall and the early morning. We reach the park, and Riley sits down in the snow and faces the sun rising in the sky like he's taking it in for the first time. He looks at me as if to say, "See, isn't this worth getting up for?" before he runs full steam toward the open field.

I marvel at his energy and wait for it to run its course. As he jumps like a jackrabbit into the snowdrifts, sticking his nose into the cold, fresh powder, I feel an enormous sense of gratitude that he's my best friend. My family has named him the fifty-thousand-dollar dog. Two knee surgeries, one cancer operation, and now monthly medication for diabetes, but he's still running in the park and getting me up at first daylight.

How much would you pay to save your best friend? What is his life worth? He is the one constant in life that never lets me down. His unconditional love greets me at the door every day after work and helps me forget how much my lousy day doesn't matter.

He races toward me now, his tongue hanging out, and I know he's expended all his energy and is ready to walk back home together. The coffee in the pot is still hot. I pour myself another cup. He snuggles up beside me on the couch, where we read the paper and enjoy the solitude of Saturday morning. Mornings like this are priceless.

— Lucy Wetherall —

A Birthday for Our May

Never trust a dog to watch your food.
~Author Unknown

Our dog May understands us way too well. Any talk of playing with a b-a-l-l, going for a w-a-l-k, taking a b-a-t-h or even the mention of a b-i-r-d in the yard has to be spelled out if we don't want her to bound into action! Every Sunday, when it is time to pull the garbage cans out to the road for pick-up, you better call it trash or she'll be ready for her job at the mention of g-a-r-b-a-g-e.

Everyone in the house was aware of the words we had to spell, but we didn't realize we also had a problem with her recognizing a certain song.

After several of her own birthday celebrations, I guess May came to learn that something delicious waited as soon as we were finished singing the "Happy Birthday" song to her. One year, we prepared a dog-recipe cake. When she turned nine, she got to eat a hot dog with a real bun! And last year she was shocked to find a dog-safe pizza. (The only other time she tasted pizza was when she pulled the end of a slice out of the kitchen garbage!)

We didn't realize May had made this birthday connection until we gathered in the kitchen to celebrate my sister's birthday. May was resting upstairs. We lit the candles and began to sing when we were interrupted by a thundering sound. May raced down the stairway and into the kitchen like a kid on Christmas morning. With her big tail wagging, she looked expectantly at me for her big treat! Through the laughter, I headed for the refrigerator to grab a complimentary piece of cheese. It wasn't her birthday, but I couldn't leave her empty-handed! Now, every human birthday, I come prepared with a small treat to satisfy her because we cannot spell out the whole song!

As I write this, today is the morning of May's eleventh birthday. She is lying on her pad next to my chair, arms crossed and eyelids fluttering between sleep and awake. Everything is calm and quiet, yet she is keeping an ear out for anything of note. She is unaware that later today we are going to gather in the yard. It will be like any other day, but the difference is we are planning to catch her off guard and burst into song. I can already laugh as I picture her unable to contain her excitement, especially when she realizes that a dog submarine sandwich is waiting at the end of her favorite song. And something tells me she is not going to be able to wait until we finish singing to e-a-t it!

— Penny Blacksand —

64

Staring Dog

*The greatest pleasure of a dog is that you may make a
fool of yourself with him, and not only will he not scold
you, but he will make a fool of himself, too.*
~Samuel Butler

"Mom! That dog is out there again!" I stopped my
work and swept aside my office curtains to con-
firm my son's announcement. Yup. There he was.
Again. Standing in the front yard. Again.

I set down my pen and rested my chin on my hand, settling in
for a moment to watch. The questions once again flooded my mind as
they did every time this beautiful creature showed up on our property.
Whose dog was this? Did he have someone who loved him? With
his brilliant coats of reddish brown and white and a perfectly fluffed
tail that curved gracefully over his back, it was clear that while not
purebred, this dog had Husky flowing through his veins.

I adored Huskies. However, I was married to a cat person, and
had one kid who was also a cat person and another who was allergic
to dogs. My nostalgia for my own beautiful Husky, Lady Cheyenne,
may she rest in peace, was overwhelming.

This husky mix was intriguing. We had tried to find out who he
belonged to. We had asked neighbors, posted on social media, and
watched for missing-dog alerts. Nothing. He was too skittish to let me
approach him either. The second I even opened the door to go outside,
he ran away, coming to a complete stop at a safe distance and turning

back to watch my next move, in true Husky style.

I watched him watch us. He stood in the middle of the street and watched my neighbor's house for hours. He watched the fence in my yard from across the street. I watched him stare at a random tree until dark. I spent hours watching that dog stare at things for no apparent reason. It had become a running joke around my house.

"I have decided to name him Staring Dog," my son now proclaimed, "since all he seems to do is stare at everything. That is the weirdest thing I have ever seen."

I turned back to the window. Yup, still there. Staring. *Hello, Staring Dog. What are you looking at?*

It continued for months. My welcome distraction on tough days. My familiar when life was full of change. I tried to interpret the intent behind all that staring, finding that I had become a staring human staring at a dog staring at... what? There had to be a reason.

Some days, I would go outside and stand where he had been standing, long enough to see his perspective but not long enough to freak out the neighbors. At first... nothing. Then, one day, I saw a beautiful bird singing a melody I remembered from when I was a child. Another day, I saw the wind blow the leaves into a swirling twist of floating colors, signifying the change of seasons that was coming. Yet another, I saw my exhausted but still smiling mail lady working late to make sure our mail made it here. I saw a lonely young man playing basketball. I saw a raccoon herding babies to the safety of the woods.

I saw life. I saw growth. I saw change. All things I had missed with my head down in the business of my day and the ding of my phone.

That dog might be smarter than we think. Huskies usually are.

I still have no clue what Staring Dog is staring at. He still comes around, although not as often, to stand frozen in our yard or nearby, staring off at something that I cannot see.

I may never know the real secret of Staring Dog, but I know the secret that he has taught me. There is so much to look for. Even from a distance, I can see the beauty of life if I look for it. Staring Dog is pretty clever, for no matter what he is staring at, he has taught me to see.

Some day, I know he will not appear in my yard. Some day, he will not be here to teach me. I will have to hold tight to what he has shown me.

But, for now, he stares. Long live Staring Dog and the lessons he brings for us all.

—Shannon Leach—

65

Forgive Quickly

To err is human — to forgive, canine.
~Author Unknown

"**S**he needs me." Those were the exact words I spoke to my husband when I spotted Dottie, a scruffy little Terrier mix we found at a local shelter eight years ago. We picked her because she was so unpickable.

Her handler provided a bit of history. In Dottie's one and a half years she had suffered abuse, abandonment, and a broken leg. Dottie had a rough start, and it was clear she had given up on all humans. She leaned away when I tried to pet her and refused to let me hold her. While the other dogs jumped and barked, Dottie retired to the back of the cage, curled up in a ball, willing us to leave her alone.

The entire drive home, Dottie trembled in fear. So, upon arrival at our house, we got right to work. I held her as much as possible, scratching her head and softly singing in her ear. We learned that she loved belly rubs, so every time we passed by, we'd flip her over and offer a gentle sample. Eventually, we noticed her presenting her belly as we walked by her. I knew we were making real progress when I found her quietly napping on a chair one day, her head resting on one of my slippers. My heart melted as I realized she had brought it there because it contained my scent, and she wanted it nearby.

Ever so slowly, our little Terrier came to life. She began to play with toys, enjoy walks, and nap in our laps. There was no special medication, no fancy food or toys. All we did was love her. And she thrived. She was so broken when we first met her that we had no idea what her true personality would be. But as it emerged, we found a sweet, playful, loving soul. What a privilege it was to witness her transformation.

One day, a few years after her adoption, I was busy completing chores around the house, doing laundry and climbing the stairs from the basement up to the main floor. When I finished, I sat down and enjoyed a well-deserved break. That's when I realized I hadn't seen Dottie for a while. I called to her and began searching. "Dottie! Dottie!" No response. My heart raced and my pace quickened as I began checking under beds and behind couches.

Suddenly, I remembered the door to the basement. I ran and opened it. There she sat on the top step, quiet as a mouse, head down, ears sagging. She had been following me, as she always did, and I had inadvertently closed the door on her. She never made a peep. She just waited quietly for me to find her. I don't know if she assumed she was being punished, but it was clear she was traumatized.

I scooped my little girl up in my arms and held her tight, telling her how sorry I was. I scratched her head and rubbed her belly, reassuring her that she was a good girl. She let me hold her for exactly one minute and then suddenly ran off, returning with a toy for me to throw. All was well as far as Dottie was concerned.

It's funny how I believed we were the big heroes when we rescued this sad little dog, having no idea how much joy and love she would bring to our lives. The truth is, Dottie teaches me new lessons every day. But I believe during that moment, on the top step of my basement, she taught me the most valuable one of all: Forgive quickly. Life is short. There is so much love to receive and too many toys to chase.

Thanks, Dottie.

— Joan Donnelly-Emery —

Chapter 8

Miracles Happen

Bouncer

Where there is great love, there are always miracles.
~Willa Cather

have long been a runner, but my first husband was not. He didn't like the idea of me running alone because our neighborhood was not entirely safe. He suggested we get a big dog who could run with me.

At a local animal shelter, we adopted a German Shepherd/Labrador mix named Bouncer. He was medium-sized but he was still young and he had huge paws. Sure enough, he soon grew to eighty-five pounds.

He was a sweetie, and he made a good running companion — except for pulling me with him whenever he'd chase after a squirrel or another dog, which happened every time he saw one. He also loved to jump on every person who entered our house.

After our daughter Kristen was born, Bouncer was as rowdy as ever. Seeing that Kristen was scared of the huge dog, and worried that Bouncer would accidentally hurt her, my husband made the difficult decision to return him to the animal shelter.

He immediately regretted it. He returned to the shelter two days later to re-adopt Bouncer but was saddened to learn that he'd already been adopted. We prayed that he'd gone to a good home.

On a lazy Saturday afternoon a few years later, my husband suggested going to the shelter again to let Kristen pet all the cute dogs and cats, which she loved. When we got to the big dogs, however, we spotted a dog who looked just like Bouncer.

We took him out to the enclosed grassy area to play, and he acted just like Bouncer, too. His name card said "Nacho" and that his owner was moving and unable to keep him. We called him "Bouncer" and he responded. Kristen was not afraid of him anymore, either.

We had not planned to adopt a pet that day, but we did anyway. When we got "Nacho" home, we ran to our photo albums and compared pictures. Bouncer had distinct facial and body markings. Nacho's were exactly the same.

"Welcome home, Bouncer! Please forgive us for letting you go!"

Why did we go to the shelter, we wondered, when we were not even planning to adopt a pet, and on the very same afternoon when his second owner had dropped him back there? We felt that it was meant to be.

Bouncer was as exuberant and goofy as ever, forcing his way out of our fenced yard more times than we could count. He loved to roam the neighborhood, but then he'd come home for food.

One time, though, he didn't come home. A few weeks later, my husband claimed he heard Bouncer's bark. Climbing on the roof of our garage to look around, he spotted Bouncer in someone's back yard a few houses down. We knocked on their door many times, but no one answered.

Finally, one day, I asked the neighbor whose yard was behind this one if I could go through their yard. They let me do so, and I found Bouncer securely leashed to a storage shed. I unhooked him and took him home with me.

Then I called the police, worried that I could get in trouble for dognapping. They assured me that, as long as it was my dog, it wasn't a crime to take him back.

A few years later, my husband and I divorced. My ex and I shared custody of Kristen, but I let him keep Bouncer full-time; he just seemed to need him more than I did. After a few years in his new neighborhood, Bouncer disappeared again. Almost a year went by, and then Bouncer showed up again on my ex's doorstep.

I have no idea what to make of the miracle of this dog, running in and out of our lives time after time. Maybe he's showing us that there is a season for everything, and we should just enjoy each one without clinging too tightly.

Or maybe he just wants to prove that dogs can have nine lives, too.

— Margaret Lea —

67

Joyful

In times of trouble, be strong. And wait patiently
for God to rescue you.
~Lailah Gifty Akita, Think Great: Be Great!

had dropped off my dog at the vet in the morning, and I was worried. Joyful, my beloved Miniature Dachshund, had six mammary tumors. Today was the Big Day: surgery. I was pacing back and forth between the living room and dining room of my little apartment, waiting for the veterinarian to call me with the first update.

Joy is fourteen years old and has Cushing's disease, which means she is at high risk under general anesthesia. To make sure that Joy was a candidate for surgery, the vet was doing bloodwork and taking X-rays of her lungs to verify that her cancerous tumors had not metastasized. I was urgently hoping that Joy would be able to have her surgery when my cellphone rang.

Dr. Salazar was on the line. She had good news and bad news. The good news was that Joy's lungs were clear; the cancer had not metastasized as far as she could see. The bad news was that Joy's bloodwork was on the borderline of acceptable. At her age and stage of Cushing's disease, Joy was at risk of an adverse outcome under general anesthesia, including cardiovascular collapse and death.

"But if we don't do the surgery," I said, "what is Joy's prognosis with these tumors?"

"Six to twelve months," Dr. Salazar replied.

Her answer was like a blow to my heart. I felt like I was making an end-of-life decision for Joy. If we proceeded with the surgery, Joy could die that day under anesthesia. If we didn't, she could die in months from her tumors. It was a hard choice, and I wasn't sure what to do.

Some of the tumors were small, but one was large — the size of a small lemon — and it was toward the back of Joy's body. It looked especially big on my tiny dog. I was concerned it would start to affect the functioning of Joy's other organs, especially her bladder, kidneys, and liver, which were already enlarged from Cushing's disease. Dr. Salazar had also warned me that the tumors themselves could become infected if not removed.

"What would you do if she were your dog?" I asked.

"I would be concerned about the anesthesia," Dr. Salazar said cautiously.

I wasn't sure I was ready to give up on the surgery, however, especially if it meant Joy would essentially be on hospice care until she passed away.

"Can I think about it and call you back in fifteen minutes?" I asked.

"Of course," Dr. Salazar said.

Luckily for me, my neighbor is a vet tech. I thought I could call and ask her for help, which I did. Unfortunately, she couldn't talk right away.

Distressed, I went to talk to my friend and apartment manager, Kristen, to ask for her advice. She has two dogs who she loves, and she loves Joy, too. She has a deeply compassionate heart and a generous nature, and I knew she would understand my dilemma. When I got to the apartment complex's main office, I explained the situation to her.

"I know how much you love your dog," she said, her green eyes full of sympathy.

Then her office phone rang, and she had to take the call. I stepped out of the room into the clubhouse waiting room and sat down on the couch. Still feeling anxious, I picked up my cell phone and called my mom. I told her what was going on and asked what she thought I should do.

"Jane, if it were me, I would let Joy have the surgery," she said.

"God can see her safely through it, and he can heal her afterward."

My mom's words had a powerful impact on me. My mom is a cancer survivor herself. Several years ago, she underwent radiation therapy for malignant stomach cancer, and she fully recovered. She has been living a happy, fulfilling life ever since. For her to say that she would do the surgery meant so much to me.

"I love the grand-dog," my mom said, her voice full of compassion.

"I know," I said, still uncertain about what to do. "Let me pray about it, and I will decide."

We ended our call, and I went back into the office with Kristen. She was off the phone, so I asked if she would pray with me. She agreed.

Kristen and I held hands. I closed my eyes and prayed out loud, asking, "God, if you could just give me one word, or a song, or a simple picture in my mind to help me to know what I should do, that would help me so much."

Suddenly, I had a clear picture in my mind. It was a picture of Joy with no mammary tumors on her belly, only a long scar. Her face was radiant with happiness as she looked right at me!

I opened my eyes.

"Kristen," I said. "I know what to do."

"Okay..." she said hesitatingly, surprised by the sudden shift in my attitude from worry to confidence.

As I was sitting there with Kristen, I picked up my cell phone and called Dr. Salazar again.

"It's okay," I said, my voice firm. "Let's go ahead and do the surgery."

"Okay," Dr. Salazar said, her voice equally confident.

A couple of hours later, I got a call from the vet. Joy had made it safely through surgery! Dr. Salazar had removed Joy's tumors, and Joy was recovering just fine in a post-operative kennel. I could pick her up later that same day.

The next day, my neighbor Ayana, the vet tech, came over to check on Joy. We could see that she was tired but strong. Joy even got up to wag her tail when she saw her friend, Ayana.

As I write this story, Joy is fully recovered from her surgery. She has no tumors — only a long scar where her veterinarian cut to remove them. Every day, she looks at me with a happy, delighted expression on her sweet face. I am so thankful!

—Jane Beal—

68

War Dog

There is no faith which has never yet been broken,
except that of a truly faithful dog.
~Konrad Lorenz

L ast night, my wife and I watched the film *Marley and Me*. I was a fan of the author, John Grogan, during the four years he wrote a column for *The Philadelphia Inquirer*. His writing always touched a nerve in me, but because I knew that Marley dies at the end of his breakout book, I had purposely not read it. With some hesitation, I watched the film.

Most of my life, a four-legged animal has been close by. Over the past fifty-one years, my wife and I have had dogs of various sizes. There was our Irish Wolfhound, whose only fear was overhead airplanes and whose bristly muzzle served as support for sticky-fingered toddlers. There was our rough-coated Collie, who had a long nose she tucked into your crotch while she stared up into your soul. Our last dog, a Bichon Frisé, stole candy out of pocketbooks and never deemed to look, let alone bark, at another dog. She was convinced she was human, a grand dame of some rank and privilege. She died in my wife's arms, her last heartbeats matching my wife's as she slipped away.

But, in watching the twenty-two dogs that played the part of Marley in the film last night, I thought of only one animal from my past: Buster.

My father rescued Buster when I was in third grade. He was a short-haired, big-boned fellow, maybe a mix between a Boxer and a

Lab. He responded to a leash, as though someone had trained him. He seemed gentle, which was good because he looked a tad scary when he barked. He also had scars that ran down the side of his right rear leg. We had no idea what caused them.

My brothers and I fancied ourselves accomplished animal trainers. So, one day, when the weather was turning a tad cold, we took his leash off his collar, walked a couple of steps, and called, "Come." But Buster didn't come. He looked at us, turned his head, and ran like the dickens. Within twenty seconds, he was gone from sight. We rushed home and told our parents, who weren't at all impressed with our training skills. We searched and searched. We couldn't find him.

Snow came and then more snow. It was bone-crunching cold. And then, a month later, the phone rang one night. A stranger said he had Buster and asked if he could bring him over. We were stunned. An hour later, a tall man in his late thirties arrived with Buster in tow. Buster was much thinner, and his paws were in bad shape.

The man said he was recently out of the military and had served in Korea. He said he had contacted the shelter to find who had adopted Buster so he could return him. He had come home that day and found Buster at the door to his apartment.

"But how did Buster find you?" my father asked.

"Buster is an unusual dog," the man said.

We just stared at him.

"When I came home from Korea, my wife had given birth to our son," he said. "We had to find an apartment. None of them allowed dogs. When I took Buster to the shelter, we lived two towns over. I've since found a nicer apartment ten miles from there."

"Are you telling me that Buster made his way, in freezing cold and snow, without knowing where he was going, and found you miles from here?" my father asked.

"Yes," said the man. "Buster is used to a harsh environment."

My mother nodded. The truth hit her first.

"Buster served with you in Korea," she said.

"Yes," the man said. "I was in recon. Buster was a courier dog, among other things. You may have noticed the scars on his rear leg.

He was dropped by machine-gun fire, but he kept going."

He looked down at Buster, who had not moved from his side.

"I brought him back with me from overseas. He is a trusted soldier and my best friend. But I can't keep him. I don't have the money for a house, and I'll get caught if I try to hide him in the apartment."

He looked at my tall, lanky father, my tiny mother, and my two brothers and me.

"I sense you're a good family. I know you'll care for him and love him."

He knelt down and took Buster's large head in his hands.

"Goodbye, my friend," he said.

He stood and walked to the front door.

"Buster," he said in a firm voice. "Down."

Buster immediately dropped to the floor.

"Stay," he said.

And he walked out our front door.

Buster never ran away again.

We moved to another house with acres of woodland behind us. At the bottom of a very steep descent, a creek cut lazily through pines and an old mill toward a county park. With Buster in the lead, my brothers, friends and I explored trails, sniffed spoor, and lay in the coolness of rotting leaves during the summers. One time, Buster blocked my dad's path when he was carrying my younger brother to his bedroom. My brother's body was limp with sleep, and Buster, fearing that something was wrong, would not let my dad pass until he shook my brother awake to prove that all was right with the world. Buster once chased off a dog twice his size that was nipping at our heels while sledding, and he wouldn't allow trash collectors on our property if they wore red bandanas — the color of the armband and star on Communist soldiers' uniforms in Korea.

As much as Marley barked, damaged and disobeyed, Buster protected and embraced. Just as Owen Wilson struggled to find the courage to carry Marley to the vet for his final visit, my father had to carry Buster, who had been dropped by cancer and could no longer keep going. And just as the three children of the movie family struggled to find the words for their goodbye at Marley's gravesite, my two brothers and I have never forgotten the privilege of sharing our home with a good soldier and our best friend.

—James Hugh Comey—

69

Parvo Pup

*Just being there for someone can sometimes
bring hope when all seems hopeless.*
~Dave G. Llewelyn

A big cardboard box sat outside the post office in our tiny mountain hamlet. Inside squirmed thirteen whining, yipping puppies.

Twelve of them were lively, furry balls of energy. Products of a Dane/Shepherd/Chow union, they were big, brown-and-black, long-haired fluff balls, and all were boys. But there in the corner of the box hovered unlucky number thirteen. The only girl, she was clearly the runt. A pale, short-haired, scrawny thing with a slight sheen of reddish-blond across her back, she was curled up in the corner, shivering and hiding. And yet she had clearly swept my son totally off his feet.

"Please, Mommy, please. Can I have her?" he whispered. "Look how afraid she is. She needs me."

My son, too, suffered from crippling anxiety. As I looked in his eyes, I could see that he had found a soul mate in this terrified runt. How could I say no?

As we walked home with our new prize, I held her against my chest and felt her little heart fluttering. Matthew held my shirt and made a litany of promises. "…And I'll feed her and pick up her poop every day, and she'll sleep with me, and I'll never let her be bad…"

But, as we walked, I couldn't imagine this miserable creature ever harnessing enough energy or gumption to do anything remotely mischievous. For, in this little package, there was only fear and desperation. And as if to punctuate my thoughts, at that very moment she released both bladder and bowel down the front of my shirt as she struggled to climb up my chest and into whatever safer hiding place she thought my body could provide.

Even after we got home and bathed and dried her, she would not stop shaking. But by then Matthew's love had totally enveloped her as he searched the closet for a bow for her neck and pulled out his own hairbrush to comb her fur.

"I'm going to call her Peaches," he announced. "Look, she's the color of a peach. It's a perfect name."

But, as his eyes glowed, my heart sank. I stood her up to a bowl to drink water, and Peaches fell over. Her shivering had gotten even worse, and now she couldn't stand. Something was terribly wrong with this little puppy.

I wrapped her in a blanket and went back to the post office. I was going to talk to the owners and find out what they could tell me. But, when we got there, they were gone.

I then drove to the local vet. When I walked in to tell him the problem, he told me to leave the pup in the car. He'd check her there. When he did, the news was devastating.

Peaches had parvo. It was far along. She would probably die later that night. He gave her virtually no chance to live past the morning. He told me to take her home and let her die with our family.

I asked him to put her down right then. "My son is only five. My daughter isn't yet three. This can't be their first experience with a dog."

"No," said this seemingly cruel man. "You adopted the dog. She's yours. I will not put down a puppy like that. Your children will just have to learn a tough life lesson at a young age."

He then gave us a syringe and a bag of saline solution with instructions to try and push as much of it as we could under the skin at the back of her neck every three hours. It might give her a little chance to live or would make her death more comfortable.

And, with that, I took her home to break the bad news.

Of course, the kids were devastated. Matthew held her and loved her, begging his dad and me to find a way to fix her. His baby sister, Mary, kissed and kissed the puppy, positive that her kisses could heal Peaches' "owies" just as surely as mine cured hers.

With tears in our eyes, Steven and I held this desperately ill puppy and squeezed saline solution under her skin as she whined and wiggled to escape.

As soon as we let her go, she darted across the room, moving faster than we'd ever seen her go, and ducked under our antique armoire.

Enormously heavy and built low to the ground with a decorative filigree along the bottom, it was impossible to reach under. Even Matthew's little arms could not coax that frightened dog from her hiding place.

"Let's go to bed," Steven offered when all our attempts to pull her out had failed. "We'll just leave her to the angels." So, we stood in a circle in front of the armoire and prayed for her doggy-angels to save her and then sadly headed off to bed.

Once there, Steven laid out how we'd dismantle the armoire in the morning, and then we could bury her body in the garden. We planned a little doggy funeral that we thought would offer the kids some solace and drifted off to a troubled sleep.

At dawn, Matthew and Mary came running into our room. "Where's Peaches?" they shouted. "Have you seen Peaches?"

Bleary-eyed, Steven and I sat up in bed. "No darlings, we haven't seen —"

But we got no further.

Suddenly, out from under the armoire popped a puppy like none we'd ever seen before. Her fur was fluffy, her ears were up, and her tail was curled. Peaches strutted out from under the armoire and ran straight to the kids. I swear the pup had a smile on her face! She jumped on the kids, and the three of them tumbled around the floor in a whirlwind of giggles, squeals and utter joy!

"I knew she'd be okay!" Matthew yelled as he pulled the puppy to his heart. Mary echoed, "Kisses work! Kisses work!"

For the next sixteen years, Peaches was a beloved member of our family. We'd soon find out that not one of her twelve brothers lived — all being struck down by the same awful disease that nearly claimed their sister.

I'm still grateful for that vet who refused to let me put down my parvo pup. In so doing, it opened up our lives with the wonderful Peaches.

— Susan Traugh —

Our Miracle Dog

There are only two ways to live your life.
One is as though nothing is a miracle.
The other is as though everything is a miracle.
~Albert Einstein

Capilano Suspension Bridge Park in Vancouver, B.C., provided the backdrop for the closing event of the conference I was attending. It was a beautiful location to spend time with the work colleagues I'd come to cherish. The conversation turned to dogs, and I pulled out my phone to show off a picture of my adorable Cockapoo named Roman. At three and a half, he still looked like a puppy.

That's when I noticed I had missed a call from my husband Randy. Over the din of 350 lively attendees, I hadn't heard it ring. His message said, "Call me." I decided to wait until I returned to my room. While I was on the bus back to the hotel, he called again, and this time I answered. "What's up?"

"Where are you?"

"Still on the bus on our way back to the hotel."

"Okay, call me when you get back." He sounded more agitated than he had in his voicemail.

Back at the hotel, I saw a note for me on the conference message board. "Call your husband." Now I was getting worried. Back in my room, the red message light flashed on the hotel phone. It was Randy. Once again, the only message was, "Call me as soon as you can." A

Miracles Happen | 217

million scenarios of what might be wrong — because something was definitely wrong — flew through my mind.

I pulled my cell phone from my purse and hit redial. "What is going on? You have me worried."

"Everything is okay," he said, "but Roman got run over by a car."

My heart sank. How could everything possibly be "okay" when the unthinkable had happened to my sweet little puppy? I wished I could sprout wings and fly home right then or rent a car and drive like crazy, but I had to wait until the next day for my one-hour flight home.

"Tell me what happened." And so, Randy recounted the tale of Roman's accident.

Randy and our son Benton were having a water-balloon fight in the front yard. They were going in and out the front door to reload their store of neon-colored water balloons. One of the times the door was opened, Roman caught sight of a big dog walking by with its owner. He didn't allow other dogs on "his road."

Before Randy could stop him, Roman made a beeline for the dog, running across our lawn, between the rosebushes, up over the retaining wall, and in front of our Kia Rio parked on the street. He never made it to the dog.

At that exact moment, a Volkswagen Beetle drove up the street. The driver never saw the tiny ball of fur run in front of her. And because he had a cataract and was mostly blind on that side — and was keenly focused on the offending dog on his road — Roman never saw the VW.

Our neighbor, who is a fireman, was out in his yard when it happened. He rushed over and checked Roman for broken bones and found none. Randy then carefully picked him up and laid him in the back seat of our Ford Escape. He drove to the emergency vet clinic while Benton sat beside his injured friend, gently petting his head.

At the clinic, Randy carried Roman in and said, "My dog got run over by a car!"

"Bring him back this way," the vet tech said. The vet ordered

X-rays, which revealed Roman had no internal injuries. The incident cracked but did not break two of his ribs.

"We do not see dogs who have been hit by a car come in like this," the vet said. "I can't believe he is even alive, much less has no serious injuries. He'll be in pain for a few weeks but should heal without further veterinary intervention." The vet sent Randy home with pain medicine and orders to make sure Roman got plenty of rest.

When I got home from my conference the next day, it was the first time in three years that Roman didn't come running to greet me. He lay sleeping under our china hutch. I got down on the floor next to him and kissed his nose. He barely lifted his head and looked at me.

"Don't get up, sweetie," I said. "I'm so glad you'll be okay."

Four days later, Roman brought me his tennis ball to play fetch, tossing it up on the couch next to me like he always did. I wanted to throw it for him, but because the vet ordered no running or playing fetch for at least two weeks, I just dropped the ball on the floor in front of him. He didn't seem to understand.

The following week, I spoke to a neighbor who had watched the whole incident from the nearby intersection. He said both the front and back tires of the Beetle rolled right over the top of Roman — over 3,000 pounds on top of a mere twenty-four pounds. It's a miracle his guts weren't all over the road. As the neighbor recounted what he had witnessed, I imagined an angel hovering over Roman at the point of impact, protecting him from harm. Perhaps it was the very hand of God that held off the full weight of the car.

Out of this potential tragedy came a blessing. The incident taught Roman that if you run out the front door without permission, you're likely to get hurt. This was helpful the next year when we remodeled our house. Contractors went in and out the front door, often propping it wide open to haul in materials. Roman never once ventured across the threshold without one of us. I wonder if his guardian angel stood beside him, reminding him to stay in the safety of the house.

Fifteen years later, people often mistake Roman for a puppy, albeit a puppy with a bit of gray around the edges. He still doesn't like other dogs on his road, loves to play fetch, and is quite oblivious to cars when we are on a walk. He still has no idea what hit him that day or what a miracle it is that he's alive.

—Linda L. Kruschke—

Wrong-Way Maggie

Nobody can fully understand the meaning of love
unless he's owned a dog.
~Gene Hill

ix days before Christmas, the phone rang. "Maggie ran off, and I can't find her," Jerry said in an anxious voice. He'd driven to the town park with our Puggle, Maggie, and Toy Poodle, Polly.

"Why'd she run away?"

"A smaller dog scared her, and she took off over the footbridge."

I shook my head. Maggie was eleven years old, overweight, and afraid of her own shadow. "You'd better find her before she roams too far."

Our daughter overheard my end of the conversation. Jennifer had moved out years ago but often cuddled up on the couch with Maggie. I didn't have to tell her which dog we were talking about. She knew how skittish our Puggle was. "Maggie's lost? Tell Dad I'll help him look for her." She flew out the door.

"Jennifer's on her way," I told Jerry. I wanted to go, too, but my MS would only slow them down.

At first, Maggie's tracks were easy to follow because a couple of inches of snow covered the ground. But her prints stopped at the parking lot where the snow had melted. My husband brought Polly home, and then he and Jennifer searched for hours into the night.

Before leaving the park, Jerry hung his jacket from a rainspout on the concession stand and placed Maggie's bed below it. He hoped the wind would carry his scent and Maggie would find her way back.

But there was no sign of her the next day. Both my daughter and her father took off from work. Jennifer made flyers and distributed them to houses around the park. We posted Maggie's photo on all the "Lost Dog" sites and social media. Friends and family promised to keep an eye out for her.

I waited at home for calls. A girl reported that she'd tried to catch Maggie near an electric transfer station. Jerry and Jennifer had been looking in the wrong area, so they changed course. Jerry spotted fresh paw prints by the transfer station that looked like Maggie's.

Jennifer made new flyers, and I contacted M&M Pet Rescue. They offered to help. But there were no sightings, and we were all worried. Winters in western New York are brutal. How could Maggie survive another night?

Our house was too quiet. Maggie's spot on the couch was empty and Polly waited for her by the door. With our kids grown, these dogs meant everything to us, and we'd spoiled them rotten with belly rubs and good food. Jerry always cooked them breakfast and dinner. Maggie loved to eat. We lost our appetites knowing how hungry she must be.

On the third day, Jerry and Jennifer went door-to-door with Maggie's picture, asking if anyone had seen her. They looked in empty barns and sheds. A lot of people joined them. Pet Rescue said Maggie was probably scared and hiding. That was an accurate description of our Puggle all the time. She was a shy dog who hid in the corner when strangers came to the house.

On the fourth night, a couple discovered Maggie in their back yard, but their dogs spooked her. Jerry and Jennifer grabbed flashlights and headed out. Maggie's prints led into the woods. For two hours, they yelled her name and squeaked her favorite chew toy, but she didn't come.

Jennifer took a week off from her job to look for Maggie. Jerry tried going back to work on day five, but he couldn't concentrate with our dog missing. He and Jennifer returned to the place where Maggie was seen the night before. Again, they had no luck. They came home wet and covered in mud, much the way I imagined poor Maggie was by now.

Weather forecasts predicted a foot of snow. Knowing a bad storm was on the way, friends and even strangers reached out to help look for Maggie. I was grateful but wished I could go, too.

On Christmas morning, our family didn't open gifts. Jennifer and her brother met their dad and continued searching. They were surprised to run into friends who'd taken time away from their holiday to look for Maggie. The snow started coming down, and we prayed our sweet girl was somewhere safe.

The flurries continued. By December 27th, two feet of snow blanketed the ground. Maggie's legs were only five inches long. "There's no way she'll be able to walk in this," I said, looking out the window. "How will she keep warm?" Both Jerry and Jennifer had horrible colds from searching endlessly in freezing temperatures. I wondered if Maggie was sick, too.

Finally, the snow stopped, and the sun shone brightly. If Maggie was still alive, maybe she'd come out of hiding. A woman messaged us and said her eight-year-old grandson bought a leash, bowl, and can of dog food. They rode around calling for Maggie. Having such good neighbors warmed my heart.

Jerry and Jennifer looked for Maggie every day after work. No one was ready to give up, but we were all losing hope. How could she have survived that fierce storm? Heartbroken, we waited for a new lead.

On December 29th, a man who lived near Maggie's last sighting noticed dog prints on his property. That gave us reason to hope again. But trudging through deep snow for hours exhausted everyone. Pet Rescue set up video cameras in that area and then moved them when a farmer thought he saw Maggie running through his field.

On New Year's Day, Pet Rescue set traps with food and captured a video of a dog—Maggie! She looked thinner and wasn't wearing her harness. One paw appeared to be bleeding. But it was her, and she was alive! She ate all the food around the cage but didn't go in.

On January 3rd, the phone rang, and a woman yelled into my ear. "We've got Maggie!"

"You've got her?"

"Yes, she's down in the ravine. My neighbor has her cornered inside an open log."

The ravine was four miles from our house, two from the park. Pretty far for an old, lazy dog to travel in thick snow. Was it really Maggie? My husband and I rushed over, and the woman showed Jerry where she was. I couldn't risk following him on the icy ground.

As Jerry came toward me cradling our Puggle like a newborn, I cried tears of joy. I don't know who was happier: Maggie or us. She covered us with kisses. She was filthy and smelled awful, but none of that mattered. We had her back!

Polly was as happy to see Maggie as we were. She raced to her "sister" and licked her all over. We gave Maggie a bath, fed her a feast, and set up an appointment with the vet. She was ten pounds lighter and had a fever and ear infection. But it could have been so much worse.

Maggie returned to her spot on the couch. She'd proven herself to be a tough, old dog. Our timid, pampered Puggle somehow survived sixteen days against all odds. If only she'd come this way as far as she'd gone in the opposite direction, she would have made it home!

— Deb Penfold —

For the Love of a Dog

My dear old dog, most constant of all friends.
~William Croswell Doane

y husband and a neighbor were standing in the yard talking when a little dog walked up to them. He was a ragged-looking little fellow who looked like he had been neglected for some time. He wore a rabies tag from a veterinarian some thirty miles from where we lived. My neighbor decided to take him home and drive to the vet on Monday to see if the owner could be found.

When my husband told me about the dog, I went to my neighbor's house to see him. When I entered, the little dog ran to me, jumping up and down, and wagging his tail in excitement. I clapped my hands and said, "Okay, Scooter," and sat down on the sofa. I don't know where the name Scooter came from. It just popped out of my mouth. The little dog immediately jumped in my lap and made himself comfortable. When I got ready to leave, he wanted to go with me. I felt bad about leaving him.

The next day, on Sunday afternoon, I went back to see Scooter. Again, he did his happy dance. He fell asleep on my lap until I had to leave. Something about that little dog tugged at my heartstrings. When I said goodbye this time, my eyes welled up with tears. He didn't want me to leave and kept trying to follow me out the door. I knew he would be going with my neighbor the next day to the veterinarian so his owner could be found. As I walked out the door, I glanced back to see him watching me as he whimpered. My heart was breaking.

After returning home from work on Monday afternoon, my neighbor called and asked if I was sitting down. He said, "Guess what the dog's name is." I had no clue to the dog's name but was totally surprised when he said, "It's Scooter!" I couldn't believe my ears nor what followed. My neighbor had checked the neighborhood prior to taking the little dog to the vet and learned a lady who lived a street behind us had found him on Friday wandering in the street just a short distance from where I was working. He escaped from her yard on Saturday morning. The vet informed my neighbor that Scooter had belonged to a physician who didn't have time for him and gave him to someone else. When that person was called, he did not want the dog, so my neighbor brought him back to his house. Scooter was a Schnoodle — part Schnauzer and part Poodle.

When my neighbor told me he was taking Scooter to the shelter, my mouth opened, and the words flew out, "No, I want him!" My husband and I had two Golden Retrievers, and now I was adding another dog to our family.

I didn't know then what an impact Scooter would have on my life. After taking him to my veterinarian and the groomer, they both told me that Scooter had been abused. I knew then that I had made the right decision to give him a home where he could feel safe and loved.

Scooter trusted me completely and found his space next to me on the bed. We played hide-and-seek in the house and, running from room to room, he was determined to find me. When he did, he jumped up and down, and rolled on the floor. It was as if he was saying, "I found you!"

His favorite spot was sitting beside me no matter what I was doing. When he wanted play time, he stood on his hind legs and looked directly into my eyes. He loved to go for rides, and each time I opened the car door, he ran as fast as his little legs allowed and jumped in the back seat. When I sat on the porch, he was right there with me. He followed me everywhere and even sat on the bathroom floor when I took a bath or shower.

Scooter and I were downstairs one day when I suddenly fainted.

He went upstairs and kept barking and turning toward the stairs. My husband realized something was wrong. He followed Scooter downstairs to find me lying on the floor. Scooter always knew when I was sick and would lie beside me, occasionally licking my hand or face as if to tell me everything was going to be alright.

Scooter was around seven years old when he came into my life, and we were together for three years. My heart filled with sadness when he was going blind and deaf. Age had not been kind to him, and he was in pain from other medical problems. The day came when I was told it was time to let him go. I knew that I loved him too much to let him suffer, but my heart was filled with anguish. For the love of a dog, I had to do what was best for him. Letting him go meant loving him enough to say goodbye when it needed to be said.

I know I was chosen by a Higher Power to give that little dog the happiness he deserved until his time on Earth was done. He gave me love and joy, and left his little paw prints on my heart.

— Carol Gentry Allen —

Mud Soup Miracle

Gratitude; my cup overfloweth.
~Author Unknown

The frost was setting in. It was cold and time to go home. I could hear her sniffing, but I could barely see her in the twilight.

"Diana!" I yelled multiple times with every tone of voice possible to see what might work. But, as she crackled through the undergrowth, I knew she was deliberately being naughty.

It had been about nine months since we got Diana, our chocolate Labrador Retriever. She was the runt of the litter and a ball of energy. The day that my mother let me choose her from the kennel, she came over and started biting my shoelaces. She was playfully bounding around and licking me every chance she could find while the other puppies sat stoically in the sun.

"This one," I had said, pointing at her.

"Are you sure? She looks like quite the handful!" my mother had said.

But I knew from the moment I set eyes on her that she was the perfect dog for me. And, for some reason, that feisty energy was everything that I needed in my life.

On this particular night, however, that feisty energy was making me frustrated. I whistled to her again, blew into my cold hands, and zipped my coat up tighter around my neck.

We lived in a remote area, and my mother didn't like me walking

Diana too late after school. Mother often got home late and didn't want me in the woods past dark. But I was a teenager and loved defying the rules, so I disregarded her warnings and set out later than usual that day.

But, as the sun set and the encroaching night began casting eerie shadows through trees, I couldn't help but feel nervous. Thoughts started flooding my head about losing my way. Or, worse yet, some frightening creature coming out of the dark unexpectedly. The hairs on the back of my arms stood on end.

"Diana!" I yelled again, this time with true fear in my voice. She finally came trotting back over.

Relief set in as I tied her to the leash, giving her a small treat and rubbing behind her ears. Diana seemed oblivious to my fear of the dark. She was playful and drooled all over me.

I took a moment to calm us both for our different reasons, and then we set off in the direction of our home — or so I thought.

After about ten minutes, we had lost the path. I took a deep breath to try to calm my nerves.

I looked around and could just about make out the open surface of a dried-up lake. I knew that home wasn't far away.

I'd never walked across the lake before, and my mother had warned against it, but I felt afraid and just wanted to get home quickly. So, rather than going all the way around, I decided I'd feel safer taking the shortcut across the lake.

Diana went first. In the dimming light, I could see that the mud directly below her paws was dry and brittle.

I stepped out onto the lake, and my foot went in a little deeper than expected, but I was heavier than Diana. Cautiously, I took a second step.

Diana unknowingly pulled me forward, and I lost my balance. I stumbled, but this time I was sinking. Below the hard-looking surface was wet-mud soup, and it was pulling me under.

"Help!" I cried feebly.

I tried to pull my legs free, but that only sucked me further down. The lake was relentlessly pulling me under like quicksand.

"Help me!" I yelled loudly this time.

Diana started to bark. She knew something was wrong and moved away from the muddy space that was now beginning to pull at her own feet. With relative ease, she leapt back to the side of the lake. I saw her reach the safety of the shore.

I was about to let go of the leash but stopped in the nick of time.

To my amazement, Diana grabbed the leash in her mouth — something I'd only seen her do with that feisty energy of hers when she was playing — and stuck her paws into the hard ground beneath her, pulling ferociously.

She was trying to save me, and it was working. Her pulls were enough to help me inch forward.

"Yes, Diana, you can do it!" I shouted with tears in my eyes.

She was young but had grown strong enough to counterbalance my weight. Once she had pulled me close enough, I reached forward and grabbed at the bulrushes that had been out of reach. I dragged myself out of the mud with all my might.

In a state of shock, I can't remember the walk that we took — this time around the lake — to the safety of our home. My mother was there when I walked in the door with mud all over me.

"What on earth happened?" she asked.

"I didn't listen to your warnings. I'm sorry, Mother," I replied sheepishly while scratching the back of Diana's head.

My mother gave me a frustrated look, but she knew that I had learned a lesson and didn't push me to say more at the time, for which I was thankful.

I looked down to Diana's loving eyes and knew that I had been right to trust my intuition on the day that I chose her.

But I realized that her feisty energy was more than something I just needed in my life. Because of it, I had been saved.

Diana had saved my life.

— M.J. Irving —

Sometimes You Just Have to Laugh

The Arithmetic Teacher

*If you think dogs can't count, try putting three dog
biscuits in your pocket and then give him
only two of them.*
~Phil Pastoret

watched my dad scowl as he listened to the voice coming through
the telephone receiver. I heard him say, "Yes, Miss Beisner," and
"I understand what you're saying, Miss Beisner. I appreciate you
sharing this information. We'll see what we can do about the
situation. Thank you for calling. Goodbye."

Miss Beisner was my first-grade teacher, and I loved her. I thought
she felt the same about me, but now I was beginning to wonder.
The tone of Dad's voice, the redness in his cheeks, and his repeated
clenching and unclenching of fists made it pretty clear. This was not
a warm and fuzzy good-news-from-the teacher call.

As I was deciding whether I should lock myself in my bedroom
for the rest of my life or run away from home, Dad hung up the phone.
"Jacquie, come here and sit down. We need to talk."

Uh-oh. When Dad said, "We need to talk," it meant *he* needed to
talk, and *I* needed to listen.

I shuffled over to the well-worn brown chair in the corner of the
living room, plopped down, and waited to hear the nature of my crime.

Dad told me that Miss Beisner thought I was bright but not working up to my ability. She said I had strong verbal skills but weak study habits. Translation: I never closed my mouth, and I seldom opened a book. Apparently, my failure to memorize the addition facts, or even attempt to, was more than she was willing to put up with. Hence, the telephone call.

Dad ended our one-way conversation with a verbal outline for his plan of attack. Bubbles, our Toy Manchester Terrier, was going to teach me math. Silently, I thought, *No way is any dumb dog going to teach me how to add, not even our beloved Bubbles.* Out loud, I said, "How?"

Dad summoned Bubbles from her bed near the stove and commanded her to sit. "Bubbles," Dad said, "how much is five plus three?" Bubbles let out eight loud, crisp barks.

"How do I know if that's the right answer?" I asked. Dad told me to go to the kitchen and ask Mom. "And while you're there, ask her to give you a new problem for Bubbles to solve. You might as well get the answer while you're there; it'll save you a trip." Before you could say, "Jacquie is clueless," I was back. That time, I addressed Bubbles. "Bubbles, how much is seven plus three?" Silence. Dead silence.

"I think Bubbles will answer only if I give her the problem," Dad said. "Bubbles, sit. How much is seven plus three?" Bubbles responded with ten sharp barks, the same number Mom had told me to expect. I was incredulous… and mortified. I couldn't understand how a dog could add, and I was more than a little embarrassed by the fact that the family dog was smarter than me.

After that I would hop off the school bus each afternoon, devour a couple of fresh-from-the-oven cookies, and ask for my flashcards. By the time Dad came in I was ready for him and Bubbles to check my latest test. The results were always the same. Ten circles on the paper, a smile from Dad, a hug from Mom, and a dog biscuit for Bubbles.

Within two weeks of Miss Beisner's telephone call, I knew every one of my math facts. I was proud of my accomplishment, my parents were elated, and Miss Beisner was back to smiling. I'm not sure, but I suspect Bubbles may have been a bit less enthusiastic about my speedy turnaround because it meant one less doggie treat for her each day.

Strangely, nearly two decades went by before I thought to question

Dad about Bubbles' math wizardry. I was frantically preparing my first-grade classroom for the first day of school when I happened to think about my math-fact experience when I was a first grader. I set my bulletin-board materials on a nearby desk and walked briskly to the office where the one and only phone was housed.

Mom answered. "Jacquie," she said, "is something wrong? I thought you were at school getting your new room ready." I assured her nothing was wrong, but could I please speak to Dad? Within seconds, I heard Dad's quavering voice say, "What's wrong?"

I ignored the question and said, "Dad, did Bubbles really know how to add?" After a moment of silence, I heard a low chuckle. "I wondered if you'd ever get around to asking." He laughed. Then, he told me his long-kept secret.

He said he had been teaching Bubbles "how to add" for several weeks prior to Miss Beisner's telephone call. He had planned to wait for perfection before unveiling the trick to the family, but the teacher's call prompted him to put his plan into action sooner than expected.

He said he taught Bubbles to sit perfectly still, to fixate on Dad's eyes, and to remain silent until Dad stopped speaking. At that point, Bubbles was to start releasing slow, measured barks. When she had barked the same number of times as the correct answer, Dad would shift his eyes sideways without moving his head, and Bubbles would stop barking. Trick performed. Kid fooled.

"No, Bubbles couldn't add, subtract, multiply or divide," laughed Dad, "but she sure could teach."

—Jacquie McTaggart—

75

For Whom the Bell Tolls

Humor is merely tragedy standing
on its head with its pants torn.
~Irvin S. Cobb

The frantic ringing of a bell woke me from a sound sleep in the dead of night. Skylar, our Border Collie, was trained to ring a bell hanging from the doorknob if she needed to go outside for an emergency potty trip. Unfortunately, she quickly learned that her "staff" would jump and open the door anytime she rang. Sometimes, she just wanted to go out and roll in the grass or chase rabbits.

But this was different. This was the middle of the night. She didn't usually ring the bell in the middle of the night.

I pulled myself out of bed, grabbed my cell phone to use as a light so I wouldn't disturb my husband, and stumbled to the back door as the ringing got louder and more persistent. Something wasn't right.

I opened the door and whispered, "Go, Skylar! Hurry up! Fast potty!"

I couldn't see her clearly in the dark. Aiming my cell phone's flashlight on Skylar, I asked her, "Are you going to go potty?" Rather than go out the door, she sat and stared at me. I could have sworn she was tapping a paw.

I turned off the flashlight and was plunged again into darkness.

In fact, it was too dark. The only sound I heard, not counting my husband's gentle snoring, was the ticking of a wall clock. There was no refrigerator or air-conditioner whirr. I tried flicking on a light. Nothing. The only illumination I saw was coming from my solar lights out in the yard.

Skylar gave me the "I-told-you-so look" from where she sat, got up and went back to her bed. It was obvious she felt her work was done. She'd informed me that the power was out, and now I had to figure out what to do about it.

At 3:00 in the morning, you don't always think clearly. I went outside in my pajamas, gathered up any solar lights I could find from the back yard, and placed them in the bathroom, family room and kitchen. I figured this would get us through until the sun rose.

I got on my phone and saw that the electric company estimated it would be two hours before the power would be back on. Great. I was now wide awake, and the house was getting warm. I tried opening windows, but there was no breeze so I closed them. I decided to try and sleep on the sofa since it was leather and felt cool. It soon felt hot and sticky from my body heat. I tossed and turned before heading over to a cloth recliner — and then realized it was an electric recliner so there would be no reclining. I almost went back to my bed, but I didn't want to disturb my husband, so back to the sofa I went — this time armed with a cool sheet to lay over the leather.

The power came back on just about the time I finally drifted off to sleep, which was also the time Skylar decided to ring the bell again. This time, she did have "business" to conduct outside. Her mission accomplished, I closed the door and lay back down on the sofa to try and get an extra hour or two of sleep.

My husband, who slept blissfully through the entire night, woke me up to ask why there were solar lights all over the house and why was I sleeping on the sofa. I gave him the same exasperated look that Skylar had given me, told him to go reset all the clocks, rolled over, and went back to sleep — just like Skylar had taught me.

— Donna Anderson —

76

The Milk-Bone Dance

Dogs act exactly the way we would act
if we had no shame.
~Cynthia Heimel

I rarely set an alarm clock anymore. Inevitably, five minutes before it would go off, the guardians of the grounds pad quietly into my bedroom and arrange themselves closest to any unprotected areas of flesh. My skin contracts as three very cold noses dig in. If I try to cover myself and slip back into sleep, they institute phase two.

Joe, the German Shepherd, has a bark that would put a Marine Corps Master Sergeant to shame. He maneuvers closest to my head and lets go.

"UP!" he barks. "YOU DARE TO SHIRK YOUR SACRED DUTY TO YOUR GUARDIANS AND PROTECTORS!!! GET OUT FROM UNDER THAT BLANKET — NOW!"

Of course, once he starts, the two girls join in, and an overwhelming cacophony forces me to draw back the blankets. Once I am sitting up, the yips, barks and pathetic moans drive me to my feet. Then, the Milk-Bone Dance begins.

One German Shepherd and two big fluffy Chows encircle me, leaping and spinning. They prance and prod, herding me toward the kitchen. I don't even think about making a side-step to my dresser, bathroom or closet as two hundred and twenty pounds of canine steer my course.

I stumble down the hall. They twirl, long tongues dripping with anticipation. Three strong tails pound the furniture and walls as we pass. If I slow down, I am licked until my steps go forward again.

The frenzy suddenly stills as I approach the pantry. Loud panting heightens the anticipation as I reach into the large Milk-Bone box and draw out three identical treats. Joe grabs his first and disappears through the extra-large doggy door to his spot on the front-porch rug. Ginger steps up and firmly claims her prize, also disappearing outside. Lucy hangs back and waits for me to walk to her, and then delicately draws the Milk-Bone from my hand and pads over to the carpet in the entryway to nibble away.

I might go back to bed, but most of the time I make a cup of Earl Grey tea with honey to clear the fog from my brain and enjoy the silence before they notify me it is time for breakfast.

—Rose Marie Kern—

Domesticating Woodrow

*A door is what a dog is perpetually
on the wrong side of.*
~Ogden Nash

own a $15,000 dog. His name is Woodrow (aka Woody), and he's an eight-year-old mutt we rescued over eight years ago. But if you ask him, he never needed rescuing. Actually, I have often wondered if this dog was meant to stay with us at all. He's as wild as the dingoes of the Australian Outback and looks exactly like one, too. He's not a cuddler but allows you to pet him. He doesn't obey most commands but will reluctantly come to you when he's ready. He's an awful leash dog. Between his wildly loud yelping and the consistent pull of my shoulder out of the socket, he does not make a good walking partner. If he is let off leash, you can pretty much say goodbye because he has much better things to do. Yet, when I look into his sweet brown eyes, something takes hold of my heart, and he can do no wrong. Plus, he makes an awesome co-pilot and tremendous watch dog, and he is my daughter's sleeping partner.

But, boy, has he given us a run for our money.

In his younger years, Woodrow tended to escape our large fenced yard and roam about the neighborhood. He never did any harm but loved to run with the many lady pups that lingered about our property. Several times, we were called by someone who found our escapee, and we'd go and retrieve him. Other times, we'd have to bail his sorry butt out of doggy jail and pay some ridiculous fines. We became tired of the shenanigans and needed to get serious about keeping him constrained. We couldn't afford it anymore!

We searched the fenced perimeter again and again for the weak spot, to no avail. He was smart enough to escape when no one was looking! One day, Woodrow got sloppy and left behind the rickety tool he used to chip away at a secret hole in the fence, *Shawshank Redemption* style. We secured the spot, and he remained in the yard. Ha, success! He then learned that with the proper velocity he could easily scale the rickety old fence. We learned this after another expensive, off-leash ticket.

It was time to bring out the big guns.

The electric-fence consultant taught us how to properly train Woodrow on the system. After a major hole in our bank account and a considerable amount of time spent training him, Woodrow was actually a quick study. He learned how to run through the invisible fence line at harrowing speeds, willingly trading the zap for his freedom. We'd hear a loud YIP and knew he had escaped... again. We could host a ticker-tape parade for the number of tickets we've accumulated, each becoming more and more expensive for our repeat offender.

We began to wonder: Should we just let him run free? Does he need to be on a farm? What a choice to have to make. He was a part of our family. You don't just give away a child if he keeps acting up. My mother-in-law always said, "A dog is for life," and with her words echoing in our ears, we couldn't give up on Woodrow.

For the next attempt at domesticating Woodrow, we tried electric fence tape for horses around the top of the fenced area. It took a weekend to install and about $500 in supplies. We now had both the top and bottom of the fenced enclosure secured. We let him in the back and watched as he sniffed the newness of his grounds. He looked up at us with remorse-filled eyes. We had won! Then the call from Animal Control (who knew me on a first-name basis) startled me awake.

"Hey, Sandy, we found Woodrow again and are required to bring him to the shelter this time. There will be a $500 fee to get him out."

The move to our new home threw Woody off his game. We didn't have a fence at all, just a large lot of land with room to roam. Oh, how he basked in the compliments on his good behavior as he lounged about our property. Each belly rub fed his ego, and in no time, he was back to his old tricks. So, we had a $7,000, five-foot fence installed with a thin shock wire on top. When all was finished, we waited for Woodrow to summon his inner Houdini. As expected, he did. But after one serious zap, he never attempted it again.

Woodrow has been a challenge from the beginning. He's just wild at heart. He has taught us that there is a reward for patience and compassion and to not give up on someone or something because they aren't perfect. We've come to look beyond his shenanigans, accept his indifferent personality, applaud his tenacity, and laugh at the stories we'll be telling forever.

— Sandy Hoban —

78

The Porch Pirate

Every dog must have his day.
~Jonathan Swift

ylan trotted up our driveway with the Sunday *Los Angeles Times* gripped between his jaws. When he spotted me, he slowed his pace to a proud strut, wagging his tail, milking the moment until he laid his hard-won treasure at my feet.

I patted his silky head and sighed. I'd just gotten off the phone with our neighbor. "We saw your dog stealing our paper again," he had growled.

This was the third copy of the Sunday *Times* that Dylan had fetched that morning. At least this time I knew who to return it to.

Being a Golden Retriever, it was in Dylan's DNA to bring things to his humans. It was a job he took seriously. He had no idea why we wanted the newspaper, and he had no idea that we wanted only our own copy.

Teaching Dylan to fetch the paper had been easy. I merely led him to the bundle at the bottom of the drive, waggled it at him until he understood that I wanted him to pick it up, and praised him when he did. "Good boy," I told him as he followed me, paper in mouth, to the front door. We did this a couple of times until the light of understanding twinkled in Dylan's eyes.

The next Sunday, I summoned the rest of the family to watch as Dylan headed down the driveway and came back with the *Times*. With the flourish of a showman, he dropped the paper at our feet and sat back to receive our adulation.

This worked beautifully for a couple of weeks. But soon a problem developed. It's in a dog's nature to believe that if a little of something is good, then more of it must be better. Alas, it hadn't occurred to me to teach Dylan to distinguish between our newspaper and our neighbors' newspapers.

At first, our neighbors took the fact that our dog was filching their Sunday paper every week with good humor. Soon, however, the charm of seeing Dylan make off with the news had worn off. For us, it was both embarrassing and a chore to return the stolen goods to their rightful owners.

The Sunday after my phone conversation with our disgruntled neighbor, we closed the gate to the driveway, cutting off Dylan's access to all the newspapers on the block, ours included. Of course, we still let him outside for his morning constitutional. But I soon noticed that it was taking Dylan considerably longer than usual to take care of business.

When I stepped outside to call him in, he trotted up to the door looking very pleased with himself. His fur was wet and matted with globs of dirt. So were the two newspapers that sat in sodden lumps by the door. He had gathered them by digging his way under the wrought-iron fence that surrounded our yard, shoving his bounty with determined zeal through the muddy hole that resulted, and dragging them up to the porch one at a time.

The look on Dylan's face said plain as day that he wasn't going to let anything stop him from bringing us every copy of the Sunday *Los Angeles Times* that he could find.

How could we do anything but thank him? We petted him, praised him, and fed him treats as his tail thumped with pride. Clearly, though, our dog's newspaper piracy had to stop.

Getting Dylan to give up his career as a newshound was more complicated than teaching him to fetch the paper. My husband had to repair the hole under the fence and rig up a length of chicken wire to defeat further excavations. We revised our Sunday morning routine so that Dylan was no longer allowed out of the house without supervision.

We didn't have the heart to tell Dylan that bringing us the newspaper, previously his crowning achievement, now made him a bad dog. We needed to find something else he could retrieve.

Our yard contained several avocado trees. It didn't take long to train Dylan to bring us their fallen fruit. That worked out great. The yard was cleaner, we had plenty of ripe avocados at the ready, and Dylan again had a rewarding task. Everyone was happy.

But he soon discovered that those bumpy, green things were delicious. From the number of empty skins and pits we found scattered around our back door, it became clear that he was eating as many of them as he delivered to us. And he was putting on weight.

We hated to do it, but we had to put Dylan on a diet. Golden Retrievers love their people above all else, but food comes in a close second. None of us enjoyed restricting Dylan's intake, least of all him.

Managing Dylan's weight was necessary for his health — after all, he was an old dog — but it didn't seem fair. After all, he'd learned two new tricks! It took a lot of petting and tummy rubs to console him for his reduced rations.

But we'd learned something, too. Dogs, especially Golden Retrievers, are like genies. Your wish is their command — but you'd better be careful what you ask for.

—Jan M. Flynn—

79

Partners in Crime

*We could have bought a small yacht with what
we spent on our dog and all the things he destroyed.
Then again, how many yachts wait by the door
all day for your return?*
~John Grogan

Summer was quickly coming to an end. August, when I would
have to go back to my teaching job, loomed ahead. I had
gotten my rescue pup, Sonny, from the shelter at the end of
the previous school year and had spent the summer months
getting him potty- trained and used to our routine.

Now that I had to go back to work, Sonny would have to spend
his days in the large, shaded kennel in our side yard. I tried to make
it as comfortable a place to hang out as possible. I bought a large dog
igloo to put in the kennel with a soft bed inside it and a large pad
outside it. I also bought him a large water bucket and a child's plastic
play pool, which I wedged in a corner.

A couple of weeks before I had to go back to work, I attempted
a few trial runs. At first, all I had to do was throw a large dog biscuit
inside the kennel, and he would run for it while I shut the gate. While
he was eagerly chomping down, I would make my getaway in the car.
It wasn't until I turned the corner of our street that I heard his barks
and howls of protest and injustice.

It wasn't long before he figured out my ploy and would grab the
biscuit and then race back to the gate as I was shutting it. That meant

I had to look into his eyes, try to explain the reasons for my departure, and point out enthusiastically all the amenities of his kennel. I then tried throwing in another biscuit, but he remained standing at the gate, his eyes full of sorrow and recrimination.

When I returned home the second time, having been gone maybe an hour, he had been busy demonstrating his displeasure. The pool was practically emptied. Only an inch of muddy water remained, and teeth marks and broken plastic were scattered about. His water bowl had been knocked over and flipped upside down. His outside pad had been ripped, and pieces of cloth and stuffing covered the ground. His inside igloo bed had been dragged outside, but apparently he had needed to rest before tearing that up as well.

After scolding him, though he showed not a hint of remorse, I cleaned up the filling, threw away all the pieces, and crammed the plastic pool in the recycle bin. I cleaned his water bowl and then brought it inside. That night, I went online and ordered a large water bucket that I could hang on the fence so he wouldn't be able to knock it over.

The night before the dreaded day, my husband and I went over the following morning's plan. Since he left for work after me and got home much earlier, he would be in charge of putting Sonny in the kennel and then letting him out. He worked a short distance from home, so I asked if, at the beginning, he could go home at lunch to make sure Sonny had water and hadn't done any major damage. He assured me he would and everything would be just fine.

I went outside for one final check of Sonny's outside lodgings. Even though it went against rational thinking, I had bought a new larger pad to replace the one he ripped. My husband would fill the water bucket in the morning. Everything looked ready.

When I returned from a long first day of school, I pulled up the driveway and craned my neck to see if there was any damage inside the kennel. I didn't see any. I parked my car in the garage and then raced over for a closer look inside the closure. Nothing. I couldn't believe my eyes. The igloo looked untouched, the pad outside was still pristine, the water bucket was intact. My heart flooded with love for my "good boy."

When I got inside the house, the stars were still in my eyes as I witnessed the peaceful scene. There on the couch sat my husband doing his crossword puzzle and at his feet, sound asleep, was my Sonny.

I rushed over to Sonny and hugged him, praising him for being such a good boy. I looked up at my husband with a smile and asked if he had cleaned the kennel before I got home.

"Nope," he said. "That's the way I found it."

"You don't know how relieved I am," I told him.

"That's great, honey," he replied.

I put away my school stuff, got into my sweats, poured myself a glass of wine and took it into the living room. I sat down on the couch and leaned back.

"Where's the pillow?" I asked my husband.

"What?"

"The pillow. The one on the couch. I put it behind my back for support."

"Oh, yeah. I'm so sorry. I spilled a cup of coffee on it, and it soaked totally through. I had to toss it."

Not wanting to put the kibosh on my glow, I let it go, deciding it was a good excuse to buy new couch pillows.

The next two weeks were the same. When I arrived home at night, the kennel was pristine, and the dog and husband were comfortably ensconced in the living room. I couldn't believe I had worried and fretted so about leaving Sonny caged.

Then, one day, I got to leave school early. We had a shortened day due to parent conferences. Since I would be home before my husband, I planned to take Sonny for a nice long walk.

When I pulled into the driveway, I didn't hear any barking. I craned my neck to see Sonny, but there was no sight of him. I parked and raced over to the kennel. The door was closed, but no dog. I couldn't see any holes around the bottom that he might have dug, and I knew that the contractor had sunk the wire walls pretty deeply into the ground. All I could think was that he must have been stolen. I ran to the house wondering who to call... 911? The police? The pound?

I unlocked the front door and stood frozen, my mouth open to scream. Scattered around the room were torn pillows, their stuffing tossed about. My soft throw had been pulled out of the basket and dragged around before being ripped. And there, gnawing on the wooden chair leg, lay the culprit.

"Sonny!" I cried.

He happily ran up to greet me, a look of pure innocence on his furry face.

When my husband got home, he confessed all. He took Sonny out that first day, but then as he heard the dog's heart-wrenching whines and cries, he was unable to walk away. Instead, he brought him back inside and put anything that he could tear on top of the table. Then, at lunch, he'd let Sonny out before returning home a few hours later and putting everything back in its place.

Looking at the two of them, eyes downcast, quivering for forgiveness, I knew I was beaten.

— Martha Roggli —

80

I Was Just Being a Dog

You can trust your dog to guard your house but never
trust your dog to guard your sandwich.
~Author Unknown

You left me home all afternoon; I got a little bored.
I thought I'd check the pantry out; it begged to be explored.

You left the door wide open, and that was very kind.
I therefore went and helped myself; I didn't think you'd mind.

I ate the bag of candy, consumed the peanut mix.
I gobbled up those suckers, and then spit out the sticks.

I finished off the cookies and sampled whole-grain rice.
I then enjoyed some honey… with the crackers, it's quite nice.

I gulped it down and swallowed it, extremely fast and quick.
My stomach didn't like it much, I suddenly felt sick.

I needed to be let outside; I ran straight to the door.
I scratched and waited, squirmed a bit; my tummy was so sore.

I stood right there, I didn't move, unsure of what to do.
I needed that door open now; I really had to poo!

You weren't home, I couldn't wait, I had to let it go.
The diarrhea shot right out, I couldn't stop the flow.

And then my stomach started up, it wasn't feeling good.
I threw up all that junk I ate, got rid of all I could.

You came home and looked around, and seemed extremely mad.
But I'd forgotten what I'd done; forgot that I'd been bad.

You didn't greet me nicely or smile and say hello.
You stormed around and shouted, "The mess, the smell. Oh, no!"

Who is that dog named Naughty, whose name I heard you yell?
I was home all by myself, as far as I could tell.

It puzzled me to watch you fume; I could not comprehend.
I did my best to comfort you because you're my best friend.

I love you more than life itself; I'm loyal, faithful, true.
If you were ever threatened, I'd risk my life for you.

So, when you've done your mopping up, let's go out for a walk.
You seem to be a little stressed, and it always helps to talk.

—Maureen Slater—

81

The Great Pretender

A well-balanced person is one who finds
both sides of an issue laughable.
~Herbert Procknow

We adopted our mutt, Zeus, from our local animal shelter three years ago. As sweet as he is, there are a few things Zeus doesn't do. One is ride in cars. He not only gets sick but manages to throw up as soon as we arrive at our destination. Another is noises. From popping a can of soda to running a leaf blower, Zeus hates them all.

However, the last phobia trumps all others. Zeus doesn't like his paws being touched by unfamiliar people. As you can surmise, this is a problem when he visits groomers.

The visit to the last local groomer within a ten-mile radius for a pedicure appointment went like this:

I warned the kennel over the phone while making the appointment that Zeus and his seventy pounds of muscle didn't like his nails clipped. When we got there, and after Zeus threw up in the passenger seat, the youthful groomer with immaculately coiffed hair assured me as I relinquished Zeus's leash to him that he could handle any recalcitrant dog, and the clipping would only last a few minutes.

I gave Zeus five minutes before all chaos broke loose. It turned out that I had underestimated Zeus's hatred of all things paw-related.

A scant two minutes later, there was a boom, a screech and a cacophony of animal noises. The groomer's hair was sticking up, and a triumphant Zeus sauntered gracefully into the waiting room as if he had won the Westminster Dog Show.

"He faked a heart attack," the groomer snarled, no longer looking as confident as he had minutes ago. "He faked a heart attack and fell off the table. When I went to pick him up, he jumped up and ran down the cat kennels and upended tables. He's not allowed back here."

I'm not sure, but I think Zeus gloated until we got home and he threw up in the back seat.

— Christy Breedlove —

82

The Freakout

Humor is emotional chaos remembered in tranquility.
~James Thurber

"Hi, honey, I'm sorry to call you. I know it's early in California, but it's an emergency," I said anxiously through the phone to my husband, Vishal.

"What's wrong? Are you okay?"

"I think I lost the dog. I'm freaking out!" I said while running up and down the stairs, looking from room to room.

"Sirius! Sirius, where are you?" I yelled. "I'm so scared. I left him alone in the house for fifteen minutes while I dropped the boys off at baseball practice. He didn't run over to greet me when I returned, and now I've been all through the house. I searched the yard, and I can't find him! SIRIUS! SIRIUS, WHERE ARE YOU?" I screamed.

"Were any of the doors left open? Do you think he ran out of the house? If he did, he should have his collar on. I can't imagine he would run through the electric fence," my half-asleep husband reasoned.

"Yes, his collar is on, and the doors were closed. I should call the police. He must have been kidnapped or dognapped or whatever it's called!" I pronounced.

"What? You think someone broke in and took the dog? Does it look like we had a break-in? Are things missing?" Vishal asked.

"No, nothing is missing. Dognappers just take dogs!" I said, jogging to the back of the house, still searching frantically.

"SIRIUS, TO ME!" I commanded, listening for the sound of my

giant dog galloping toward me. In the continued silence, my heart started beating more rapidly as my stress level went up.

"Vishal, I'll call you later. I'm going to call the police right now," I said quickly.

"Wait, wait, wait, calm down. Let's just think this through. I don't understand why you think a robber would break in our house and only take the dog," said Vishal.

"This is what dognappers do! This happened to Lady Gaga's dogs. Dognappers nab the dog. Then, they wait for a reward offer or ask for ransom! That must be what happened. Some dognapper saw our big, beautiful, special dog and knows we'll do anything for him. They might have been watching us, spying on us for weeks. I'll call the police. They can start a search and begin negotiations with the dognappers. I'm so upset that we didn't neuter him and get the GPS chip in him yet. If he was microchipped, we could track his location, and then the police could storm into the dognappers' evil lair and rescue him. I'll call you back after I file a report with the police. I know you have a client meeting later. It's okay. Don't cancel your meeting. I'll let you know.... Oh, Sirius! I FOUND HIM! I'VE GOT HIM! Sirius Black, you scared me. Oh, thank God," I shrieked, hugging and kissing my big, fluffy dog.

"He's there?" asked Vishal.

"Yes, thank goodness. I just found him in the guest bathroom. His big body must have accidentally closed the door behind him, and he trapped himself in," I said with relief. "I'm so sorry I woke you," I added.

"It's okay. I'm glad the dog is safe with you. But, listen, I'm seeing a pattern here. When I landed in California for this business trip, you said you were worried my plane got hijacked because my phone died, and I didn't answer your call right away. You were about to call the hotel manager to check on me. When Ryan asked if he could bike around the neighborhood with his friends, you practiced with him for weeks, decided he was ready, and then panicked the whole time he went out with his pals. You thought about calling our neighbors to keep an eye out for him and report his location. When Leo had his first day in a new school, you almost cried because you were worried he would be lonely during recess and might be sitting inside all by himself. You were about to call the teacher to get an update. Now, you almost called the police because you couldn't find the dog in our own house because you heard Lady Gaga's dogs were dognapped," he said patiently.

"You're right. I do see a pattern. This is a problem," I conceded.

"I'm so glad you see it. This has to stop," he said.

"Yes, it really does. I'll ask the vet if he can microchip all of you."

— Kelly Bakshi —

The Itch

A dog will quickly turn you into a fool, but who cares.
I'm a fool for my dog and proud of it.
~Author Unknown

n her younger days, Sassy had been nervous about visiting the vet, but now she stood motionless on the examining-room table and endured Dr. Barkasy's prodding and poking with the quiet dignity one would expect from a dog of her years. He had examined her ears to satisfy himself that there was no recurrence of the ear infections she'd had a couple of months ago. He had taken special care to check the condition of her skin since that could be an issue from time to time. He asked about her appetite and bathroom habits and reviewed the results of some blood tests she'd had not long ago. Then he shrugged. He could find nothing wrong with her at all.

Normally, this would have been good news, but obviously he had overlooked something. There had to be some explanation for her recurrent bouts of itchiness. Now Sassy, a rather stout Boston Terrier, had a blocky physique that didn't allow for much by way of bending or flexing. When she had an itch, she could rarely reach it. She would make scratching motions, but her hind leg would not make contact with the source of the irritation. If you were completely heartless, you might even find her efforts amusing.

I had taken a video of Sassy when she was having one of her spells so he could see the problem for himself. On camera, Sassy could be heard giving a sharp bark or two and then frantically scrabbling, her hind foot waving in the air an inch or so away from her body. Where was the intended target? She gave another yip and glared at the camera. "Don't just stand there taking pictures! Can't you see I need help?"

Dr. Barkasy laughed. I was shocked by this heartless response.

"What do you do when she does this?" he asked.

Since Sassy was standing there in front of us, I was able to demonstrate as I explained the efforts that I went through to find and ease the mysterious itch. I started with her ears. (They'd been itchy when she had the infection.) I inserted an index finger into each ear and rotated it a bit, more of a rub than a scratch since I didn't want to irritate the skin. Then I scratched behind the ears. With one hand on each side of her body, I worked my way down and around her neck. When her ruff had been thoroughly dealt with, I moved on to her shoulders, then down her sides, stopping along the way to give special attention to what would be her armpits if she were human. The rump area also got a vigorous scratching.

Dr. Barkasy got the picture. "So," he said, "every time she yips and does this scratching motion, you give her a full body massage." It was a statement not a question. He was right, of course, but I'd never thought of it that way.

He put her chart back into its folder and turned to leave.

"Stop it," he said. "Just quit doing that."

So I did, and would you believe the itch went away all by itself?

— Carole Lazar —

Brandy's Shoe

*Dogs are great. Bad dogs, if you can really call them that,
are perhaps the greatest of them all.*
~John Grogan

went for a walk around our property one fine spring day. The
sun was warm on my shoulders, and a slight breeze was blowing. I strolled toward the wooded area that borders our land and
noticed the path leading off into the woods. I assumed it was an
animal trail and only briefly glanced up the path. But then I noticed
something pink just to one side of the trail. My curiosity got the better of me, and I ventured up the trail to see what it was. Buried almost
completely in the leaves was a shoe. The sight of that old tennis shoe
took me back to a time many years ago.

I'd been in the kitchen when my husband came home and told
me to ride with him to his father's house. When we got there, he told
me to wait in the car. After a few minutes, he opened the car door and
put a little reddish-brown puppy in my lap. She looked up at me with
her big brown eyes and laid her head on my chest. She was trembling
at first but calmed when she snuggled up to me.

"Where did you get it?" I asked.

"It's a stray that someone dropped off here yesterday. She's been
sitting on the side of the road ever since then. Poor little thing must
think they are coming back for her."

It broke my heart to think of that tiny puppy sitting by the road
all night waiting for someone who wasn't coming back.

We took her home, fed her some leftover wieners, and made a bed for her in a cardboard box on our porch. We even picked out a name for her: Brandy.

I was afraid we would be kept awake by the puppy's whining during the night, but she never made a sound. I worried that she might leave and was relieved that she was still in her bed the next morning.

I stopped on the way home from work that day and bought some dog food and a flea collar. I was very disappointed when I got home and she wasn't there. It was amazing how attached I had gotten to her in such a short time.

Not long after I got home, the phone rang, and my husband's grandmother told me the puppy had gone back to the spot where she had been dumped.

I was so glad to see her but sad that she was still waiting for the inhumane person who had discarded her like a piece of trash.

I took her home and fed her. She settled down in the box after eating and went to sleep.

She returned to that spot three times before she gave up and settled in with us.

She wasn't supposed to be an inside dog in the beginning, but we just couldn't leave her outside when the weather was really cold. It turned out that she was a good inside dog. She never chewed anything but her toys and she was already housebroken.

We noticed early on that she loved shoes. If we left the closet door open, she would take out all the shoes. Some would be in the living room, with a few in the kitchen, and I even found one in the bathtub. She didn't chew on the shoes; she just loved carrying them around.

When summer came, she stayed outside a lot during the day when we were home. She never wandered far. One day, she came walking up, proudly carrying a large work boot. It was almost as big as she was, and she had to stop every few feet to get a better grip on the boot with her teeth. I knew the boot probably belonged to our neighbor, and I took it back.

The next day, she brought a man's shoe. It also belonged to our neighbor. When I took it back, I suggested that he might want to take his shoes inside. He didn't leave shoes out from then on. Brandy brought several other shoes home; we never found out where some of them belonged.

I thought she might not steal shoes if she had a shoe of her own. I gave her one of mine. I told her it was her shoe, and she didn't have to give it back. I think she understood because she never stole another shoe.

She loved that shoe and carried it with her everywhere she went. She even slept with it in her dog bed. Sometimes, she would misplace it for a day or so, but she always found it and brought it back.

Brandy had a long, happy life with us, and I grieved when she passed away at the age of fourteen. We buried her in the yard under the walnut tree. I wanted to put her shoe with her, but we couldn't find it.

I thought I would never see that shoe again, but there it was on the trail. I sat down beside the shoe and shed a tear. Then, I got up and left it there, a memorial to a sweet little dog who loved shoes.

I feel sorry for the people who dumped Brandy on the side of the road. They missed out on a wonderful, gentle dog.

— Linda Tilley —

85

Rommel's Retrieve

Dogs got personality. Personality goes a long way.
~Quentin Tarantino

Years ago, I lived in a sleepy, southern town with Rommel, my Doberman Pinscher, a handsome and most faithful companion. My neighbors were friendly but guarded around Rommel, a sweet-natured, albeit fierce-looking boy. Leash laws were not an issue then, so Rommel enjoyed an unaccompanied romp to the end of the cul-de-sac and back every day.

One morning, as I was just about to take my first sip of coffee, there came a loud pounding on the front door. Alarmed and frightened, I mustered the courage to shout, "I do not answer the door for strangers!"

An angry voice replied, "I'm not a stranger. I'm your neighbor, and your dog just stole my newspaper!"

Still in my fluffy robe and slippers, I cautiously opened the door to find a burly man in a flannel robe and leather slippers.

"Lady, you need to give me my paper. Your doggone dog stole it off my porch!"

"Oh, I don't think so," I retorted. "Rommel is right here, and he does not have your newspaper!"

"Well, I don't know what he did with it, but he got it. I saw him with my own eyes!"

I caught Rommel by the collar so I could control him in case he tried to defend me against this angry man. I told my neighbor he could have my paper but to wait for a moment while I closed the door to get it from the kitchen. I picked up the paper from the kitchen table. The back door was open, so I reached to push it closed when, lo and behold, I could not believe my eyes. There on the back stoop was not one but a half-dozen copies of the daily newspaper.

Apparently, Rommel thought they all belonged to me and had no business on other people's porches. So, faithful friend that he was, he simply gathered them up one by one and deposited them on the back porch. I gathered them all in my arms and opened the front door.

"I'm so sorry," I said. "I guess my dog thought they were mine, and he brought them home," which I thought was hilarious. He did not. He grabbed them out of my arms and stomped off, spouting some command to keep my dog in my own yard. I assumed he distributed them to the rest of our neighbors as I did not receive another angry visitation.

Rommel was promptly scolded, after I lovingly thanked him, of course, for bringing to me what he thought was a treasure. It was a difficult conversation to have with a dog, but an intelligent animal understands his master. And it never happened again.

—J. Lynn Thomas—

Get On with Life

86

Saving Shadow

The best therapist has fur and four legs.
~Author Unknown

For months, I had done little but lie on my sofa. My husband and Labrador Retriever had both died Christmas week. I was trying to muster the willpower to go on, but it was slow going. Grief had become my constant companion.

Off and on, I thought about getting a new dog, but I just didn't have the energy. *A female Mini Doodle,* I thought to myself—small enough to handle easily, with hair instead of fur, adult so I could skip the puppy stage.

The following summer, I heard a little voice in my head that said, "Your dog is ready now."

Okay, I thought, *I have officially lost it.* But, within a week, I was looking for *her.* I checked websites for Doodle-type dogs, but they were expensive, not in my budget.

The next week, I went to an adoption event at a pet store. There was a lot of slobbering and barking in the large circular pen where thirty dogs were gathered. It was chaos!

When I picked up one dog, she gazed at me, her eyes probing and loving, deeply curious. Few humans had ever looked at me that way. "Who are you, my friend?" her eyes conveyed. And yet the environment was clearly stressful to her. She was anxious and panting but still interested in me. Her physical condition was sad. She was very skinny, had been shaved all over, and had scars on her face.

I asked the rescue worker to tell me about this little doggie. She said the dog had been rescued two weeks before from a puppy mill, where she was a breed dog and had lived her first two years in a cage. Her hair was completely matted when the rescue group got her, which is why they had shaved her. A vet had spayed her and repaired a hernia. The poor little thing hadn't had pleasant interactions with humans yet.

I was already sure she was the dog for me. I asked what type of dog she was and was told, "The tag on the cage said Mini Goldendoodle." I started to cry. It had been exactly two weeks since I had heard the voice telling me my dog was ready. This mysterious universe had made it easy for me to find the dog of my dreams.

The next weeks were hard. She was afraid of other people and cried most bitterly at being put in a crate. From the second night, she slept with me. I named her Shadow because that is what she was: my shadow. She was afraid to be away from me.

We started to walk in the neighborhood, and Shadow began to see a larger world. Gradually, she became more confident. She held up her curly tail, and it bounced up and down as she strutted down the street. Her crazy Doodle fur grew back and covered the scars on her face. She learned that the people in my world wouldn't hurt her, and she greeted everyone she met as if they would adore her. Most did.

As I worked to rehabilitate Shadow, she helped me recover from my losses. If I cried, she looked into my eyes compassionately and licked my hand. I came off the sofa and resumed life. Every day, Shadow fixed those big brown eyes on mine, letting me know I was loved and no longer alone.

Seven years later, you would never know this friendly, outgoing dog who loves all humans and dogs was ever abused. Only if you smooth the pretty hair off her face can you see the scars. She has a brief look of fear as I start to put on her harness. Sometimes, the nightmares come, but I'm there to wake her gently and remind her all is well in our world now.

I'm grateful to the voice that led me to my best friend. I began a new life with her. I knew my life would not be the same as it was before, but with Shadow by my side, I knew I could be happy again. She saved me as much as I saved her. All she asks in return is a belly rub.

— Linda Healy —

87

The Dog with Two Names

When I look into the eyes of an animal, I do not see an animal.
I see a living being. I see a friend. I feel a soul.
~Anthony Douglas Williams

Strays often paused briefly at my house before climbing the steep hill past our property, but the spotted dog lying under my carport looked worse than most. He could barely raise his head, his rib cage protruded through his skin, and he was filthy.

My husband offered water to the dog, and he gulped down an entire bucket. "He's starving," Tim said as he grabbed some food from the refrigerator. The dog shyly accepted three hot dogs from Tim's hand and swallowed them whole.

"You know we can't keep him, right?" I asked.

"I know," Tim said.

The stray stared at me.

"I'm glad you're feeding him, though," I said. "He must be miserable."

I figured he would depart in a few hours, but at bedtime the emaciated dog slept in the same spot. When the morning alarm sounded, I peeked out the window to find him awake with his head resting on his front paws. Tim fed him again, this time treating him to leftover chicken casserole. Throughout the day, I checked on the stray and felt hopeful when he stood. Much to my delight, he walked around a few times.

Because my job as a tour director kept me on the road many weeks of the year, owning and nurturing a dog was not an option. Therefore, I couldn't allow an emotional connection to begin as we nursed the dog back to health over the next several days. Eventually, he moved around the yard a bit and made his way up the steps of our front porch. He was a timid dog, perhaps the victim of abuse. He lay silently at my feet, seemingly content to be near me, and occasionally nudged my leg with his nose. I reluctantly reached down and petted him. Against my better judgment, we were becoming friends. I even gave him a temporary name: Fred.

I needed to find a long-term home for Fred to assure that he'd be loved. My cousin Julie had a big heart for rescue animals and agreed to take him when she heard his story. A twinge of separation anxiety crossed my heart as Tim loaded Fred into the truck for the seven-mile ride to Julie's house. The trek included four miles on a four-lane highway, five winding county roads, lots of barns and cows, and a gravel driveway leading into the woods.

Julie wasn't home, but her deaf dog, Keller, and donkey, Itchy, were happy to receive visitors. Tim scratched under Fred's chin and wished him a wonderful life surrounded by pine trees, rippling creeks, and bluffs. Then Tim retraced his route home, and we settled in for a quiet evening.

Not realizing Fred had been delivered, Julie and her son Graison dropped by to pick him up three hours later. We visited indoors for a few minutes before walking outside for them to leave. Graison pointed to my carport and asked, "Is that the dog?"

I laughed. My family is filled with pranksters, so I didn't even look. "Yeah, right," I said.

"Really," Graison insisted. "There's a dog under your carport."

I slowly walked toward the carport and then stopped. "No way!" I said.

Fred was lying there, relaxing as if he had never left.

How had he found his way across unknown territory he'd traveled only by truck? That kind of determination merited a more meaningful name than Fred, so I renamed him Mo (short for Moses). He deserved the strong and honorable name after "crossing the desert." Since Julie's unfenced paradise was too much freedom for him, my son Isaac and his fenced yard became Plan B. And the best part was that Mo got to remain in our family!

Mo traversed a long and unfamiliar route, maneuvering curves and crossroads along the way. In the end, he successfully reached his desired destination. That spotted dog and his tenacity stirred a question within me:

On a scale of "one to Mo," what was my determination level to reach life goals? Mo became my example to follow when traveling the winding roads that led to where I wanted to be.

— Becky Alexander —

88

A Dog's Guide to Divorce

Happiness is a warm puppy.
~Charles Schulz

Unless you have personally experienced divorce, no one can really explain that feeling of spiraling backward into a black hole, where the foundation you stood upon disintegrates. The hundred-year-old historical house you bought and loved with your partner, initially filled with unlimited possibilities, now feels like an empty carcass of wood. The friends you had in common stand divided on either side of each partner, not wanting to get involved. Nevertheless, the friends end up as collateral damage. During holidays spent with grandparents and family, the seat at the family table normally reserved for your partner is now filled with someone else.

I understand now why people say divorce is like death. So many mornings, I would lie in my bed and go back in time, wondering how I ended up here. If it weren't for my girls, I probably wouldn't have left my bed for an entire year.

But one Saturday morning when I woke up I realized that my mind was completely clear, and the only thing I could think of was getting a dog. A dog — me? Why was the universe whispering this to me? I had always been a cat person, and I had never owned a dog. I tried to push this thought out of my head, but it was so strong and compelling that I wondered if it was a sign. I got out of bed.

"Girls, let's go! We are getting a puppy!" I could hear the girls mumbling to each other about how their mom had really lost it this time. "Mom, you don't even like dogs." My girls seized the opportunity to call their friends and invite them to witness the official insanity of their newly divorced mom. Before I knew it, the car was filled with a few very excited giggling girls ready for this crazy mom to get a puppy.

I heard on the radio that there was a puppy-adoption event at Kmart, so I drove there. As we walked toward the outdoor event, we saw a white Labrador-mix puppy. I picked him up, and he squirmed in my arms. I stared at the girls, and they stared back at me. Then, I heard another lady calling her husband to come and look at the dog. It was now or never, so I blurted out as loudly as I could, "We will take him!"

As the pet-adoption person began to fill out the paperwork, I pulled out my wallet for the sixty-dollar adoption fee. My wallet was empty. As my eyes began to water, my youngest child, age nine, proudly declared, "Mommy, I have sixty dollars." She walked back to the car and triumphantly returned with her life savings. And off we went with our squirming ball of fur.

We named our new little brother Baxter. A good friend of mine had a wonderful husband named Baxter who was loyal and dependable, so Baxter seemed like an appropriate name.

When we went to buy him supplies at the pet store, we had to clean up the mess he made in the cart. When we took him to the veterinarian, he ran through what seemed like a thousand diseases a puppy could catch, and I began to feel my confidence waning. At nighttime, Baxter howled in his crate, and the girls became distraught because they couldn't sleep. After a sleepless night of howling, I began to sob. I called my good friend, proclaimed defeat, and declared that I was not meant to be a dog owner. She rushed over with books, a leash and toys, and convinced me that I could not give that puppy back. I could do this!

One night, as I carried our crying pup outside, I stopped and looked up at the stars. In the stillness and peace of the night, I realized that there was truly something much bigger at work, and the girls and I would be okay. I felt a force moving me forward. Call it Spirit, God, or the Universe, but somehow I knew to trust my intuition and follow the signs that were leading me forward.

Baxter was, and is, a leading force. He got me out of the house for walks and kept me active when all I wanted to do was sleep all day. When my girls were sad that their father no longer lived with us, they would play with Baxter, and everything seemed to be better. We even went to puppy-training class, and I will always love the photograph of Baxter, me, and my girls holding up our certificate of accomplishment.

When the girls got older and were out on a Saturday night, Baxter and I would sit together and watch a movie. When they went away to college, my nest was not truly empty because Baxter was always there waiting for me when I got home. At nighttime, he would walk up the stairs and sleep next to my bed. The next morning, I would always find him downstairs. I knew that he would stay with me until I was asleep and then go back down to guard the house. I never felt alone, and I always felt safe.

The quieter we are, the more we really "see." The more we live in the moment and out of our heads, the faster we will heal. Divorce can be an opportunity for rebirth. It is an opportunity to really look at our life and the choices that we have made. It is often an opportunity for a "cat person" to be a "dog person." We often discover we are more resilient than we think. In my case, I was lucky because I had Baxter to force me to live in the moment and guide me.

—Marie A. Saleeby—

89

Tiny's Magic

Life is funny... We never know what's in store for us,
and time brings on what is meant to be.
~April Mae Monterrosa

s a young child, I was given a baby Chihuahua as a gift. Because of this dog's teacup size, it seemed only natural to name her "Tiny," and she quickly became much more than a pet. She became my best friend and faithful companion.

I often dressed Tiny like a real baby and pushed her around the neighborhood in a baby carriage. Whenever I pulled out her bonnet and blanket, she knew she was going for a ride, and she never tried to escape or get out of the carriage. In fact, Tiny was very tolerant of all my maneuvers to make her into a doll, fairy, mermaid, or unicorn. I read books to her, performed songs and dances for her, and told her my secrets. We were together constantly, and I regarded her as my special friend and magical playmate.

When I was eleven years old, however, our companionship abruptly ceased. My mother informed me that she was going to remarry, and we would be moving five hundred miles away. I would have to leave the only home I had ever known. Much more devastating was the news that we would be living in an apartment, and the apartment did not allow pets. I was heartbroken at this news. I cried until I had no more tears, but it did not change anything. We were moving, and Tiny could not go.

Eventually, I decided to give Tiny to my grandfather because I knew he would take good care of her. When the day for our departure arrived, I thought it was the end of the world, but Tiny had more magic in her than I knew. It just took me a while to appreciate it.

Leaving my home and Tiny hurt terribly, but I was a soon-to-be teenager and almost ready to enter middle school. I was growing up, making new friends, and getting involved in new activities. My world was expanding.

My elderly grandfather, on the other hand, was slowing down. He was limiting his activities, and his circle of acquaintances was growing smaller. His world was contracting. In this smaller realm, however, Tiny became the reigning queen.

As soon as we were settled in our new apartment, my grandfather began to write me letters about Tiny's activities and how she was doing. Occasionally, he would even send me a picture. From the beginning, it was clear that Tiny was enjoying my grandfather's company, and it was even more apparent that he was enjoying hers.

When we returned home on holidays to visit my grandfather, I was able to see, with my own eyes, the companionship and love that he and Tiny shared. I think my grandfather thought he was taking care of Tiny for me, but I am certain she was actually taking care of him. It was part of her magic. Once I realized how happy my grandfather and Tiny were together, the ache in my heart eased.

Tiny had been an affectionate, entertaining, and loyal friend to me, but for my grandfather, Tiny was a soul mate. He adored her, and she adored him. We could see it in the way she followed him around, watched his every move, and cocked her head to listen to every word he said.

My grandfather and Tiny were inseparable. They worked, played, ate, and slept together. Tiny would sit in my grandfather's lap when he read and curl up by his feet when he watched television. It took time, but I eventually realized that my grandfather and Tiny were meant to be together.

Had Tiny accompanied me to my new home, her life would have been confined to an apartment. She would have gotten outside for an occasional walk, but most of her days would have been spent waiting on me to get home from school or return from activities with friends.

On my grandfather's small farm, however, Tiny was able to roam at will. She could be inside with all the comforts of home or outside exploring all the pleasures of nature. Either way, she knew she had a close and protective friend nearby.

Because of this companionship, Tiny's last years were spent in happiness, peace, and security. When she eventually passed away, my grandfather buried her on his farm. He made a special grave and adorned it with a marker he made himself. He would show Tiny's grave to everyone who came to visit him. Not too long after Tiny's death, my grandfather also passed away.

Tiny taught me to be grateful for every minute we have with those we love. She helped me to understand there are times in life when we may lose our most prized possession, but we may find it is even more highly prized by someone else. And she taught me that to truly appreciate the value of something, we may have to give it away.

— Billie Holladay Skelley —

90

Totally Worth It

The life of a good dog is like the life of a good person,
only shorter and more compressed.
~Anna Quindlen

I began an online search for our next dog six months after Hootie, our Terrier mix, died of a heart attack at sixteen. My husband Lee and I were still grieving and might have waited before adopting again, but our eight-year-old Roxie needed a friend. I can't explain how, but the moment I saw Milo on the Muttville senior-dog rescue website, I knew he was our dog. Muttville contacted Milo's foster mom, who quickly arranged a meeting.

How could anyone not fall in love with Milo — a tiny gray-and-white eleven-year-old gentleman in need of a forever home? The funny old fellow looked more like a tiny mountain goat than a dog, with his pointy face and ears, beady eyes, and mane of soft white hair. He stood uncertainly on spindly legs and looked up at me cloudy-eyed. His foster mom explained he'd recently been treated for an intestinal parasite in addition to having dental work. The poor little guy looked like a fur-covered skeleton and weighed just seven pounds. I looked at Lee, who nodded, and then we both looked at Roxie, who sniffed Milo with interest. He went home with us that day.

At first, Milo, who'd barely adjusted to his foster home, was bewildered to find himself in still another household. He was quickly won over by love, affection, and home-cooked meals of meat, sweet potatoes, brown rice, and vegetables, which he gobbled with gusto.

It took three weeks to teach this old dog the new trick of using the dog door to our fenced-in backyard, but once he caught on, he was one happy guy.

Six months later, Milo weighed almost nine pounds. He and Roxie were pack members who often curled up together on the couch or their dog bed during the day. At night, we helped him into our bed to sleep with his bony little body snuggled between the three of us. The next morning, or sometimes during the night, his sharp little bark alerted us to his need to go out. We never begrudged him any lost sleep. We'd fallen in love with his endearing way of pressing his head against our legs, and with his wagging tail and joyful bark that let us know he was content with his forever home.

After eighteen months with us, Milo showed signs of confusion, loss of balance, and diminished eyesight. He fell often, thrashing about frantically while attempting to right himself, striking his head repeatedly, until I reached him and scooped him up in my arms. He got lost in our yard, wandering, unsure where to turn. Three times, he darted mindlessly off the bed without warning, crashing to the floor.

Our vet attributed his behavior to pressure from a mass in his brain. The prednisone she prescribed helped, but not enough. One day, while watching him struggle to maintain his balance while pooping, Lee and I recalled that when two of our other dogs, Conan and Penny, were finally put down, we later regretted having waited too long.

"It's time then," Lee said, and I couldn't disagree. Milo's life had become more struggle than enjoyment. Rather than prolong it, we had him put down that day.

The vet and her assistant were all we could have wished for. By pre-arrangement, we parked our van in their lot, and they came outside to administer the shot. Milo was asleep against my chest when the sedative was injected and then the second shot that would send him on his way.

We were all there together. Lee and Roxie were watching. I don't know what Roxie was thinking. Lee's eyes were wet with tears. I looked away when the needle pierced Milo's skin, concentrating instead on the soft, little body I was holding. The last thing he felt was my heartbeat and the warmth of my arms.

Lee and I have no regrets about adopting Milo, even though we had less than two years together and caring for a special-needs dog like him was no easy task. We were the third family he gave his heart to. Someone gave him up due to "time constraints" after eight years, and someone else after two-and-a-half. He was already old and frail when we adopted him. We take comfort in knowing we gave him everything he might have wanted: the freedom of a dog door, a canine companion, home-cooked meals, daily walks, and unconditional love.

What he gave us was far more than that.

— Lynn Sunday —

91

Lessons in Grieving

The one best place to bury a good dog
is in the heart of his master.
~Ben Hur Lampman

W e all have a "thing." Mine? I always expect the worst. My husband doesn't answer the phone? He's probably dead. My childhood friend didn't message me on my birthday? Definitely dead. The gardener didn't show up to blow the leaves? Very dead. The only way I can be sure some- one's not dead is to have them right in front of me.

Sadly, my husband has to go to work, and my best friend lives 6,000 miles away in Western Siberia. The only creature that yearned for my around-the-clock surveillance was our dog, Spoon.

An Entlebucher Mountain Dog—imagine an oversized Corgi with a Beagle's face — our pup Spoon was what they call "a lot of dog." From day one, he stalked me around the house, issuing a deafening bark at every minor noise outside. He nipped at my jeans, driven by an ancient herding instinct, and he tried to chest-bump our docile cats.

A Google search revealed that Entlebuchers need a job, or worst- case scenario, they'll eat the cats (and I like my cats). So, I went ahead and signed Spoon up for a local dog agility class.

You've seen it before — likely at 3:00 A.M. on Channel 149. An athletic canine navigates through a numbered obstacle course consisting of jumps, tunnels, seesaw and weave poles, directed by a considerably less agile human, aka the "handler." The stoic judge closely observes the run, calling faults and bestowing points.

Held indoors, with lowered jumps and a scaled-down seesaw, our first agility class was amateurish and low-stakes. The instructors had no agenda to turn their students into the next National Agility Champion. My only objective was to tire out a dog, but instead I accidentally gave his life meaning.

Soon, Spoon's erratic behavior gave way to a wise, contained presence punctuated by only an occasional bark. The cats descended from their cat trees and roamed the house like antelopes without their natural predator. My remaining pair of jeans stayed intact.

Within a year, Spoon reliably crushed Thursday's "Agility League," and it was time for us to turn pro. I put my social life on pause and fully gave in to my calling of becoming a cuckoo Dog Sports Aficionado.

Every weekend, Spoon and I would get up at the crack of dawn, hop in my dented Prius, and head to a destination like City of Industry, California, where I would squeeze in between formidable camp trailers, armed to the teeth with industrial-strength dog crates and backup lawn chairs. Spoon and I would sail through the crowd of middle-aged, hyper-focused, ribbon-grasping competitors and settle on the bleachers. From there, we would watch born-to-run Border Collies, bear-like Bernese, and peppy Papillons as they ran the course.

Then, our turn would come, and for a handful of seconds, the world would stop spinning and go out of focus, leaving nothing but my dog kicking the cloud of dirt, tongue flipping in the wind, screaming with excitement or frustration, depending on how timely I communicated to him the order in which to take the obstacles. When we messed up, it was usually my fault.

No matter. Even when we didn't qualify, we had a blast. Spoon lived for the sport. He whimpered every time we pulled into the parking lot, charged toward the ring like a young bull, and howled at me at the start line, basically calling out, "Can we go already?" Once, he barreled through the set of weave poles with such herculean force that he snapped off one pole with his rock-hard head — and kept going. I still have that broken weave pole on a shelf next to a garbage bag full of ribbons.

I never came to love agility the way Spoon did. What kept me coming back was the deepening of our bond. An agility dog is trained to take cues from its human. Spoon began to mirror my energy and emotions. My husband rolled his eyes. "You two are the same," he said. I liked hearing that. I also liked that I no longer pictured my husband dropping dead at work. My brain was too busy visualizing winning ribbons.

Eventually, agility wasn't enough, so Spoon and I pursued the farcical sport of K9 Nose Work, where you actually spend money to teach your dog how to sniff. You do that by taking a handful of scented Q-tips and setting them up in a large barn or an open field. The dog's job is to identify the exact location of each Q-tip and communicate its findings using a distinct body language known as "alert."

Within a few years, my commitment to dog sports yielded unexpected results. Spoon became the number-one agility dog in his breed nationwide. His skills and discipline led him to working behind the scenes of a high-profile TV hit. He was even written up in American Kennel Club's publication, to the chagrin of his dog-show frenemies.

Then, suddenly, Spoon lost the ability to walk and was diagnosed with aggressive bone cancer in his spine. My husband and I scavenged for all the options until there was only one option left. It was time for me to say goodbye to my unstoppable partner in dog sports.

We saw Spoon off on an unusually windy Los Angeles night. He bounced back, if only for a moment, devouring a whole bag of deli meats, a banana and a cherry yogurt. I placed a few scented Q-tips from his Nose Work kit on the blanket so he could sniff them out for the last time.

Spoon faded, licking a peanut-butter-filled rubber Kong, while my husband and I held him and sang to him. (Mind you, we're both terrible singers, but Spoon was into it, just like he was into anything we did together.) After the first euthanasia shot, while Spoon could still hear us, I told him to "weave, weave," sending him off on his final agility course. The second shot stopped his heart.

My dog's death crushed me. I couldn't write, eat, or tie the proverbial shoes. One night, my husband found me crouching on the kitchen floor, clasping the urn with Spoon's ashes like some non-homicidal Medea. Instead of walking over and giving me his usual uplifting spiel, he mumbled something about getting fresh air and made a beeline for the front door. I watched him leave. Was I turning into an emotional vampire? Maybe this wasn't just about Spoon anymore. Maybe I was processing another, deeper loss from when I was sixteen years old, back in my hometown in Siberia.

I'll never forget that day: The outside temperature was negative forty. Feeble sunlight barely streaked past the monstrous layer of ice plastering our window. Primordial, blotched wallpaper adorned the living room where I sat eating mealy potatoes dipped in sunflower oil with a pinch of salt. My mom was reclining on the couch, dressed in the faded cotton nightgown that she wore around the clock.

The phone rang, and Mom picked it up.

Then, her voice cracked and became unusually high-pitched. "Dead? He's dead?"

I knew immediately from her reaction that she was talking about my father.

Mom collapsed on the couch, wailing. I spit the half-chewed potato back on the plate and promised myself I wouldn't cry. There was room for only one to grieve, and my mom had called dibs on it.

I should have been weeping, too. After all, Dad was my favorite person. He taught me how to read, speak broken English, and play chess. A coal-mining engineer on the verge of getting his dissertation, he used to wear neat, ill-fitting suits, smell of pungent cologne, and draw me pictures of bunnies. He would only get drunk every other month or so, nothing to write home to your babushka about.

Then, Dad had a falling-out with his mentor, a distinguished member of the still-powerful Communist Party. The dream of dissertation had been squashed, and with it the hope of a sizable, government-issued, new apartment, steady paycheck, and a tolerable marriage.

Worst of all, Dad's drinking took a dismal turn, even by Russian measures. He would forage the cabinets for a hidden bottle of vodka, cheap wine, or even the cologne that once resided on his skin — anything to dull the Dostoevsky-level pain of self-loathing. Mom tried to make him stop, but who could stop a force of nature?

Eventually, Dad gave up on people and civilization and moved to live a hermit's life deep in the thicket of taiga, where he could drink in peace. He'd visit every few weeks, looking less and less like my father, carrying a sack of gnarly beets and potatoes he'd farmed with his freshly callused hands. We had nothing to talk about — and I started drawing my own bunnies.

And now he was dead. Dad's neighbors discovered his frozen corpse in the pile of snow outside his dilapidated farmhouse. He had been drinking and had a heart attack. According to the coroner, if Dad had survived, his limbs would have had to be amputated.

Two days later, my mom, now a ruin of a human being, had an idea.

"Dochka, you're not going to the funeral. It's too far, too cold," she told me.

That wasn't the main reason, and we both knew it. It was Mom's offer to help preserve me in my tearless state. With no mental image of my father's corpse, the idea occurred to me that I could skip over the whole grieving process. I agreed in a heartbeat.

Over the past several years, I've moved to Los Angeles where I've shed some of my thick Siberian skin and gone partially woo-woo with LA's yoga and meditation. I've yet to achieve enlightenment, but I have become aware of one thing: I never got to cheat the grieving process. Instead, I harbored it close to my heart, allowing it to shape me into a fretful person filled with survivor's guilt. And now, with Spoon's death, I was finally feeling it all.

Here's how it would go. I'd be laughing about something with my husband and then, suddenly, a thought would strike me: Laughing is just a way for me to ignore the fact that Spoon is gone. Oh, and you know who else is gone? My dad, who never got to hear me singing to him off-tune on his deathbed, or even have a deathbed. Laughing, then, was an act of betrayal, a selfish attempt to feel joy in the face of the universe's ultimate truth.

But then, the same day, I'd stumble on a loose agility ribbon or a picture of Spoon levitating over a jump, his expression that of pure bliss, and realize that the only way to challenge death is to live full throttle, whether by snapping off a weave pole mid-run or laughing your heart out.

Eventually, I learned to integrate both losses into the multitude of experiences that comprise me. I now allow myself to cry—about Dad or Spoon. Afterward, I saddle up and go on living.

Don't get me wrong. I'm not comparing the loss of a parent to that of a pet. But my dog's final gift was giving me the space to grieve—not only his death, or even my dad's death, but all the time I've lost being terrified of death, when I could be doing life.

There's a small silk pouch sitting on my writing desk. Inside it is a fistful of soil from my dad's grave. For decades, I hid it in the drawers, afraid that seeing it would send me off into an endless loop of anxiety. Now, from time to time, I pull it out and hold the slinky fabric in my palm. It brings me comfort: I had a dad. He is still with me.

—Sasha Feiler—

92

The Joy of Jeremiah

*Until one has loved an animal, a part of one's soul
remains unawakened.*
~Anatole France

The small black-and-white dog lived in a tiny wire cage. No name, just a number. He and the other little dogs on the property received no affection. No vet care. No toys. They didn't play in the grass or live in a home. There was little shade from the hot sun, almost no protection from the wind, rain, and cold, and not much interaction with one another.

After almost three years, the male Shih Tzu and the other thirty-five dogs were removed from the Missouri puppy mill by an animal-rescue organization. Little did the canines realize the joy their newfound freedom would bring — to themselves and to others, including me.

Each dog received a name for the first time. The male Shih Tzu's moniker became Stormy. For nearly a year, he and the other dogs lived at a Nebraska rescue sanctuary. Staff and volunteers provided compassion and care, restoring the abused creatures' spirits and giving them the medical treatment the "owners" neglected. They also received nutritious food, although that wasn't enough to save Stormy's rotten teeth. The sanctuary's veterinarian had to extract twenty-eight of them.

Sanctuary staff and volunteers interacted with the rescued residents, sitting in the rooms that held the dogs, offering gentle pets and loving cuddles. The hesitation and fear experienced by the dogs transformed into acceptance and excitement as the once-neglected canines evolved into adoptable, lovable companions. As weeks turned into months, walks on leashes and romps in the grassy play yard became daily joys for Stormy and his surviving puppy-mill companions.

On a warm August day, I was perusing the Petfinder website in search of a small dog. Stormy's almond-colored eyes reached from the computer screen into my heart. His round furry face reminded me of an Ewok from the *Star Wars* movie series. I submitted an adoption application and, after approval, my husband and I drove 600 miles one way to bring the little dog home. I had no clue how much this once-neglected pup would impact my life, how much he needed a loving home to call his own, or the challenges we'd encounter — and eventually overcome — during the first few months.

The first change came when we christened him Jeremiah. New home, new life, new name. The adjustment took time for him. However, consistent repetition over several weeks helped him respond to the new moniker.

Never having lived in a home before, the small dog knew little of house training. Puddles and "prizes" were often left overnight. Noises, such as a phone ringing, music playing, the television chatting, or the doorbell chiming caused him to jump and tremble.

However, my husband and I soon learned we had an antidote to many of these challenges: a Springer Spaniel mix named Mary.

This stocky black-and-white beauty had also come to us via a rescue organization. Her previous owner had died, and Mary needed a new family. My husband's favorite breeds are Springer and Cocker Spaniels, so when we learned of Mary's need, we stepped in to fulfill it. We learned she had been trained as a therapy dog; therefore, I often took her to libraries, schools, and nursing homes. She became our new dog's teacher and best friend.

A few months after Jeremiah's adoption, when I returned home for a lunch break from work, I released both dogs from the inside of the house into the back yard. I observed them from the deck. Mary, our mellow, sweet seven-year-old, explored the scents of birds and squirrels. I noticed Jeremiah following her around and appearing to imitate her actions. I realized Mary's ability to be our asset and Jeremiah's advocate. Before I left the house to return to work from my lunch break, I placed a baby gate across the entrance from the living room into the kitchen; we used that wooden barrier to keep our charming Mary from becoming a monster garbage hound. I also closed doors to the other rooms in the house. This allowed Jeremiah to have some freedom and yet kept him from disrupting and disturbing too many things in the house… and less room to leave me "gifts."

It worked. When I returned home at the end of my workday, I found no "presents" except one: Jeremiah and Mary curled together on the green recliner in the living room. That became "their spot," a place of companionship and comfort.

Jeremiah's confidence grew. A few weeks later, as I sat on the couch reading, a squeak caused me to glance up from the book. There was Jeremiah chewing on one of the soft squeaky toys we'd purchased several weeks before. His nearly toothless mouth gnawed on the multi-colored, fleece-covered duck while his paws wrestled to hold the toy in place. He clamped his jaws on the soft plaything and shook it with vigor.

Tears formed in my eyes as I realized this was the first time since he'd come to live with us that he engaged with a toy. I remembered just a few hours prior when Mary had taken one of her toys from a nearby basket and chewed on it, rolled across it, and squeaked it with her mouth. Jeremiah had learned the joy of a toy from his canine companion, just as he had learned to walk on a leash around the neighborhood and to go to the bathroom in the back yard instead of our kitchen. Mary was Jeremiah's mentor, and she helped bring joy into his life through the new experiences of living in a home.

Not long thereafter, I again stood on our deck observing Mary and Jeremiah in the back yard. The late autumn sun immersed the tan grasses with light, and though I needed to return to work, I basked in the warmth and hesitated to call the dogs inside. But I had to, so I did. When Jeremiah heard his name, his head perked, his ears peaked, and his eyes darted in my direction. He sprinted across the yard, experiencing the freedom to run likely for the first time in his life. He seemed to smile, showing his remaining teeth. His wispy ears folded back like wings as he raced toward me. A grin dawned on my face as I experienced his apparent joy once again.

This puppy-mill survivor's early life caused harm emotionally and physically. However, his rescue and adoption surpassed the abuse, bringing love and joy not only to him but to me. I believe that's also the case for his former puppy-mill companions… and for all animals that are rescued.

Jeremiah's joy is my joy, too. Each day we share is a blessing. Author Louis Sabin is quoted as saying, "No matter how little money and how few possessions you own, having a dog makes you rich." It's so true. With Jeremiah sharing life with me, my cup indeed overflows!

— Gayle M. Irwin —

93

The Dog I Didn't Want

*There is nothing truer in this world
than the love of a good dog.*
~Mira Grant

y dog Connor was *that* dog. The one you never forget. The one you talk about and think about for years after he's gone.

And, for me, he was the dog I didn't want.

My husband had brought him home, a rescue dog he'd found online. I objected to no avail. I tried not to become attached, but Connor quickly broke down my defenses and wormed his way into my heart. And, several months later, when I became a widow, he became the rock I leaned on.

A Mastiff mix, Connor was close to 150 pounds, and his head was higher than my waist. He gave me a sense of security as I became accustomed to living alone. He was smart — scary-smart, I called him — as his intelligence exceeded any dog I'd ever encountered.

But he was even more.

One afternoon, I let the dogs outside to romp in the yard a bit. I was feeling sad. It was one of those days in which the melancholy hung around my neck like a pendant. I did laundry, swept floors — my typical weekend chores — and tried to make myself feel normal.

When the dogs asked to come back in, I opened the door. As Connor came in, he dropped something at my feet and sat down to wait.

I looked down to find a perfect bloom from the bush by the patio.

The large pink flowers filled the plant each year, an abundance that bloomed and then fell to the ground as new buds pushed their way in. Connor had picked up one of these and brought it to me.

My heart lifted a little. *How cute,* I thought, rubbing his ears and expressing my gratitude. He couldn't know what that little trick did for my heart, but I was happy for the gesture.

Or could he?

Could this dog, who I had accepted was incredibly intelligent, be emotionally aware as well?

Over the next weeks, as the bush continued to bloom, he continued to occasionally bring me a flower. And I soon began to realize that he brought them on the days I needed them. It wasn't a random trick, a learned behavior designed to get a "good boy" and an ear scratch. Regular, normal days in which I wasn't mired in malaise did not include a gift from my scary-smart dog. But on the days in which my mood was somber and my heart was sad, I found the cheerful bloom dropped at my feet, and loving eyes sought mine. *I'm here, Mom,* they said. *You've still got me.*

As time passed, I began to feel more like myself. And the stronger I became, the fewer gifts were dropped at my feet. He was the smartest dog I ever knew, and the sweetest as well. The dog I didn't want was absolutely the dog I needed the most.

— Tammie Rue Elliott —

94

Two Little Wolves

An animal's eyes have the power to speak
a great language.
~Martin Buber

'm retired and not responsible for much these days. I don't have school-age children who require help with their homework. I sleep in when I choose, do a little writing, tinker with my motor-cycle, and repair a few things around the house. That's about it.

My wife's work, on the other hand, is never-ending. Diana takes care of her parents (both in their mid-nineties), tends to home and garden, volunteers for various civic organizations, and is a gold-star grandmother. She is also a dedicated feline lover. Throughout her life, Diana has surrounded herself with cats, usually two or three at a time. Sometimes, a dozen or more. She has never owned a reptile, bird, or tropical fish. Cats have always been her pet of choice.

All that changed when two small black-and-brown dogs scampered into our yard and melted Diana's heart.

It happened not long ago. The dogs appeared unannounced, materializing from the dense forest behind our home. They were little mixed-breed mongrels, part Chihuahua, part Miniature Dachshund, and part something else. They had been seen by hikers on numerous occasions, roaming the woods like tiny lost souls. They were homeless dogs, as wild as the wind. No one could get within 100 yards of them. In their struggle for survival, the two had figured out a way to avoid people and find food and shelter in the wilderness.

They were undeniably cute and appealing. Many of our neighbors tried to lure them in with treats, but the tiny dogs remained unapproachable

My wife began leaving tasty tidbits out for the dogs, slowly moving the food bowl closer with each feeding. As days passed, they ventured closer and closer. Diana made a conscious effort not to frighten the skittish dogs. She called them to dinner with a soothing voice and let them know they were safe. It was important that they trusted her. Why? She was looking for something to mother. For Diana, love is the medicine to everything, and nothing tugged at her heartstrings more than a hungry and homeless animal.

She called the dogs her "little wolves."

Initially, they would not let her touch them. As days turned into weeks, their bond slowly grew. Soon, Diana was petting them. Next, they were eating from her hand. Before long, she had them sitting in her lap and following her around the yard. And poof! My wife was instantly transformed from cat lady to cat/dog lady.

It wasn't long before the dogs were sleeping in the house and assuming their role as "watchdogs." They became fierce protectors of our home, a comforting presence. Each day, they would police the property, chase deer from the flower beds, and run down birds, butterflies, and other phantom creatures that Diana and I could neither see nor hear. The little animals put their hearts into their work and would return to the house expecting a treat and a pat on the head for a job well done. They always received both.

Our little wolves didn't ask for much. Diana christened them "Emma" (after her grandmother) and "Daisy" (a wildflower in a field). Their love and devotion were unquestioning and fierce. They quickly became entwined into the fabric of our daily lives. We bought dog food and flea medicine, and took them to the vet for a checkup.

For Daisy and Emma, every day is the best day, and every snack is the best snack ever. The dogs are totally in the moment, completely innocent and, above all, happy. They are intelligent and have strong personalities; it must be how they survived. Where did they come from? That was a question I never stop asking myself. Maybe an unavoidable tragedy brought the little wolves to us, an illness or death that caused them to become instant orphans. Or maybe they had been adopted by a misguided human and eventually ran away. Whatever it was, our furry friends are the essence of happiness. They display absolute joy in simply being alive.

Their wagging tails and cold little noses always lift my spirits.

Time in the yard feels like a second childhood with Daisy and Emma frolicking about our feet. They constantly try and outdo each for attention and, in the process, ratchet up their cuteness to nearly unbearable levels. The dogs take their cues from each other and are filled with so much energy that it can't be contained. They race around the yard at top speed, barking and chasing each other, and then sprint back to us, tongues and tails wagging, for another love session of pets and hugs.

If Diana steps inside the house for a moment, she returns to find several of her gardening shoes missing (Daisy and Emma's way of scolding her for leaving). And when my wife goes shopping, she comes home to find the dogs waiting patiently in the driveway, perched on a nest of her shoes. The message is perfectly clear.

Those who rescue stray or abandoned animals are the best people in the world. Diana is one of them. She is nothing short of amazing. My wife was able to win the hearts of two wild animals with love and kindness. Daisy and Emma serve as a reminder that we don't choose our pets so much as they choose us. They are now so omnipresent in our lives that we can't imagine being without them. The dogs have taught us to savor every moment spent in their company.

I've also learned that it's highly possible to turn a cat lady into a cat/dog lady with two little wolves and a whole lotta love.

— Tim Martin —

Chapter 11

Saying Goodbye with Gratitude

95

Never Alone

Blessed is the person who has earned
the love of an old dog.
~Sydney Jeanne Seward

work from home. From the time I kiss my husband goodbye in the morning until late in the day, I am alone. For many years, my only companion was our dog, Sno.

A small but mighty Bichon Frisé, our dog may have looked fluffy, but he was smart, creative, and always ready for mint ice cream and rolling in mysterious stink. While I worked, he slept, rousing only to chase the red cat from next door, greet a delivery person, or sit in the sunshine.

We didn't agree on everything, especially when to get up, when to go to bed, and mint ice cream. He sighed with boredom when a project was due and I didn't have time to play. He didn't understand weekends, deadlines, and visitors who left him. However, we both agreed on walking.

At least once a week, we took a long walk to the beach. For him, there were swaths of tall grass and exciting smells. For me, there were other dog walkers and neighbors to catch up with. We returned tired, thirsty, and very happy.

Being a dog with huge ambition and short legs, Sno needed several breaks along the way. The one at the entrance to the beach was his favorite, possibly because he knew we were circling back home.

There, on a windy summer day, he looked up at me just as I was looking down at him. We both grinned. This was the best walk ever.

When he was old and dying, our walks were shorter and closer to home. I'd take him for a walk and then go out for my own walk, looping around the beach like we used to do. I always grinned when I got to the entrance to the beach, remembering that summer day when he was young and energetic.

In his final days, Sno still insisted on walking. It took twice as long to take even the shortest walk, but we savored every step.

Then came that Sunday when he leaned hard toward the beach walk. How could I refuse his last-walk wish?

We took the walk. It took an extra hour to take that walk. He needed to rest, sniff, and pause at his favorite places.

He sat down when we came to the entrance to the beach. He looked up at me the way he had that long-ago summer day.

I don't know if dogs can cry, but if they can, that made two of us sobbing at the entrance to the beach.

After he died, I went for a long walk. I felt like part of me was missing. I kept looking down as if he were there beside me enjoying the sun, warmth, and fresh air. When I came to the place where we'd turn for the beach, I turned the other way.

Months later, I came to the place of decision. I asked him to be with me when I took our walk by myself for the first time.

My eyes filled at the stopping place near the tall grass. Tears flowed when I came to the yard with his dog friends, who raced to say hello and stopped when they saw he wasn't with me.

Approaching the entrance to the beach, I braced myself. If the other places were bad, this was where I'd have my breakdown. I clutched my tissues and walked faster.

He was with me when I walked past the entrance, thinking of that smiling day when we shared our best walk ever.

Instead of crying, I grinned. It was a warm, windy day with a bright, blue sky just like our magical walk.

I was the only one standing there, but I wasn't alone.

That walk to the beach is now my favorite. I grin every time I come to the entrance to the beach and tell him I love him.

I may be walking by myself, but I'm never alone.

— Louise Foerster —

96

Mosby's Rainbow

The rainbow is a promise.
~Mary Clark Dalton

y husband Sam and I had loaded up our truck and camper as we did every long weekend in May. We would be heading out to our favorite lake for a three-day camping trip, a special annual event that marked the first outing of the season.

We had planned to take off early Friday morning, but on Thursday afternoon our Terrier Mosby took sick. He hadn't had much of an appetite for the past couple of days, so we decided it was time for him to see the vet. But since the clinic was already closed for the long weekend, we were only able to speak to our veterinarian by telephone.

After a long talk, the doctor said our little dog had probably eaten something that didn't agree with him. The best thing we could do was to give him plenty of water and keep him comfortable. She also gently reminded us that Mosby was nearing his eighteenth birthday. However, she assured us that if he was not better by Tuesday, she would be back in town and able to see him in person.

So, instead of sitting on the sandy beach enjoying the sunshine, and taking long evening walks along the lakeshore with Mosby dodging in and out of the water, we spent the weekend at home tending to our sick little guy.

Mosby would not attempt to drink water from his dish, so I dug out one of the kids' old baby bottles from the attic and filled it with water.

I was able to get him to take enough water to prevent dehydration.

He would not eat anything on Friday, and by Saturday he refused to take any water. Mosby just wanted to sleep and seemed most peaceful when I was holding him in my arms. Ever since he was a pup, he loved to be held and cuddled, but even more so during the past couple of years after he lost most of his hearing.

One of the things he enjoyed in his later years was laying his head against my chest and "hearing" me hum, so I held him throughout the day, gently rocking him and humming the tune of "Rock of Ages," the old hymn I had learned as a child in Sunday school.

It was an unseasonably cold and terribly wet long weekend, definitely one of the gloomiest and saddest ones I could remember. On Monday afternoon, Mosby took his last breath and died peacefully in my arms.

With heavy hearts, on Tuesday we took our Mosby to the pet-memorial center to have him cremated. On Wednesday, we went to pick up a little cedar box that held his remains.

When we returned home that afternoon, it was still raining. The house was cold, quiet and empty. Sam and I sat down on the living room sofa, and after more tears than either of us had shed in years, we were able to find words to speak about the little box that I was cradling in my lap.

We wondered: Where in our big old rambling house would Mosby's spirit be most comfortable? Where would he wish to rest? The answer came in an instant! After Mosby's hearing started to go, whenever I went to play the piano, he'd eagerly follow me into the living room and beg to be picked up to share the piano bench with me. And there he'd lie at my side for as long as I played. He seemed to really enjoy "feeling" the vibrations of the music; he wouldn't budge until the session was over and the lid was closed.

I placed the little box on top of the piano that sat in front of the living room window. I opened the drapes and noticed the rain had finally stopped. I caught a glimpse of a brilliant rainbow across the street.

Ever since I was a child, seeing the beautiful colors of a rainbow always reminded me that God was near. I called Sam to the window to share the rainbow with me.

As we patted the box, a brilliant ray of light lit up the whole room. We could feel the warmth of the sun on our hands, and we knew in our hearts that Mosby was free of pain and happy to be home.

—Linda Gabris—

Come Back to Me

A dog has one purpose in life: to bestow his heart.
~J.B. Aukerly

'd always wanted a dog. But the answer was always no. Then when I was eight years old, the stars aligned. My aunt came back from her daily run with a rescued puppy in tow.

After weeks of unsuccessfully looking for the owner and begging to keep him, "Pepper," a black-and-tan Beagle mix, was finally a member of my family. And, like many children with a new thing, I became obsessed. Dog-training classes, dog drawings, dog stories, learning about every dog breed imaginable — everything "dog" was at the center of my world.

Pepper was there for me as I grew up. Amid a home life of mental and emotional abuse, he cheered me up and gave me unconditional love. His corkscrew tail uncurled and recurled with every wag and prompted me to smile. His welcoming "tippy-tap dance" let me forget the day when I'd been bullied at school. The way he cocked his head when I talked to him made me feel as if he understood every word. He'd perform tricks to win a treat or two… or four. I even gave him a treat when I'd say "Roll over" and he'd fake the roll by lying on his back and then getting back up, never completing the trick. His pudgy belly was the undeniable proof of too many treats and his obsession with bananas.

Then, when Pepper was sixteen, I got the call I'd hoped would never come. I was twenty-four, unhappily married, living hours away,

Saying Goodbye with Gratitude |

barely making ends meet, and trying to balance life with a newborn son. The phone rang with unexpected news that it was time to say goodbye to Pepper. I desperately tried to put enough money together so I could drive home and see him one last time. But I couldn't. My spouse hadn't worked in months, and my sporadic, temporary jobs couldn't cover any additional expenses.

The realization that I wasn't going to be able to say goodbye tore my heart apart. I envisioned my Pepper wondering why I was not there for him when he had been there for me for so many years. I begged my parents to give me more time or have him cremated so I could have some piece of him with me afterward, but they refused.

Within days, he was gone.

For years, I didn't forgive myself. Every time his memory flashed across my mind, the tears returned as if the wound in my heart was fresh. That old adage, "Time heals all wounds," was a horrible lie. How could I heal? I didn't get to say goodbye. The only thing I could do was weep over his picture, telling his image, "I'm so sorry," and "I love you so much."

When my son was eight years old, another rescue dog came into our lives — a white-and-tan Beagle mix we named Preston. While Pepper still owned a piece of my heart, Preston brought back my love and obsession for dogs. He was there for me when my marriage finally crumbled and as my son and I rebuilt our own happy family. But something unexpected was in Preston. Something familiar. Something comforting. The curious way his corkscrew tail uncurled and recurled. That recognizable "tippy-tap dance." The way he cocked his head when I talked to him as if he understood every word. His tricks to win a treat or two... or four. Even the trick when I'd say, "Roll over," and he'd fake the roll by turning around in a circle, never doing the actual trick. His pudgy belly was the undeniable proof of too many treats. And he was obsessed with bananas.

It was as if Pepper had come back to me again. I thought I was seeing what I wanted to see in him, but even a high-school friend who'd known Pepper made the unsolicited comment, "It's so uncanny! His mannerisms are just like Pepper!"

This brought me profound comfort, and my heart began to heal. While I'd never considered reincarnation before, and I didn't know if I believed in it, I allowed myself to think I'd been given another chance to love Pepper again. Preston allowed me to find closure and somehow make up for not being there for Pepper. My unrelenting guilt released its grip, and I was able to put it to rest.

Preston graced our lives for almost a decade. After developing a medical condition, he was prescribed prednisone, which unexpectedly caused him to go into kidney failure. I desperately tried to save his life, admitting him into the ICU and asking the doctors to do anything and everything possible to keep him with us. But the damage was irreversible. I had to make an excruciating choice: put him down then or bring him home for his last few days. If I chose the latter, he would quickly worsen and probably suffer, and I'd risk him dying alone. I couldn't bear the thought of losing another dog, but I also couldn't bear the thought of him passing without me there. Not again. Not this time.

My son, now seventeen, and I made the choice together, and we drove in silence to the ICU. That corkscrew tail, uncurling and recurling, greeted us one final time, but he was too weak for his "tippy-tap dance." We lay on the floor together, telling him how much we loved him, how much he meant to us, promising him we'd never forget him. Our last moments were full of tears, kisses, licks, and hugs. I put my hand in front of his nose so his last inhale would be of my scent and he'd know I was there through the end.

Then I nodded to the tech. I whispered, "I love you, I love you" in his ear, over and over until the tech leaned in to check his heartbeat and touched my arm. He was gone. My old wounds tore open with a newfound rush of agony, and I was rocked again with overwhelming grief. But I was also grateful for the chance to be there this time — together through his very last moment.

I may never know if reincarnation actually happened. Maybe it was my heart seeing what it so desperately wanted to see. Maybe it was purely coincidental. Maybe there are plenty of other dogs out there who love bananas, fake the roll-over trick, and listen like they understand every word. Or maybe something bigger out there knew exactly what I needed to heal my shattered heart. In any case, if good dogs do reincarnate, and if certain souls are truly meant to be together, then I know I will find him again.

— Vicki Liston —

98

A Paw to Remember

Dogs leave paw prints on our hearts.
~Author Unknown

The empty parking lot where our local elementary school once stood became my walking track one summer. It was away from traffic and afforded me the serenity every woman craves. The first day I chose this location to exercise, I had on my headphones, listening to motivational music that would inspire me to walk faster. However, my music was being drowned out by incessant barking.

After a short perusal of the area, I saw the most beautiful black Labrador Retriever in the back yard of a quaint historic home. She was in a pen, so she posed no threat to me. She certainly didn't seem vicious, yet she was extremely persistent.

For several days, I walked in the area while my new friend barked at me. It took a few weeks, but she grew to trust me and started to quietly observe me. By this time, I was thoroughly convinced the barking had been my invitation to enter into a friendship with this onyx beauty.

One day, I approached her owner in an effort to learn more about this beautiful girl. He was a teacher who worked in another county, and during the school year he rented a house closer to his job. His dad owned the local general store, and he assumed the responsibility of feeding and caring for her in the teacher's absence. I was formally introduced to Ashley.

I was shocked to learn that Ashley was much older than she

appeared. She gave me a huge smile and a jubilant tail wag at our introduction. I was granted full permission by her owner to visit and entertain her whenever I felt compelled. Treats were certainly not off-limits!

Visiting Ashley became part of my daily routine. The minute she saw me coming, she would start a happy dance that filled my heart with joy. I never entered her pen, but I quickly discovered that I could reach through the wire and play "fetch the rock" with her. She had a rope toy but she far preferred playing with rocks.

As time went on, I could see my canine friend slowing down. While she still enjoyed treats, playtime became a little shorter and more strained. One cold February morning, after battling a virus for a few days, I ventured down the hill to visit Ashley. I hadn't seen her in a few days and felt a rush of excitement at finally feeling well enough to walk.

But as I got closer to her pen, I saw something dark lying in front of her doghouse. My first thought was that she had pulled out her rug, but as I got closer, the reality set in. It was Ashley. She was gone. I tearfully ran to the store to give the bad news to her owner's father. He was shocked as he conveyed to me that he had just fed her a few hours before and she had seemed fine.

My furry friend was gone and part of me selfishly wished I hadn't gone that day. The vision of her lifeless body haunted me for weeks, but deep inside I knew I had been led to her by a power I couldn't see to say goodbye in person.

As warmer temperatures arrived, I felt a strong urge to go back to my walking track, but I didn't know if I could bear to see that empty pen. There would be no barking, no happy dance, no rock fetching, no Ashley. Maybe more to seek closure than to walk, one evening I ventured down to the old school lot. The sun was just starting to set, and the air was crisp. I slowly walked to the pen, opened the gate, and entered — something I had never done during our years of friendship. Through the tears that clouded my eyes, I spotted a rock. For some reason, I felt very strongly it was the last rock we'd played with together. I put the rock in my pocket to cherish as a keepsake of our happy times together.

When I arrived home, I shared my experience with my husband and showed him my treasure. I expressed my interest in having her name and date of departure painted on the rock as a memorial. My husband gently took the rock from my hand and turned it over, examining it like a precious gem. His eyes widened, and he looked at me with a broad smile. "I can see why she selected *this* rock to give you!" Puzzled, I took a closer look. "Do you see it?" he said. Clear to me now on the back of the rock was an indentation that formed the perfect shape of a small paw print.

I found peace in believing Ashley guided me to her to say goodbye in person the day she left this Earth. Now she was providing me with a priceless gift to thank me for our friendship. I have since had the rock painted, and it sits prominently on my kitchen windowsill as a gentle reminder that nothing, not even death, can separate us from those we love.

— Tamara Bell —

99

Charlie's Angels

Things that were hard to bear are sweet to remember.
~Seneca

I settled into bed and felt my heart heavy in my chest. Our fifteen-year-old Beagle, Charlie, had been declining for months. We heard his hacking cough, watched him drag himself across the floor, and noticed him periodically licking wounds from the cancer spreading inside him. But, at that moment, his snoring assured me he was finally sleeping.

"We have to do this for him," I said, turning to face my husband Brandon.

In Brandon's mind, we'd take Charlie to the vet for a lethal injection, say our goodbyes, and that would be it. Me? I started plotting how we could scatter Charlie's ashes at Brandon's late wife's grave. I didn't know if Sherise would want Charlie with her. I didn't even know if it was legal. But I hated the idea of her stuck in a cemetery flanked by strangers.

Brandon and I both want to be cremated when we die. He wants his remains tossed over Key West. I'm leaving my resting place up to our three children. Sherise's family members' post-death plans are up in the air. So, where does that leave her? Alone for eternity? It didn't seem right.

Sherise had been dead for fourteen years. I never met her, but I was acutely aware of how much she'd given me. I had inherited not only her husband, but also Charlie. The "regal Beagle," as we called him, was a gift from Brandon to Sherise on her thirty-third birthday.

"After she died, Charlie camped out at the front door waiting for her to come home," Brandon said. "He stayed there for three weeks."

The first time I visited Brandon, Charlie rushed to the door to greet me and then spun circles around me like something out of a *Tom and Jerry* cartoon.

"He seems to like you," said Brandon.

"Nah, he just wants to play," I said as I wrestled with him.

If Charlie fell in love with me on the spot, it took me longer to warm up. I'm not a dog person. I even viewed Charlie as a strike against Brandon — a constant reminder of the tragedy he'd suffered.

But Charlie's playful nature, uncanny intuition, and dogged pursuit of the last strip of bacon won me over. I pushed him off my lap during *90210* reruns, only to have him nuzzle his wet nose under my elbow until I relented and stroked his ear.

After I moved in with Brandon, Charlie became my home-office mate. He kept me company while I worked and hogged half the couch during lunch breaks. Still, I insisted Charlie was not my dog; I was just his caretaker by default.

At thirteen, when many Beagles call it quits, Charlie tried to keep up with the three children we ambushed him with. He traversed rooms littered with LEGOS, lapped up every high-chair mishap, and plopped on top of our board games mid-play. If the kids' antics took a toll on him, he didn't show it, even while navigating a litany of health problems. He developed cancer at ten, lost his left hind leg at twelve, and had surgery for a bleeding growth at fourteen.

Now more white than brown, and with only three legs, Charlie turned away from his food and water bowls. We knew he was nearing the end of the road. Still, we had been flip-flopping for weeks about whether to put him down.

I cuddled up next to Charlie at night and saw my reflection in his liquid brown eyes. "What should we do, sweet boy? Is it time?" I whispered while he drifted off to sleep.

Desperate for guidance, I asked Sherise to send us a sign. The next day, Charlie vomited not once or twice, but five times.

"There's your sign," Brandon said.

Despite his easy answer, I knew Brandon was struggling. Charlie carried him through the darkest times of his life. He and Sherise had just bought a new house. They were decorating a home and planning for children when a car accident took her life. Charlie was the single tie left from their union — the only bridge between her family and mine.

"They should be together, don't you think?" I asked Brandon.

"Probably, but what does that even look like?" he said, with a million questions in his eyes.

So, I started researching our options and ultimately hired a mobile veterinarian to come to our house, deliver an injection and return Charlie's ashes to us. Half would stay on our dresser. The other half would go into the earth with Sherise.

The night before we put Charlie down, I yearned to see a picture of him as a puppy. I wanted to know what he looked like before Sherise died. After I tucked our kids into bed, I saw a box on our dining room table.

"If I have a picture of Charlie as a puppy, it's in here," Brandon said. I studied him closely as we riffled through the losses in that box — pictures of a family full of promise, her wallet with her ID and credit cards still in the pockets, the coroner's report, and court documents.

"Ugh, Brandon, I'm so sorry," I said, my stare fixed on an image of him carrying Sherise against the backdrop of a Hawaiian beach. He didn't linger in the sadness. The box reopened the wound, but it was no longer bleeding. And there among the rubble was a picture of twelve-week-old Charlie.

Almost fourteen years to the day after Sherise's funeral, Brandon put Charlie's ashes in our minivan, and we set out to reunite our dog with his first owner.

I packed up our boys along with our picnic lunches. They knew we were returning Charlie to Sherise — some of him anyway. They even imagined him in Heaven as evidenced by the drawings they carried with them.

Our six-year-old, Jack, drew Charlie next to a Rainbow Bridge with the words, "Giddy up." Eight-year-old Max's masterpiece showcased an angel welcoming Charlie to Heaven. And Brian, also eight, drew Charlie as an angel beside an old-style telephone. The caption read: "This is what you can use to call us."

I laid out the blanket, and we ate PB&Js while sharing Charlie memories. The time Brandon replanted the flower beds and Charlie lay on top of the freshly planted soil. The time he couldn't find his way out of the duvet cover. And the time he tried swimming but sunk like a stone.

As our time wound down, Brandon pulled Charlie's ashes out of the jar. "Let's do this," he said, removing the vase near her headstone. Then each of us took a turn scattering Charlie's ashes into the earth.

When the jar was empty, I saw Brandon stand back and tear up. I assumed he was missing Charlie or Sherise. Maybe both? Then I realized his tears were not of sadness, but of gratitude.

"If someone had told me fifteen years ago that my wife would die six months after we married, and then I would visit her grave with my second wife and our three sons to scatter her Beagle's ashes years later, I never would have believed it," he said. And yet, we were all there, all somehow connected.

— Amy Paturel —

100

Last Swim

If there is a heaven, it's certain our animals
are to be there. Their lives become so interwoven
with our own, it would take more than
an archangel to detangle them.
~Pam Brown

have never been fond of dogs, especially big ones. It might have something to do with when I was young. I was bitten by a large dog and still have the scar to show for it. Any dog that looks like it could take me, at 5'3" and 110 pounds, immediately intimidates me. I get shaky and scared, and I retreat as far away as possible.

When my husband Johnny and I first started dating, he would show off pictures of his two dogs to me with such pride. I would smile politely, while my anxiety reminded me that if things kept going well between us, I was going to have to meet these giant beasts eventually.

Since we were in the beginning phases of our romance, we were inseparable, but he mostly spent time at my house. After a while, the inevitable happened, and I had to spend time at his house. Embarrassed, I tried not to show my nerves as we entered the front door and these two excited dogs came bounding toward us with all the energy of an eighty-pound toddler. I forced a smile and politely introduced myself to Jackson and Duke, trying not to run away.

It had been a while since Johnny had been home, so we rushed to let the boys out with an encouraging "Who wants to go outside?" The dogs ran around the front yard with a level of excitement that only a dog can have for playtime. I sat down and tried to be out of the way so as to not be bowled over by their enthusiasm. I put down my head and tried not to panic as my boyfriend played with his pets.

Then I felt something wet on my knee. I looked up, and Duke was there with a slobbery tennis ball in his mouth, looking at me with eyes full of hope. "He wants you to throw it," Johnny said, his eyes also hopeful. So, I grabbed the gross ball from the brown dog's mouth and chucked it as far as I could, which admittedly was not far. Thinking that was it, but proud of myself for helping, I went back to my phone. Thirty seconds later, Duke was back with the same ball and the same look in his eyes. Reluctantly, I took the ball and threw it again. And again. And again. For about half an hour, we played this game until I finally admitted that my arm was tired and I could not play any longer.

"Well, he is a Chesapeake Bay *Retriever*," Johnny joked. "He will do that as long as you let him."

I went inside, no longer wanting to play their doggy games. I sat on the couch and tried to ignore the dog-slobber smell on my hands. Five minutes later, the three boys came into the house. Duke jumped up on the couch next to me and settled in with his head on my lap. Apparently, I had made a new friend.

And that was it. Duke was by my side whenever I was there. This brown slobbery dog who was almost my size became my new best friend. When I was in the kitchen cooking, he'd be under my feet. If I got sick and was in bed, he would be by my side in case I needed something. And if I was in the shower, he would be there too because he loved the water.

As his health began to deteriorate, I was by his side all the time. I would sit on the floor with him when his legs were no longer strong enough to get up on the bed. I would rub medicine on his skin that he chewed raw. I had to take care of my sick buddy, as he had done for me.

As the time to put him down grew near, Johnny and I decided to take him to my brother's house on the lake for one final swim. He was so excited about the car ride. And when he got out of the car, the joy in his eyes was obvious when he saw the lake in the distance. He bounded toward it with the energy of a puppy. Before we could catch up with him, he had already swum so far that we could barely see his brown head sticking out of the water. Worried, my husband dove in to retrieve the Retriever. They made it back to the shore with Duke's front legs over Johnny's shoulders. He retired to the grass, exhausted but enjoying the sunshine.

Later, a little girl made it about fifty feet out into the lake. Although she had on a life vest, it was a bit farther than she felt comfortable. Scared, she began to yell for help. Duke abruptly woke up from his nap and swam to her rescue. She grabbed hold of the dog, and he swam her to safety. No longer scared, the girl quickly jumped into the lake again, immediately crying for help. Duke came to the rescue again. When they got back to shore, she ran right off the dock to repeat the process. It was like their own personal game of fetch. This went on for about an hour until her parents announced that it was time for them to go home. Before she left, she hugged Duke and said, "Thank you for saving me, dog." Johnny and I just looked at our exhausted hero dog with a mixture of pride and sadness because we knew what was to come.

Duke made it another year. That day at the lake seemed to rejuvenate him. He was still an old boy, but there was a bit of a spring in his step that we had not seen in quite a while. Then came a time when his quality of life diminished again. Duke was no longer interested in playing with the ball and barely ate food (even the snacks that we would lovingly give him). He could no longer control his bodily functions. It was clear that it was time.

The night before his appointment at the vet, we took him to the lake for his real final swim. We had to help him into and out of the car. His vision was no longer good, so he did not see the lake until we were right upon it. Smelling the water and wagging his tail, he walked slowly into the lake. He made it about ten feet but was obviously struggling. It was our turn to rescue him.

We sat in silence as we drove home, dreading the next day but knowing that our decision was the right one. He came home to a steak dinner and potato salad (two of his favorites). Johnny held him as he was put down the following morning. And we both cried all day.

"Well, at least we know that a little girl is out there who will never forget what a hero he was," I whispered in the midst of tears.

Neither will I, Duke. Neither will I.

—Jodi Renee Thomas—

It's What We Do for Love

All, everything that I understand,
I only understand because I love.
~Leo Tolstoy

t's noon, and I'm changing my dog Mignon's diaper again — the third diaper so far today. She waits patiently while I layer a cotton wrap with Velcro straps over the diaper to hold it in place. I've already washed a load of bedding from the kennel where she sleeps at night. I've fed her breakfast. I've let her in and out of the house several times, although it's usually just after she has wet her diaper without warning.

She trots off to one of her beds in the living room or to the kitchen to see if I have dropped some tasty food on the floor. Her spine sticks up like a row of teeth despite two meals a day and several treats. She has pulled out chunks of her own fur, leaving her looking more like a hairless Egyptian cat than a Beagle.

This has been my routine for the past eight months: I change diapers. I make daily meals for Mignon of boiled rice and, recently, canned cat food. I do one or two loads of laundry a day. I spread plastic sheeting on the floor for the accidents her diapers can't contain. I swaddle her in warm blankets and place her near me on the sofa so I can pet her and stroke her long, silky ears while I'm watching television or reading. And I do it gladly, happy for more time with her by my side.

But I'm realistic. I know her time is limited. She is about fifteen years old. She is deaf, and cataracts cloud both her eyes. She has terminal cancer.

Months ago, during a routine exam, my veterinarian, Dr. Alexander, discovered it. She removed the tumor, but the pathology report indicated it was aggressive. After a consultation with a veterinarian who specializes in oncology, Dr. Alexander very gently told me that if Mignon were her dog, she would keep her as comfortable as possible and make these weeks — or months, if we are lucky — the best of her life. Further treatment, if it were successful, she said, would not cure the cancer and only extend her life slightly. And there certainly were no guarantees that the treatment would be successful. If Mignon had been human, Dr. Alexander would have advised her: "Time to take that cruise you have always dreamed of."

There was another issue. Mignon does not like riding in the car or leaving the house, so trips to the vet's office for treatment would be both physically and emotionally traumatic for her. Even before her cancer, before she became a senior dog, she refused to take walks. After a trip to a nearby dog park a couple of years ago ended with Mignon hiding under a bench until I coaxed her out and carried her back to the car, I have come to accept that she is a homebody. A couch potato. A couple of laps around the back yard are enough for her, and then she scampers back inside to the safety and comfort of her bed or the sofa.

For the first few months after her diagnosis, I fed Mignon boiled rice and chicken or ground beef. There was even a steak or two. But she soon began to refuse these foods. A neighbor suggested I try wet cat food, and it proved irresistible. Mignon wolfs the cat food, the fishier the better. Today, the *plat du jour* is Fisherman's Catch atop a scoop of rice warmed in the microwave.

In the beginning, I was using dog diapers, which are convenient and fit well. But as I began having to change the diapers five or six times a day, the expense was mounting, so I started buying baby diapers and cutting holes for the tail. (Mignon wears a size 6 baby diaper.) She tolerates the diapers and doesn't try to scratch or rub them off. Occasionally, when she squirms on her back in one of her beds, the diapers slip down her legs. But, for the most part, the diapers and wrap stay in place on her thin, hairless rump.

At night, I let Mignon sleep in her kennel without diapers, which means the two or three layers of blankets are soaked by the time I get up in the morning. Since her kennel is near my bed — she is more content when she can see me — I keep an air freshener plugged in to help keep the room from reeking of urine.

***

When I'd seen a woman sitting in a lawn chair by the side of the road, with a black-and-white Beagle mix on a leash near her feet and a sign saying "Free Dog" next to her, I started to drive by. I already had three other dogs, and the city limit, which I'd always regarded as merely a suggestion, was two. I told myself to keep driving. Not my problem. Not this one.

Then I decided the least I could do was to warn the woman about adopting the dog to a stranger, so I stopped. I advised her to ask questions: Does the adopter have a fenced yard? Does he have any experience owning a dog? Who is his vet? Then, feeling like I had done my duty, I got back in my car and drove another few blocks before I knew I could not let this dog go to anyone else. I went back.

I fully intended to find a good home for Mignon, but after a week of her living with me and my other dogs, I was hooked. She did not bark or dig holes in the yard. She did not fight with the other dogs. She did not chew on shoes or furniture. With the exception of shredding the newspaper and tissues she stole from my purse, and grabbing hunks of my hair occasionally, she was perfect. She was mine, and I made a pact with my dogs that once they were mine, they were mine for life — in sickness and in health.

Mignon has been at my side through a couple of my own health crises, the deaths of my parents, and a move to another city. She is loving and devoted. She has outlived several other dogs I took in as strays, each one submitting to her sometimes autocratic rule of the household.

For now, Mignon seems to have a quality of life worth preserving.

She follows me through the house and loves her belly rubs, wriggling on her back and kicking her legs. Although she can no longer jump onto the sofa, she stares at me until I boost her up. Then, wrapped in a blanket, she falls asleep on my lap. I don't know how long I will have with Mignon, and I don't really want to know. When she is in pain, or when she lets me know somehow that it's time to let her go, I will. It will break my heart, but I will do it.

For now, I don't mind the inconveniences of caring for a dying dog. I am willing to walk on plastic sheets and sleep in a room that sometimes smells more like the local dog shelter than a bedroom. When she tires of cat food, I will experiment until I find something else she will eat. I will keep cutting up hot dogs for treats and breaking Milk-Bones into bite-sized pieces to keep her from losing more weight. I will do my best to make her last days the dog equivalent of a cruise to the Bahamas. I will wake up in the morning and do it all again.

That's what we do for love, isn't it? Whether who we love is a family member, a friend, or a fifteen-year-old Beagle in a diaper, it's all for love.

— Nancy Lines —

Meet Our Contributors

Becky Alexander is a tour director, leading groups in Charleston, New York, Toronto, and other destinations. When not on the road, she writes magazine articles, devotionals, and inspirational stories. She loves volunteering year-round with Operation Christmas Child. Send Becky a happy message at www.happychairbooks.com.

Carol Gentry Allen is a national Christian women's speaker and writer. She is a grief counselor, dementia and Alzheimer's practitioner. She teaches Sunday school in South Carolina where she lives with her husband and four fur babies. Carol has a book published and two manuscripts waiting for publication.

Donna Anderson lives in Texas with her husband and dogs: a Border Collie who could rule the world if she had opposable thumbs and access to a smart phone, and a tennis ball-obsessed Golden Retriever. She is a mom to three and grandmother to four. All boys! Her hobbies include genealogy, photography, antiquing, and writing.

Katie Avagliano has raised guide dog puppies for the Seeing Eye for over fifteen years. She teaches college writing at universities throughout the Mid-Atlantic region. Katie spends her time volunteering with therapy dog programs, reading outdoors, and exploring the Pine Barrens of South Jersey.

Dave Bachmann is a retired teacher from Arizona who taught writing and reading to special needs students for thirty-nine years. He now lives in California, writing stories and poems for children and grown-ups with his wife Jay, a retired kindergarten teacher and, of course, their dog Scout, who is a young fifteen-year-old Lab.

Kelly Bakshi is a freelance writer and frequent contributor to the *Chicken Soup for the Soul* series. She and her dog Sirius Black are almost equal in size. You can follow her (and Sirius) on Instagram @kellybakshibooks.

Jane Beal has a Ph.D. from UC Davis and is a professor of English literature at the University of La Verne in Southern California. She writes and publishes poetry, fiction, creative nonfiction, literary and cultural studies of literature, and music. She enjoys reading, walking, dancing, cycling, birding, singing, and playing the flute.

Lainie Belcastro is blessed to have her eighth story published in the *Chicken Soup for the Soul* series! She is a published poet and author who writes for children, women, and her heart. Lainie and her daughter Nika are also creators of Mrs. Terra Cotta Pots, an eccentric storyteller for children. Visit her at www.lainiebelcastro.com.

Tamara Bell lives in Cooperstown, PA and is enjoying restoring a 1930s cottage in Ashville, NY with her husband. She is honored to be featured four times in the *Chicken Soup for the Soul* series, and has also been featured in *Angels on Earth*, *Good Old Days*, and *All Creatures* magazine. Her greatest joy is her family.

Penny Blacksand lives in Oregon with her family. Her mom has always been her best friend and biggest supporter. Together they homeschool and their dog May, who has attended class since preschool, is in the eighth grade! Penny has loved dogs, writing, crafting, learning and nature for as long as she can remember.

Jeanne Blandford is a writer/editor who is currently working on a new children's book series with her husband. When not in their Airstream looking for new material, they can be found running SafePet, a program that fosters pets of domestic violence survivors while they search for new homes for themselves and their pets.

Christy Breedlove is a middle school educator as well as part-time author living in Georgia. She has published the *Dixie Days* cozy mystery series and is a frequent contributor to *Walton Living Magazine*. She is married to her best friend, Dave, and has two human kids and two canine kids.

Jill Burns lives in the mountains of West Virginia with her wonderful family. She's a retired piano teacher and performer. She enjoys writing, music, gardening, nature, and spending time with her grandchildren.

Blanche Carroll received her Bachelor of Science, with honors, in Business Administration in 2008. She is a mom of three, and lives in Massachusetts. Her first story, "I Wouldn't Be Caught Dead in That," was published in *Chicken Soup for the Soul: My Wonderful, Wacky Family* in November 2022. E-mail her at blanche68@comcast.net.

Lisa C. Castillo is a retired elementary school teacher, a freelance writer, and volunteer. She enjoys visiting seaside towns with her family, reading, and watching British panel shows. She is grateful for the work of animal rescue organizations and their dedication to finding loving homes for animals in need.

James Hugh Comey is an award-winning freelance writer and retired educator. His novels are available on Amazon; his blog has 29,000 page views; and he holds a doctorate from the University of Pennsylvania. When not writing, he can be found riding his motorcycle on winding country roads.

Gwen Cooper received her B.A. in English and Secondary Education in 2007 and completed the University of Denver Publishing Institute in 2009. In her free time, she enjoys traveling, gardening, and spending time exploring the outdoors with her husband and Bloodhounds. Follow her on Twitter @Gwen_Cooper10.

Terry L. Cooper was born in Salisbury, MD. She has published over sixty eBooks on Amazon, in six languages. In 2021 she was interviewed by *The Washington Post* about her story on 9/11, anthrax, and the D.C. snipers as a part of their twentieth anniversary coverage.

Mary DeVries has lived on three continents, in four countries, in fifteen cities, and in seven U.S. states. Along the way she has raised three children and remained married to the handsome guy she met at college freshman registration. She loves to write about anything and everything. E-mail her at marydj03@gmail.com.

Kathy Diamontopoulos lives in northern Massachusetts with her husband Lou and several pet family members. She enjoys exploring the outdoors with her camera and capturing the beauty of nature. When she's not snapping photos, you can find her in her garden.

Dottie still enjoys plentiful belly rubs from **Joan Donnelly-Emery** and her husband Alan at their home in Franklin, TN. She's unimpressed with Joan's BFA from Syracuse University but gives high marks for her toy-throwing skills. Dottie's passions include treats, squirrels, and Georgie, the Terrier next door.

Tammie Rue Elliott studied business at Marshall University, but writing has always been her first love. She is a previous contributor to the *Chicken Soup for the Soul* series, and has published several short stories and one mystery novel. Her current work in progress is a thriller set in rural Virginia.

Jean Ende is a former newspaper reporter, publicist for New York City government, bank marketing VP and college professor. Now retired, she has published over a dozen short stories based on her immigrant family. Jean recently completed her first novel and is looking for an agent or publisher.

N. Evans has her bachelor's in creative writing and English, which she received from Southern New Hampshire University. Nicole has been writing pieces since high school. She enjoys music, board games and spending time with friends and family.

Sasha Feiler is the only funny person to ever come out of Siberia, but you'll have to take her word for it since Siberia is the last place you'd want to visit. She was a writer on Adult Swim's *Robot Chicken* and teaches TV Writing at Script Anatomy. She also hosts a comedy podcast "Shut Up I Love It."

Jan M. Flynn writes novels, stories, and essays, and hosts a weekly podcast, "Here's a Thought" (for people who overthink). She and her husband now live in Boise, ID and are still highly influenced by the thinking of the animals in their lives.

Louise Foerster writes novels, stories, and blog posts expressing a deep curiosity and life experience. Her career in product development, publishing, and consulting began with degrees from Rutgers University and NYU. Louise enjoys hiking, gardening, reading, and living on the New England coastline with her family.

Linda Gabris instructed creating writing and international cooking courses for over sixteen years. She has written several outdoor cooking and foraging books and is currently working on a new one. Linda is a feature writer and columnist who works for numerous magazines in Canada and the U.S. E-mail her at inkserv@telus.net.

Becca Hardwick is a transcriber who lives in a small town called Yelm, WA. She has three dogs and four cats. She enjoys reading, writing, art journaling, rock painting, and spending time with her fur babies.

Kim Harms is a freelance writer, speaker, breast cancer survivor and author of *Life Reconstruction: Navigating the World of Mastectomies and Breast Reconstruction*. Harms has a degree in English from Iowa State University. She lives in Huxley, IA with her husband, the youngest of their three sons and one crazy loveable dog.

Linda Healy is a registered nurse who worked seventeen years as a hospice nurse. She enjoys writing poetry and legacy stories. Linda is a visual artist specializing in color pencil drawing and Zentangles. Her favorite pastime is watching her grandchildren grow.

Kat Heckenbach graduated from the University of Tampa with a bachelor's degree in biology, went on to teach math, and then home-schooled her son and daughter while writing and making sci-fi/fantasy art. Now that both kids have graduated, her writing and art time is constantly interrupted by her ninety-six-pound Boxer mix.

Nancy Hesting is a published writer and poet who lives with her husband in Michigan's Manistee National Forest where she can be found either shoveling snow, picking up pinecones, or hunting for mushrooms. Her work has appeared in *Ad Hoc Fiction* and *The Pangolin Review*.

Laurie Higgins is an award-winning journalist who writes about health, food, gardening and family. She currently writes for *Cape Cod Health News*. She and her chef husband live in Brewster, MA with their two Miniature Dachshunds. Laurie enjoys writing, hiking, cooking, photography, and spending time with her grandchildren.

Sandy Hoban has two undergraduate degrees — theater arts from Rutgers University and English education through the University of Wyoming and will be finishing her creative nonfiction graduate program in the spring of 2023. Sandy is passionate about tacos, reading, nature, dogs, traveling, family time, and live music.

Meadoe Hora is a writer, working mom, dog rescuer, and lover of beautiful words. She writes books for teens with strong female leads and classic mythology. She lives in Wisconsin with her family, two spoiled Basset Hounds, and a sweet black Lab.

M.J. Irving is an author of the YA fantasy novel *Nova's Quest for the Enchanted Chalice*. She is Canadian born and is now living in London, England with her partner. She loves all things outdoors and nature. M.J. has a Bachelor of Arts from the University of British Columbia. Learn more at www.mjirving.com.

Author and freelance writer **Gayle M. Irwin** is passionate about pet rescue and adoption. She has been previously published in the *Chicken Soup for the Soul* series, and she writes books for children and adults, including a sweet contemporary romance series called *Pet Rescue Romance*. Learn more at gaylemirwin.com.

Jeffree Wyn Itrich has been writing stories for a very long time. She attended the graduate school of journalism at UC Berkeley where she honed her writing skills, has authored a cookbook, a children's book, two novels, countless articles, and has been published in twelve *Chicken Soup for the Soul* books.

Aviva Jacobs and her husband left their lake home in the city for a hobby farm during COVID. She spends her days in her office working as a financial analyst while watching chickens wander the lawn. In addition to Luna Belle and a fat cat roaming the farmhouse, they have added a white German Shepherd. The vacuum runs daily.

Rev. Heather Jepsen is the pastor at First Presbyterian Church in Warrensburg, MO. She is married and has two kids and lots of pets. When she is not pastoring or writing, Heather likes to garden, quilt, and play the harp. She also writes for *Guideposts*. Read more from Heather at thisdaysblessing.com.

Vicki L. Julian, a University of Kansas alumna, is an award-winning writer and an editor who loves to do both equally. She is the author of ten books and her work has appeared in twelve anthologies, including the *Chicken Soup for the Soul* series, and various newspapers and magazines. E-mail her at vickijulian@sunflower.com.

Kiesa Kay, poet and playwright, writes and plays fiddle in her cabin in the woods with a panoramic view of the Black Mountains. Her good dog Rosa is by her side. Kiesa's plays have traveled to five states. Her first children's book, *The Warming Stone/La Piedra de Calentamiento*, was illustrated by Dania Ramirez Lopez.

Sally M. Keehn loves to explore, whether it is the past, another country, her own back yard or the lives of the sweet animals and people who populate it. The fruits of this love have led her into writing a number of novels for young people, including the award-winning *I Am Regina*.

Judy Kellersberger has written several hundred stories, songs, and poems. Pete Seeger featured her poem/song "Tribute to the Hudson River" for the Quadricentennial. *Tribute to a Firefighter* hit #1 on Cash Box. Judy is completing a book of her collected short stories and adventures.

Rose Marie Kern lives in the high desert of Albuquerque, NM. She is a solar cook, a master gardener, and a member of SouthWest Writers. She enjoys canine companionship and prefers to offer a new life to larger rescue dogs usually two to three at a time, though there have been as many as five.

Heidi Kling-Newnam holds a doctorate in nursing from West Chester University in Pennsylvania and works as a nurse practitioner. Her writing has been published in *The Upper Room* and other titles in the *Chicken Soup for the Soul* series.

Abigail Krueger earned her Bachelor of Arts in Linguistics and Spanish Interpretation in 2021. She enjoys hiking with her sweet puppies, canoeing with her two best friends in the entire world, and playing board games with her gal pals. She plans to write speculative fiction novels involving lots of neat aliens.

Linda L. Kruschke writes candid memoir and fearless poetry. She aspires to show women that God's healing is just a story away. She blogs at AnotherFearlessYear.net and has been published in *Fathom* magazine, *The Christian Journal*, *Bible Advocate*, *Calla Press*, *Divine Purpose*, iBelieve.com, and several anthologies.

Carole Lazar is a retired judge who lives in a friendly and walkable community. She always carries dog treats and is easily convinced that any pup she meets on her walk is starving. When not walking or sympathizing with her canine friends, Carole reads a lot and writes a little.

Margaret Lea is a writer, musician, music teacher, wife, and mom of three beautiful girls. To join her e-mail list, e-mail MargaretLea.author@gmail.com with "Join" in the subject line. Her weekly uplifting e-mail is centered on letting parents know they are not alone in their struggles.

Shannon Leach lives in Tennessee and is the owner of A Repurposed Heart. She writes stories about leadership, life, and loving people to encourage others and remind them they are not alone. She holds a bachelor's degree in social work and is the co-founder of the nonprofit The Fostered Gift.

Nancy Lines received a Master's in English from the University of Missouri at Kansas City and taught composition part-time while working as a legal assistant. She is a lover of all animals, especially dogs. She has adopted many stray and rescued dogs over her life. Nancy also writes short stories and essays.

Represented by five talent agencies, **Vicki Liston** is a multi-award-winning voice actor, producer, and writer with several national companies among her many credits. She's most proud of her award-winning YouTube how-to series, "On the Fly… DIY", which raises money for no-kill animal shelters and rescue organizations.

Jamie Lomax graduated from Union High School in 2009. She lives with her husband, in-laws, two dogs, and one cat in sunny Florida. Jamie enjoys reading, writing, and video games and loves animals. She aspires to be a short story and children's book author.

Corrie Lopez lives in her favorite place in the whole world — a small town in the rural Midwest with her favorite people in the whole world — her family and friends.

Joyce Styron Madsen has, over the years, adopted twenty-two rescue dogs and fostered many others as well. She could have written a story or two about each and every one of them — their special needs, their healing process (both physical and emotional), their intense love and devotion to their rescuer. "Rescue — Foster — Adopt!"

Brittany Marasciulo-Rivera is a writer of science fiction, fantasy, and space opera who spends most of her time daydreaming. She plans to write novels and screenplays so that she can share the worlds that live inside her mind.

Tim Martin's work has been featured in over two dozen *Chicken Soup for the Soul* books. He is the author of *There's Nothing Funny About Running, Wimps Like Me, Summer With Dad, The Legend of Boomer Jack,* and *Why Run If No One Is Chasing You?* E-mail Tim at tmartin@sitestar.net.

Allison McCormick lives in the charming town of Bend, OR just east of the Cascade Mountain range. She retired in 2017 after a thirty-year career in healthcare and research administration. Allison is a self-proclaimed introvert who loves to boldly and enthusiastically encourage, mentor, and support women.

Jacquie McTaggart lives in Independence, IA with her ten-pound Shih Tzu, Willow. Her writing career began at age sixty-two following an enjoyable and successful forty-two-year teaching career. She has authored two books, contributed stories to five anthologies, and written numerous articles for a wide range of parenting publications.

Linda L. Meilink is a former newspaper editor and award-winning writer and poet. She has also taught English and journalism at college. Linda is married and lives in Northern California. Her hobbies include cooking, gardening, and piano.

Brittany O'Connor is a small business owner who runs a made-to-order baking company that provides her rural community with an assortment of southern-inspired treats. She enjoys writing songs, poems, and short stories in her spare time.

Amy Paturel is a writer in California whose work frequently appears in the *New York Times, The Washington Post* and *Good Housekeeping.* An award-winning essayist, Amy teaches personal essay writing to students across the globe. Her family adopted a pandemic puppy in 2020 and named him Bosley as a nod to Charlie.

Deb Penfold loves reading, crafting, and camping — of course her dogs are always with her.

Jan Pezarro uses the power of storytelling to create compelling corporate communications materials. A favourite assignment was working with BC SPCA to launch the BC SPCA AnimalKind accreditation program. She is an MFA student at the University of Kings College and is partial to Shih Tzu Bichons.

Mary T. Post resides in rural Oregon with her husband of thirty-four years. She enjoys hiking, gardening, cooking, and sharing time with their four sons and their families. As a life-long Lutheran, married to a pastor, Mary enjoys writing stories that weave together her faith with ordinary (and oftentimes humorous) life experiences.

Winter D. Prosapio is an award-winning novelist and humor columnist. She's also a big fan of caves, small dogs, waterparks, wooden roller coasters, and funnel cake, not necessarily in that order. You can learn more about her, read some funny stuff, and even hear from her at wprosapio.com.

Connie Kaseweter Pullen lives in rural Sandy, OR, near her five children and several grandchildren. She earned a B.A. with honors, at the University of Portland in 2006, with a double major in Psychology and Sociology. Connie enjoys writing, photography and exploring nature. E-mail her at MyGrandmaPullen@aol.com.

Sallie A. Rodman's stories appear in various *Chicken Soup for the Soul* anthologies. She loves writing about the foibles of her crazy pets. She enjoys reading, writing, and raising Monarch butterflies. Sallie also teaches writing at Cal State University, Long Beach's OLLI campus. E-mail her at writergal222@gmail.com.

Since retiring from teaching, **Martha Roggli** joined two writing groups. She always looks forward to hearing the group's stories and sharing her own. They inspire her and keep her "on-task." Dogs have always been an important part of her life and she loves writing about them.

Maria Ruiz is a retired woman who has traveled around the world for ten years. She lived in Puerta Vallarta and was the moderator for the Puerto Vallarta's Writers Group. She has published stories in several magazines and is currently a contributor for Kings River Life Magazine, an e-zine. Her books are available on Amazon.

Marie A. Saleeby received her Bachelor of Arts from Skidmore College and her Master of Arts in 2014 from UNC Wilmington. Marie lived in Paris, France for several years, and her two daughters were born there. Marie has lived on many continents, and she is currently writing a food memoir exploring memories through food.

Kristine Schuler has been writing and teaching for as long as she can remember. She currently lives with her husband Stew, dog Sunny and cat Minou. She has adult children sprinkled across the country and enjoys visiting them when she is not with her other children... her students.

MK Scott is part of the cozy mystery team of Morgan and Scott. Morgan pens the tales, while Scott serves as first editor and webmaster. Daughter Sarah handles the social media and Jane the Lab supervises all digging in the garden. Learn more at www.morgankwyatt.com.

Patricia Senkiw-Rudowsky received a B.A. in English/Communications from Kean University. She is a writer/educator/artist. She is the former director of the Livingston Youth Community Services. She has one book titled *Believe?* published and her second memoir, *An Inevitable life*, is nearly completed. E-mail her at Storyteller1012@aol.com.

Pat Severin, a retired teacher, has been writing poetry since the third grade. She has two children and three grandchildren. She loves writing poems of encouragement and sending them every week to people going through difficult health struggles. Touching someone with her words is her greatest joy!

Laurel L. Shannon is the pseudonym of a NW Ohio author and writer. She enjoys writing about memorable characters and family members both currently and from her past.

Alison Shelton earned her B.A. degree in English and history and an M.A. in education. She taught high school English for thirty years. She has two daughters and five grandchildren. Alison enjoys her work as the Neighborhood Watch Pet Coordinator, reuniting lost pets with their people. Alison also enjoys card making and other crafts.

Billie Holladay Skelley received her bachelor's and master's degrees from the University of Wisconsin-Madison. A retired clinical nurse specialist, she is the mother of four and grandmother of two. Billie enjoys writing, and her work crosses several genres. She spends her non-writing time reading, gardening, and traveling.

Maureen Slater is a wife, mother, and grandmother. She loves writing poems and short stories.

Heather Spiva is a freelance writer from Sacramento, CA. She is a married mom and has two grown sons. When she's not reading or writing, she loves selling (and wearing) vintage clothing online, thrifting (AKA treasure hunting), and drinking coffee. E-mail Heather at hjspiva@gmail.com.

Christina Ray Stanton is a Florida native who has lived in New York City for almost thirty years. She is a licensed New York City tour guide and co-founder of a nonprofit called Loving All Nations. She has written two books and over fifty articles, many of them about 9/11.

Diane Stark is a wife, mom to five human kids and two canine ones, new grandma, and freelance writer. She is a frequent contributor to the *Chicken Soup for the Soul* series. She loves to write about the important things in life: her family and her faith.

Stuart Stromin is a South African American writer and filmmaker living in Los Angeles, CA. He was educated at Rhodes University, South Africa, the Alliance Francaise de Paris, and the University of California, Los Angeles.

Lynn Sunday is a writer and animal rights activist who lives in a coastal community near San Francisco. This is Lynn's eighteenth story to appear in the *Chicken Soup for the Soul* series. E-mail her at Sunday11@aol.com.

Heather Sweeney is a freelance writer who writes about military discounts at her day job. Her work has appeared in *The New York Times*, *The Washington Post*, *Newsweek*, *Insider*, *Healthline*, and elsewhere. She lives in Virginia with her boyfriend, two kids and their dog Gunner.

Believer, dreamer, storyteller **J. Lynn Thomas** enjoys her 1930s writing cottage in Virginia where she loves exploring ideas and business ventures around the kitchen table with good friends, good food, and good music while fielding sloppy kisses from her rescue Lab Sugar. A published children's author, Lynn has several books in the works.

Jodi Renee Thomas is a retired fashion designer/party girl. She has been thrilled to be part of the *Chicken Soup for the Soul* family for almost a decade. She lives happily in Florida with her husband and two dogs who like to bother her while she's writing.

Nancy Thorne is an award-winning author inspired by the courage of youth. Her novel, *The Somewhere I See You Again*, won first place for the 2021 Dante Rossetti Award for Young Adult Fiction. She lives and continues her writing journey just outside of Toronto with her family and two dogs. Learn more at www.nancythorne.com.

Linda Tilley is a retired radiology secretary. Her novel, *Mary Princess of Ayri*, was published in 2003. Linda enjoys traveling with her husband and creating digital art as well as traditional painting.

Award-winning author **Susan Traugh** writes curriculum for special needs teens for work and *Chicken Soup for the Soul* stories for fun. Her works include *The Edge of Brilliance* — a hero's tale about a bipolar teen, and seventy workbooks on adulting. She lives in Oregon with her husband, adult daughters, and spoiled dog. Learn more at susantraugh.com.

Constance Van Hoven holds an MFA in writing for children and is the author of several picture books and short stories. She mostly lives in Bozeman, MT with her husband and their twelve-year-old Lab, Peg, who still thinks she is a puppy. Learn more at www.constancevanhoven.com.

Dorenda Crager Watson has a BFA degree from CCAD and was a "Saturday Morning Art Classes" second grade instructor there, co-teaching with her husband for thirty-two years. She is pursuing her love of writing creative children's poetry that is about silly characters in colorful worlds doing lovely things. E-mail her at dcwatzworld@gmail.com.

When his wife died, **David Weiskircher** was thrown into a torrential storm. But he had a unique group of friends by his side: herding dogs. They helped him find peace. His books, including *A Thin Place* and *A Healing Way: Two Dogs, A Coyote and An Old Soul*, are available through Amazon.

Janet Wells and her husband share their Western Pennsylvanian log house with their son and three tabby cats. Mother of two and retired teacher of children of learning differences, Janet revels in retirement.

She stitches quilts, photographs nature, listens to audiobooks while doing chores, and writes, writes, writes.

Lucy Wetherall works as a law clerk in the Toronto area. Lucy was born in the UK and immigrated to Canada with her family in 1974. She is married and has two grown children. Lucy enjoys traveling, golf, Pilates, and volunteering in her community. She plans to write a novel based on her grandfather's experiences in the war.

Jerry Zezima writes a humor column for *Tribune News Service* and is the author of six books. He has one wife, two daughters, five grandchildren and many creatures. E-mail him at JerryZ111@optonline. net or read his blog at jerryzezima.blogspot.com.

Meet Amy Newmark

Amy Newmark is the bestselling author, editor-in-chief, and publisher of the *Chicken Soup for the Soul* book series. Since 2008, she has published 187 new books, most of them national bestsellers in the U.S. and Canada, more than doubling the number of Chicken Soup for the Soul titles in print today. She is also the author of *Simply Happy*, a crash course in Chicken Soup for the Soul advice and wisdom that is filled with easy-to-implement, practical tips for enjoying a better life.

Amy is credited with revitalizing the Chicken Soup for the Soul brand, which has been a publishing industry phenomenon since the first book came out in 1993. By compiling inspirational and aspirational true stories curated from ordinary people who have had extraordinary experiences, Amy has kept the twenty-nine-year-old Chicken Soup for the Soul brand fresh and relevant.

Amy graduated *magna cum laude* from Harvard University where she majored in Portuguese and minored in French. She then embarked on a three-decade career as a Wall Street analyst, a hedge fund manager, and a corporate executive in the technology field. She is a Chartered Financial Analyst.

Her return to literary pursuits was inevitable, as her honors thesis in college involved traveling throughout Brazil's impoverished northeast region, collecting stories from regular people. She is delighted to have come full circle in her writing career — from collecting stories "from the people" in Brazil as a twenty-year-old to, three decades later, collecting stories "from the people" for Chicken Soup for the Soul.

When Amy and her husband Bill, the CEO of Chicken Soup for the Soul, are not working, they are visiting their four grown children and their spouses, and their five grandchildren.

Follow Amy on Twitter @amynewmark. Listen to her free podcast — Chicken Soup for the Soul with Amy Newmark — on Apple, Google, or by using your favorite podcast app on your phone.

Thank You

We owe huge thanks to all our contributors and fans. We received thousands of submissions for this popular topic, and we spent months reading all of them. Laura Dean, Crescent LoMonaco, Maureen Peltier, Mary Fisher, and Barbara LoMonaco read all of them and narrowed down the selection for Associate Publisher D'ette Corona and Publisher and Editor-in-Chief Amy Newmark. Susan Heim did the first round of editing, and then D'ette chose the perfect quotations to put at the beginning of each story, and Amy edited the stories and shaped the final manuscript.

As we finished our work, D'ette continued to be Amy's right-hand woman in working with all our wonderful writers. Barbara LoMonaco, Kristiana Pastir and Elaine Kimbler jumped in to proof, proof, proof. And yes, there will always be typos anyway, so please feel free to let us know about them at webmaster@chickensoupforthesoul.com, and we will correct them in future printings.

The whole publishing team deserves a hand, including our Vice President of Marketing Maureen Peltier, our Vice President of Production Victor Cataldo, Executive Assistant Chris Engler, and our graphic designer Daniel Zaccari, who turned our manuscript into this beautiful, inspirational book.

About American Humane

A merican Humane is the country's first national humane organization, founded in 1877 and committed to ensuring the safety, welfare, and wellbeing of all animals. For more than 140 years, American Humane has been first to serve in promoting the welfare and safety of animals and strengthening the bond between animals and people. American Humane's initiatives are designed to help whenever and wherever animals are in need of rescue, shelter, protection or care.

American Humane is the only national humane organization with top ratings and endorsements from the key charity watchdog groups. The organization has earned Charity Navigator's highest "Four-Star Rating," the Platinum Seal of Transparency from GuideStar USA, and is one of the few charities that meets all of the Better Business Bureau's Wise Giving Alliance's 20 Standards for Charity Accountability.

American Humane's certification programs that verify humane treatment of animals are wide ranging, covering animals in film, on farms, in zoos and aquariums and even those in pet retailers. The iconic "No Animals Were Harmed®" certification, which appears during the end credits of films and TV shows, today monitors some 1,000 productions yearly.

Through rigorous, science-based criteria that are independently verified, American Humane's farm animal welfare program, Conservation program and Pet Provider programs help to ensure the humane treatment of more than one billion animals living on certified farms and ranches, in zoos and aquariums, and at pet provider locations. Simply put, American Humane is the largest verifier of animal welfare in the world.

Continuing its longstanding efforts to strengthen the healing power of the human-animal bond, American Humane also pairs veterans struggling to cope with the invisible wounds of war with highly trained service dogs, and also helps reunite discharged military working dogs with their former handlers.

To learn more about American Humane, visit AmericanHumane. org and follow them on Facebook, Instagram, Twitter and YouTube.

AMERICAN★HUMANE
FIRST TO SERVE®

Editor's Note: Chicken Soup for the Soul and American Humane have created *Humane Heroes*, a FREE new series of e-books and companion curricula for elementary, middle and high schoolers. Through thirty-six inspirational stories of animal rescue, rehabilitation, and humane conservation being performed at the world's leading zoological institutions, and eighteen easy-to-follow lesson plans, *Humane Heroes* provides highly engaging free reading materials that also encourage young people to appreciate and protect Earth's disappearing species. To download the free e-books and learn about the program, please visit www. chickensoup.com/ah.

Changing the world one story at a time®
www.chickensoup.com